The Collected Plays

VOLUME ONE

GENERAL AUDAX

HONEST URUBAMBA

LIVING ROOM WITH 6 OPPRESSIONS

A SPLITTING HEADACHE
CONCEIVED DURING THE MEMORABLE WAR BETWEEN ISTRIA AND FRIULI

THE VIRGIN AND THE UNICORN

ISLAND

VOLUME TWO

THE MONK WHO WOULDN'T

THE FATAL FRENCH DENTIST

PROFESSOR SNAFFLE'S POLYPON

THE SENSIBLE MAN OF JERUSALEM

ADAM ADAMSON

OF ANGELS AND ESKIMOS

BOOKS BY OSCAR MANDEL

A DEFINITION OF TRAGEDY, *New York University Press, 1961*

THE THEATRE OF DON JUAN, *University of Nebraska Press, 1963*

CHI PO AND THE SORCERER, *Charles E. Tuttle, 1964*

THE GOBBLE-UP STORIES, *Bruce Humphries, 1967*

SEVEN COMEDIES BY MARIVAUX, *Cornell University Press, 1968*

FIVE COMEDIES OF MEDIEVAL FRANCE, *Dutton, 1970*

COLLECTED PLAYS, VOLUME ONE, *Unicorn Press, 1970*

COLLECTED PLAYS, VOLUME TWO, *Unicorn Press, 1972*

Oscar Mandel

Collected Plays

Unicorn Press

VOLUME TWO

The Monk Who Wouldn't

The Fatal French Dentist

Professor Snaffle's Polypon

The Sensible Man of Jerusalem

Adam Adamson

Of Angels and Eskimos

Typography by Alan Brilliant
Type-set in 11 Palatino Linotype by Achilles Friedrich
Printed by Halliday Lithograph Corporation

Library of Congress Catalogue Number 70-134738
Standard Book Number 0-87775-001-7

Das menschliche Gehirn sei meine Bühne,
Mein Lieblingsregisseur die Phantasie.

Contents

Foreword

An early version of *The Monk Who Wouldn't* appeared in the Summer 1962 issue of *First Stage: a Quarterly of New Drama*. The play is based on a Kabuki drama, *Kohya-No-Hijiri*, which I saw performed in Tokyo. I recollect only that the Japanese play was built around the Circean motif that I used for my own purposes. In the years 1963 and 1964 a group of actors under the direction of Walter Bodlander performed the play for the Pacifica Network Stations in Los Angeles, San Francisco and New York. John Pearson directed a staged reading at the Astor Playhouse in New York in 1965. In 1968 Mr. Pearson directed the play for a Fine Arts Festival in Fort Wayne, Indiana.

The Fatal French Dentist was printed for the first time in the Summer 1965 issue of *First Stage,* and a second time by Samuel French in 1967. The first professional production took place at the Santa Monica Playhouse in 1966 under Ted Roter's direction. In the same year the play was produced at the Barter Playhouse in Virginia. In 1968 and 1969 it was produced by the Canadian Broadcasting Corporation for audiences in Montreal and Toronto.

Professor Snaffle's Polypon appeared in the Summer 1966 issue of *First Stage.* I am indebted to my colleague J. Kent Clark for several excellent suggestions. But I had better add that the complete *Snaffle* was in my mind several years before I joined the faculty at the California Institute of Technology.

Adam Adamson was printed in the *Minnesota Review* in the spring of 1964 under the title *The Cage Opened, and Out Flew a Coward.*

In 1969 Carl Swenson directed a production of *Of Angels and Eskimos* at Paul Kent's Melrose Theatre in Hollywood.

Once again I wish to express my gratitude to the California Institute of Technology and the Andrew W. Mellon Fund for generous assistance in the preparation of this book for the press.

O.M.

THE MONK WHO WOULDN'T

CHARACTERS

PEDDLER

HUNTER

MONK

WOMAN

IDIOT

MONKEY

PROLOGUE

(A hill, a wood, stones, trees, undergrowth, a path. Enter the hunter, carrying a rifle)

HUNTER. Who I am, and what I am,
Ladies, children, gentlemen,
Let me gradually disclose
In honest English and plain prose.
And first, to make no mystery,
I am not what I seem to be.
My open hides a hidden smile,
My genial quip, dyspeptic guile;
Round about me, as I go,
Grass hides its head under a snow,
The tiger shivers, and the mole
Declines into a deeper hole.
Only the spider with some glee
Lifts one leg to wave at me
(I taught him all his strategy).
He catches flies, and I catch men,
For each mouth gobbles what it can:
Nature is that awesome harmony
Where each kills each in due degree,
And I, Nature's own patriot,
By doing harm, fulfill my lot.
Doing harm? Not quite. I grant
All men the very harm they want!
But here I might become abstruse,
And my audience, or myself, confuse.
Instead — stop! wait; what are these sounds?
A pair of lungs, a heart that pounds,
Two legs lifting a bulk uphill
With feeble muscles, and feebler will:
It is the peddler, jolly, fat,
The merry mouse to my grim cat.
Here is set our rendezvous;
He does not know it, but you do.

(Exit)

Scene One

(Enter the peddler, huge pack on his back. He deposits it, sits, wipes his face, sighs)

PEDDLER. This is a memorable sweat. Every faucet of my body is leaking. However, I believe I have reached the top of the mountain at last. It is true, as they said in the village, that it's an odd heap of a mountain. I passed a lizard bleaching himself on a stone who pricked his ears when he saw me, and slowly turned his head to watch me go by. A bird wearing a monocle beat the air in front of me, winked, grinned with his whole beak, and flittered away. Heaven be thanked, I am steeled by ignorance and will assume that science has discussed the habits of these animals with the most reassuring Greek words. Little flask, pretty flask, where are you? *(Drinks)* Oh my, I love to fatigue myself for the sheer pleasure of resting afterward. My poor outraged pump, don't I know that uphill is the wrong way for a man? Am I not the flower of cowards and a worshipper of sofas? Come, on my way down I'll deliver myself into the hands of Nature, and let gravity do the work. Oh if a man could sweat beer! *(Sighs, sings)*

> Fiddle-high and fiddle-low,
> The sea be salt
> The sand be dry,
> Heaven be a barrel, O!

> Falalol and falali,
> A child's a cup
> A man's a bowl,
> Heaven be a barrel, Ay!

> Diddle-di and —

(A shot off-stage)

Don't shoot, I haven't got a penny, take it all, it's a mistake, I have a wife!

(He hides behind a rock. Enter the hunter, holding the rifle)

HUNTER. I thought I heard something human snivel. Oho, a fat man. Your credentials, flesh?

PEDDLER. I am a proletarian, sir. I am a peddler, a negligible peddler not worth the attention of a bullet.

HUNTER. Well, let me look at you. Stand up. I'm not a thief. I am a hunter. And I was after a doe, not flabby peddler steak. Blow your nose and let's be friends.

PEDDLER. Did the beast go the other way?

HUNTER. Yes, I missed her, but on purpose. It was our first meeting, and

I thought a hint of her future was enough. To shoot a stranger is worse than murderous, it is downright uncivil. I like a bullet to be the last rebuttal in a long, familiar discussion. But tell me, my friend, can I make up in any way for the little fright I gave you?

> You are a stranger, I know,
> While I am at home with these boulders,
> I dwell among wolves, I throw
> A bearskin over my shoulders —

PEDDLER. A bearskin!

HUNTER.
> I sleep on leaves, I dine on rabbits,
> Rough in my speech, gruff in my habits —

PEDDLER. Granted, but a bearskin!

HUNTER. Why not a bearskin?

PEDDLER. In this age of luxury? You shock me into a state of compassion.

HUNTER. You say you are a peddler?

PEDDLER. A merchant. In good standing with the Council for the Propagation of Prosperity, in whose Annual Index I am marked with two stars and an exclamation point.

HUNTER. A clothes-peddler, perhaps.

PEDDLER. Yes. I am glad you wormed the fact out of me. A bearskin in our age is a sign of antiquated thinking. You must have a wife?

HUNTER. No.

PEDDLER.
> In that case, alas, I needn't show
> My muffs and scarves and bibelots —
> Gloves dying to be dropped by flirts
> And squeezed by playboys — Cleopatra's bow —
> Salome's veils — Bathsheba's skirts;
> And — how sad! — you won't care to see
> Stoles of paramecium hair — chemisettes
> Of felted cobwebs — impudent corsets
> Amused with sequins — laces, filigree,
> Threads spun of April air, frilled hairnets —
> Or my happy Sinkiang cloth,
> My Bechuanaland brocades —
> My satins light as eyelashes of maids —
> My chintzes woven out of Dnieper froth —
> My silks dyed in twelve Patagonian shades.

Women grow faint when I name my wares. For hunters, however, I carry a serviceable coonskin jacket. Its calm solidity is matched only by its unforgivable cheapness. Allow me to open my store at Point 46, Hunters' Jackets.

HUNTER. Stop! I want the richest lady's handkerchief you have.

PEDDLER. "Richest lady's handkerchief?" So, there is something here

besides bears. Interesting. Handkerchiefs, handkerchiefs. Tablecloths, sweaters, pumps — here we are. No. This one — no. I will not
sell it. I meant to hide it. Never. Oh, this perfume! Staggering.

HUNTER. Then show me another.

PEDDLER. I cannot sell it because the Countess Melibella of Deeper Sicily
once wept in it. It is, in other words, second-hand merchandise,
though I have washed it. But to me, who, secret admirer of the
Countess that I was, gathered its precious being up after she had
waved it toward her departing husband on the shore and dropped it
in despair when the ship melted into the horizon, to me it must ever
be treasurable far beyond the three-thousand ducats' worth of gold
threaded into its tissue. Oh sweet perfume, incumbent yet!

HUNTER. Here; this is all I have.

PEDDLER. Money! I will take three out of your three coins as a token of
your interest, and then give you the handkerchief gratis. I cannot
sell it.

HUNTER. So much for that.

PEDDLER. Yes. But you have deserved my curiosity. This rich lady — this
woman — I am thinking now of your wish to compensate me for
startling me a little with your musket. Why not show me, hm, the
moral contours of these parts?

HUNTER. I will gladly show you all I know. But what exactly are you
looking for in this very strange place?

> For here is a desert of woods;
> Of redundant paths which rarely
> Find the house that they seek;
> Of boars, parrots, raw wolves and surly
> Monkeys; and a few odd souls
> Ducking nature, who harass earth
> For an unpleasant grain or two,
> And wear black at their children's birth.
> Here is a land without skeptics
> And therefore full of miracles;
> Its acorns are wise, its needles
> Guess, its roots are oracles.
> Hesitant winds meander here
> Bearing invisible noises.
> A bird weeps with fear. The rain burns
> A cottage. The dead have voices.
> And the visitor who knocks
> At the door of this anxious land
> Returns to his city trembling
> And speaks of demons at hand.

PEDDLER. I believe you. And yet, your purchase of a golden handkerchief marks this as a region to which Culture is no stranger.

> As for me, to answer your question, it was a nose for business
> Sent me this way: a flair for investments, a financier's finesse.
> What else? I was asked to leave town. Let me tell you all.
> My wife, to be plain (which she is) caught me paying a call
> On the mayor's horizontal maid. At my bistro
> The word was Money. My thirst was high, my credit low —
> The wind was against sincerity: I made my pack.
> On to new markets! Tread the virgin track!
> Wake vapid countries to the drums of trade!
> Adorn the savage in ribbon and braid!
> Thus fired, I set forth in the teeth of derision,
> Lucre my purpose and Profit my mission.

So much for the mogul in me. I disclosed a while ago a lighter side to which I would like to return. I assure you that I am not all rebates and invoices. You know the old tune —

> The bird and the bee
> Tell their secrets to me,
> And labor, and pain,
> I profoundly disdain.

I have trudged eleven days, sobbing each mile in memory of my little wife. Today, climbing this mountain — I don't know how or why — the heat of the road, and the shameless honeysuckle exhaling upon me till I gasped, the thought of my former prosperity and my explosive youth — this and that set me longing again for the long-forgotten mercies of love. Help me to these delights, hunter, and I shall account you not only a customer, but a friend. Friend: it is a word I do not utter lightly.

HUNTER. I am not a pimp.

PEDDLER. That is an impish, impudent, and impeachable word. I did not mean to pay you.

HUNTER. Then you are an honest man. But is it possible that a person of your ample means (pardon me for noticing the obvious) should be swayed by the affections, or awake them in others?

PEDDLER. Sir, a sensible girl would sooner dine on a toothpick than embrace a thin man. These lean unions are the sallow fruit of maidenly despair: we are too few, we joyous, concrete, hyperbolical lovers, to serve all women. Look at this hemisphere of skin, compare the square inches of round pleasure I command to those of your undernourished bookkeepers. I stop before you compel me to boast.

HUNTER. I surrender, my friend. Tell me you are not offended with me.
No — if you pout, I shall break down and weep. Let me be your
guide. I know my way about these wicked parts — no man better.

PEDDLER. I am in your hands.

HUNTER. Climb on this boulder. *(Helps the peddler)* Stoutly, geology!
Now tell me, what do you see?

PEDDLER. A lot of shrubs and other nondescript vegetables. Wait, here's a
path! An angular, a guilty-looking path! Where does it go?

HUNTER.
It sneaks to a hut a day's walk
Away; a jumbled, limping, scrabbled hut
In a thing you'd call a clearing
Except none ever cleared it, but
The trees have better taste than
Growing there. The house is a sty;
No door; spiders haunt it with
Their gallop, and termites wade neck-high
Into its floors. You hear beam and board
Sigh, and spinelessly agonize,
While the wind nubs his head through the walls.
An idiot rules the mansion — cries,
Groans and jabbers in the breeze.
He is overlord of mice and rats,
Of moles, porcupines, asses, goats,
Cackling monkeys, squealing cats,
And — unbelievably — a child.

PEDDLER. A child?

HUNTER.
Why not? Golddiggers sift the mud,
The desert throws up Samarkand,
The gods prophesy in a gut —

PEDDLER. The story has a moral.

HUNTER.
The idiot has a daughter. The house,
The grounds I mentioned withered
From a sheer sense of futility.
Seeing her, they frittered —
For what's the use of tidy wainscots
When a girl's perfection is the rule?
Who cares for rugs and doorknobs
In Heaven's vestibule?
Here is a woman who could turn the dead
To lechery, and the meager saints
To the reconsideration
Of their prudence. Oh nothing paints
Her but herself in the embrace

Of three-dimensional air —
Lips that leap, eyes that bite,
Shoulders like peaches rounded where
A peddler's palm can nuzzle home,
Breasts that melt to the finger's dance —
Oh and what else? I blush; thighs
Straining like two thicker arms —
And this queen, diamonded in a slum,
This danger to melancholy, this patch
Of pleasure on the world's sour face
Could be the flame burst from your match.

PEDDLER. Help me down.

HUNTER.   It happened that the moon caught sight of her
Between two parted elbows of an elm one night
When, her daily misery accomplished,
She freed the tides of her black hair
And made her body ready for her nightly bath.
The moon stood still. Time gave one cry, and fainted.
The wind, its finger fidgeting a leaf, hung
Mid-air; all life — the very ants that trot
And fuss with midget speed —
All life broke off and stood solidified.
And now the moon sent down two rays
To cup the girl's enchanted face,
He gazed at her with white surprise
And love, such love as arid moons can feel.
At last he set her free, slung time over
His shoulder, and pushing stars aside,
Marched out the night. And then the woman bathed,
Neither she nor any animal
Remembering the miracle, except
She sang, and the creatures of the bearded wood
Were less ferocious for a night; there seemed
A heartbeat in the sod, all sensing it.
Beauty strikes such peace into the universe.

PEDDLER. Help me down this rock, brother. You have wiped twenty years
off my passport. This moon-stopper, you say, lives a day's walk from
here, and she will do the foul, exquisite deed?

HUNTER. Yes, if properly asked.

PEDDLER. Properly asked — oh, there's a splinter in every board. The open
sesame to these thighs must come a fortune. And what about the
blabbering father? Bless my soul! To be lunged at by an idiot in a fit
of outraged paternity!

HUNTER. As for money, a few bits of lace out of your pack will do quite as well. The girl has not seen ten human beings in her life: the rugged path, the queer menagerie, the vacant father, everything drives off the curious. She is less spoiled than a June apple. And for the man, she will put him to sleep with wine, though for that matter he can't distinguish you from the monkeys about him. Wait! I think I hear something. Listen.

PEDDLER. I don't hear a thing except the usual jingling of the leaves.

HUNTER. But I do. Stop. Up the mountainside. He's coming our way.

PEDDLER. Who is that?

HUNTER. A monk. I can hear him. He is praying. Excellent. I want my three coins.

PEDDLER. What three coins?

HUNTER. What three coins! The three coins I gave you for the handkerchief, my good melon.

PEDDLER. Hold on! Why should I give you *my* money?

HUNTER. Because I can tell the monk about our little path, and I will send him to save the girl's soul, and perhaps mend yours on the way. Here he comes.

PEDDLER. Not a word to the godster, do you hear? All right, here are the coins. Blackmailer!

(*Enter the young monk, carrying an umbrella and psalming to himself*)

MONK.   Nine thousand fifty-seven
              Names of God, help for evil,
              Balm and spell,
              Nine thousand fifty-seven
              Avenues from Hell —

Ah! God's peace upon you, gentlemen, and good afternoon. I am a stranger, and a traveler.

PEDDLER. And I am a merchant, sir, seeking an honest living among the native populations.

MONK. A very hot afternoon, isn't it?

PEDDLER. Steaming. I recommend a little rest on this very spot. There is a breeze here of whose services I have just now availed myself. I am, in fact, refreshed enough to be leaving again. I take this very unpleasant, spiny and potholed way behind the boulder to visit a remote customer, but I will no doubt have the pleasure of meeting you again on the main road. (*Picks up his bag*) Hunter, keep your side of the bargain.

MONK. Good afternoon.

(*Exit peddler. The hunter has secretly dropped the handkerchief*)

MONK. It is good to sit down. I am not yet accustomed to long walks. Do you live here, sir? Please excuse my curiosity.

HUNTER. With pleasure. Yes, I live here. I am a hunter by profession and keep the woods free of immortality.

MONK. I am a monk. Not a very modern thing to be, but it is an honest occupation.

HUNTER. And one, I understand, with a considerable future.

MONK. He, he, yes indeed. We used to say just that at the seminary; in jest, you know.

HUNTER. You have recently taken your vows? I am guessing because of your youth and your brand new cloak.

MONK. I am almost ashamed to say how recently. One week ago. This is my first enterprise among people. I am a little frightened by it all, though everybody has been very kind.

HUNTER. Most people indulge in kindness to strangers. It is so easy. But tell me, where will you spend the night? You too must forgive all my questions, but this is quite the wilderness.

MONK. It is a kind curiosity. I sleep on the ground, anywhere, with my head on my satchel. Animals mistake me for a lump of matter, and men see at a glance that I am a pauper. I am quite safe and comfortable.

HUNTER. Even so, allow me to make a suggestion. It is late afternoon, you are tired, and the country is new to you. I cannot offer much — I live alone and simply in a small cabin not far from here. But there is solid food, strong wine — I should say clear water for you — and fresh straw to sleep on. Stay for the night, and start again tomorrow.

MONK. I accept with gratitude, and I should be glad to pay you, but I have nothing of value, except, perhaps, prayers.

HUNTER. I will take one of medium intensity, and count myself well paid. But I am really very curious about you. I haven't seen a monk in many years. May I ask what brings you to these uncanny mountains?

MONK. I will be happy to answer you, but it is difficult.
How should I put it and not be laughed at? The cloister is a screen. —
But it goes back farther, to my being, I know, such a child.
I have seen those who saw, but what they saw I have not seen.
Do you understand? It is not much to know by rote,
As I have always done; nor to hate evil by page number
In travelogues and scriptures. One must touch knowledge.
And I am a silly, uncooked, unpeppered, vague cucumber
Sort of boy. I wanted to meet misery. But you're smiling . . .

HUNTER. No. Well now, yes, I did smile a little; but not sarcastically. Actually with pleasure. "Hate, evil, misery" — these are words which we worldly men seldom use. Enviable romanticism! To meet misery! To touch knowledge!

MONK. Yes; as it were, fill my book with indecent illustrations,

Take the size of scoundrels with my actual hand,
Dip my sandal into the bloody inundation
Of the earth, weep, and think, and faintly understand.
It would be hard, I think, to fail altogether,
As, of course, it would be impossible quite to succeed.
Evil — oh yes we knew sixteen certain, thirty-odd
Probable, and ninety-two fair reasons, bead by bead,
Why God sends evil to the world. For example, what's wrong is right:
Righteous man must *wrestle* for his crown; right must wrestle wrong;
So God makes wrong, gives it beer and beef, and sends it to the world
Plump tall and ruddy, to let virtue knock it down and
    prove itself strong.
Old truths! But I, I simply said — said almost inadvertently —
"Evil, yes; but why so *much*?" I tell you, inkstands spilled!
    But "Yes," I said,
"One cancer I should understand, one murder, one blind child,
    one flood,
One storm at sea, one war perhaps, with twenty young men dead;
But why so many? Why so much? Why so often? Why so long?"
And here I journey, asking why. One average life
Of hard, collected thought and sight may yield me some first
Syllables of the reply. And others, I hope, will arrive.

HUNTER. But why should you do this? Why all this trouble?

MONK. To love a God, may God forgive me, who deserves my love.
I told our abbot I loved God the way a dog loves, one ear
Always cocked for the devil-knows-what. Dear man! He blessed me
With a complicated sigh, and left me to my slow career,
Which, being the analysis of God, who is the supreme
Junction of love and horror, must give me occupation till
I too discover heaven or do not discover
Neither heaven, hell, or continuity of will.

HUNTER. Will you think me terribly shallow if I am frightened by the austerity of such a life? For, after all, you must be careful every moment not to become your own subject; if evil were to study evil, its conclusions, I should say, would be inexact.

MONK. I pray to be helped against temptation.

HUNTER. But can you tell a temptation from an opportunity? Do you know a sin when you meet one?

MONK. I think the old catalogues are still reliable.

HUNTER. Therefore, I take it, no wines, perfumes, featherbeds and women. You hate them.

MONK. They distract. I am afraid I sound a bit starched, and even presumptuous.

HUNTER. Not a bit. But what a painful life, and alas for the wines, perfumes, featherbeds and women!

> Oh give the world a chance
> To dance,
> And give us a little sin
> To be happy in!

But I'm joking. Are you rested enough to follow me home?

MONK. I am, thank you. But are you sure I won't intrude?

HUNTER. You will give me a great deal of pleasure, I assure you. Oh,
what's this? *(He picks up the peddler's handkerchief)* A lady's
handkerchief. And an expensive one! Look, these are golden threads.
The peddler must have dropped it.

MONK. Poor fellow. Is this a handkerchief, really? Such a beautiful thing!
It may be worth a whole day's work to him, or a whole day's walk to
come back for it.

HUNTER. Well, *I* certainly have no use for it. Hunter's toughness, you
know: nothing daintier than canvas. Why don't you keep it?

MONK. Oh no. He can't be very far, carrying his heavy load. Poor fellow,
I'll catch up with him in an hour. Well, I am very thankful for your
invitation, and perhaps we shall meet again.

HUNTER. No doubt. But I still urge you to stay. I know the house our friend
is planning to visit. He will reach it tomorrow morning, and stay in
it at least for the day. Spend the night here, leave fresh at dawn
tomorrow, and if you follow my directions you will have the handkerchief in his hands that same night. And, incidentally, the house
in question is well worth a detour. A kind of old fool lives in it with
a daughter and a curious assortment of animals. Our friend was
anxious to see the whole family. He seems to be drawn to animals.
In any event, as I said, you are sure to find him there. However, if
you prefer to start at once, please feel no obligation.

MONK. This is absolutely kind of you. I will stay, then, and spend the
night here.

HUNTER. Splendid! My rifle. Are you ready? I'm looking forward to a good
conversation over the fire.

> I want you to remember the hunter you met —

MONK. Oh, I will.

HUNTER *(aside)*. And the day you stumbled into his net.

(They leave together)

SCENE TWO

(Next evening. A clearing, though there are trees at the edge, and a good deal of shrubbery. A shoddy hut, one side open so that the interior is partially visible. No one is on stage as the curtain rises, but various animal noises are heard. A chimpanzee wanders out of the hut, jumps about, and vanishes. Soon after, the idiot slouches out with a bottle and a cup, and helps himself liberally. Finally the monk appears)

MONK.   Wheel of wheels,
                          Ray of rays,
                          Sublimity of sublimities,
                          Father of fathers, —

Good evening. *(The idiot grunts)* I am a monk traveling in the name of God, and I am looking for a peddler who lost a handkerchief. Is this the house where he stopped? *(The idiot offers him wine and begins to weep)* My poor man, what is the matter? Do you understand me? Oh what a miserable creature, and what a miserable house. Has God directed me to the beginning of my work? *(Loud)* Is anyone here? *(Only the noise of animals answers)* The hunter spoke of animals. This must be the place. *(Loud again)* Is — ah *(The music of a plucked instrument is heard within, and the voice of a woman)*

WOMAN *(sings)*.   Long will be brief,
                          One becomes two,
                          Time is a thief
                          But death is true.
                          How will a mortal lover last?

                          The roses ebb,
                          The kings dismount,
                          And step by step
                          They reach the ground.
                          How will a mortal lover last?

MONK.   Seek one not mortal, immortal,
                          But I should almost sin, and say,
                          At your own lips is the music
                          Angels for angels play.

(The music stops. He calls inside) May I come in? I am a harmless monk, please don't hide.

(The woman appears. She seems about twenty years old. A pause)

WOMAN. Strange person . . . Who are you? Welcome until you dissolve. Perhaps I am dreaming you. If I gaze at you too happily, will you turn into smoke and vanish?

MONK.   Perhaps. For I am smoke in the mind of God,
And my hardest bone is his loudest joke.
Strange person. May I, shyly, applaud
What you sang, the strings your fingers trod,
And the violas and oboes you spoke.

WOMAN. Smoke would not pay me a compliment. Will you melt if I kiss you? *(kisses him)* You are still here!

MONK. How forward you are. But I must remember to thank God before I go to sleep because He improved nature with such a creature as you are.

IDIOT. Greeshur! Greeshur! Greeshur! Liquor! *(Drinks)*

MONK. The poor old man. How pitiful. But please let me state my business. I am looking for a peddler who lost a handkerchief on the road. A hunter told me that I should find him here. Have you seen such a peddler?

WOMAN. No. No one ever comes here, almost. *(Reenter the monkey. Seeing the monk, he leaps upon him playfully and pulls him this way and that)* Go away! Naughty! Please forgive me. Off with you, little beast.

MONK. He's only playing. Off with you! Tch, tch —

WOMAN. Go back to the house, monster. *(Exit the monkey, squealing and dancing)* This is my family. Oh I am so ashamed before a stranger. You are the most beautiful being I have ever met. Stay with me.

MONK. I came to find a peddler. But I won't go away at once. He may have stopped somewhere else on his way. And here is a poor soul that needs help.

WOMAN.   It is my father; I am its child.
I do for it the best I can, giving
Bread and all it cares for, wine. I keep
Harmless animals who entertain me
With their simple inapprehensions;
I have my garden, at whose breasts I feed.
Our house died long ago, and we live
In its corpse. How shall I hold the bones
Together? We are too poor. And I nail
And saw all year, but clumsily, until
I am exhausted of all skills except
The skill of crying on the shoulders
Of the wood, where no heart beats at all
And all my joy is not to be rebuked.
Oh but I am boring you, and how rude
To let you stand. Please come in. No,
        please don't!
It's so grim inside. I don't know what to say.

MONK.   I'll stay outside then. How can I help you?
                     I will teach you how a prayer is a bird,
                     And good deeds, lighter than the frankincense,
                     Fly godward. Let me wash your father's face.
*(The woman goes into the house and returns with a basin and a rag.
While the idiot grunts in annoyance, the monk washes him)*
IDIOT. Wine! Hooo! *(He slops the whole bottle over his face)*
WOMAN. Oh! It's never any use, no use ever. Let me take him inside.
MONK. I am afraid I irritated him.
WOMAN. No no. Give me your hand, nicely now, give me your hand. Stand
     up, it's good night now. Good night. *(She takes him inside)*
MONK. Please don't scold him! It was my fault. *(Alone)* How gentle this
     girl seems, and how patiently unhappy. What is the topographical
     loveliness of the thin, smoking cascade and the rumored supremacy
     of the spirits? Beside a twenty-year-old girl nothing is alive. This is
     what the abbot hinted. And I forget his documented advice. How
     should a man act in the vicinity of love?
                     Oh I should like to know the use of beauty.
                     It seems so incidental to the stuff
                     And purpose of the world. Why should creation
                     Sing when it could grumble? *(Pause)* Now let me think
                     High thoughts and place a strong hand on my brow
                     Because it is when mind relaxes that
                     The body snaps the man and God is lost.
                     What do men do with beauty when a girl
                     Smiles so problematically? Each man
                     Resorts to beauty as he will. For one
                     It is a hospital: ill from breathing,
                     And having caught the ache of blueprints,
                     Ledgers and city landlords, he betakes
                     Himself to lyric poetry, or lets
                     The meadows cure him and the mountains nurse.
                     This does not please me. I like a strapping
                     Profiteer, a bulldog over gross and net,
                     To plunk, why not, two roses on his desk,
                     And slip aromas into computation.
                     For some, again, beauty is sheer reality,
                     Reality sheer beauty, form ineffable,
                     Resplendent order: music, they will say,
                     Music speaks the truth which science stammers.
                     And yet for others what is beauty but
                     A merest humblest annex to their house,
                     A pattern on their butter, rouge on a girl,

Daffodils or shepherds stitched in tablecloths.
Snobbish and indignant philosophers
Make short work of these; and yet the case
For easy answers is not easily
Confuted: what if the universe were shallow?
Or is beauty a snare? *(Pause; softly)* Gentle, gentle snare . . .
Oh monk, collar your thoughts! Arrange! so — now,
Topic, topic, topic, lucid excellent;
My subject — Beauty — in the clean abstract.
Some — said I — stab the shrubs with snide virtue
To scare away the soft danger of nymphs.
Yes, beauty's big with sin; but is it sin?
Or a bed for the lounging of idlers
And a noble excuse for shiftlessness.
Earnest reformers tend to abhor
Its invitation to neutrality.
"A still life! Where are the vitamins of *that?*
Away with the brush; *eat* the apple; work!"
I don't know if I can answer earnest men.
And some have entered beauty like a church,
Lit hyacinths for candles and shaken
Trees, which they called priestly, with their troubles,
And lifted up the dew in prayer
Under the soft humming of the stars.
But what if beauty had no end, because
It is the end? What if morality,
Religion, business and politics — God,
Brokers, saints and senators, longed only
To pose before the artist? To place form,
Mere form, upon this protoplasmic life,
To play inconsequential harmonies
Upon a theme of tears? No. I cannot be
Voided of ethics, blowing tunes into
An ocarina world. *(Startled)* Is she coming?
Dear God, I am troubled because of this girl.
She kissed my cheek, and then what argument
Appeases or outsmarts the gorgeous blood?
When she returns, oh I must press her
For a longer kiss. How sweet, how good
The night seems, and the honeysuckle
Vaporing the air! It is the happy
Funeral of evil, and in mock mourning
The trees carry the stars aloft. She is here!

WOMAN. I have put him to bed. Dear young man, will you dine?

MONK. Yes. Thank you. And then I am going away to find the poor peddler. He may have come by and never stopped.

WOMAN. But it's too dark to find a poor peddler. Sleep here, please stay, and entertain me. Don't answer! Sit here, and drink and eat dinner. Here is a clean cup for your wine.

MONK. I don't drink wine.

WOMAN. Why not?

MONK. God tells us beware of drunkenness. Wine is a mitigated evil; that is to say, it is not scandalously bad, and several minor saints have praised it. But because it is the first step to luxury, I had rather drink water.

WOMAN. What a funny speech! Well, here is water. (He drinks) Now let me drink from your cup, the way lovers always do. Will you have meat, vegetables, and bread?

MONK. I am not allowed meat.

WOMAN. Why not?

MONK. God tells us not to kill life. Eating the meat of an animal accustoms us to the mutilation of life. I myself, quite privately, believe that a soul dwells in all beings endowed with eyes. Therefore I will eat only a little bread and these beans.

WOMAN. You speak so strangely.

MONK. I am very sober.

WOMAN. Sober indeed!

> You are like the red tempest
> Hesitating one instant
> Astraddle two waves.
>
> You are like the violent falcon
> Deceiving the sky with stiff
> Horizontal wings.
>
> You are like the tilting steed
> Stunned in his rampage by fear
> Of one new noise.

Monk, are you afraid of me? (She takes his hands)

MONK (standing up). No! We are under God. (He sits down again) I shall eat another piece of bread.

WOMAN. Who is God? You have mentioned the name several times. And you took your hands away.

MONK. My poor absent sister, is it possible? And do I have to speak of Him while munching bread? He is the invisible terrible No between yourself and sin, and the nebulous Yes which fumbles us to heaven, we hope.

WOMAN. Is it he who told you not to drink wine and eat meat?

MONK. Yes. Invisibility has written books on such matters.

WOMAN. I think invisibility is very silly. I should be sorry if *I* were invisible. Shouldn't you?

MONK. Yes.

WOMAN. Am I beautiful?

MONK. Every star in the sky, I think, is an eye admiring you.

WOMAN. What pretty things you say! I shall reward you by excusing you from meat and wine. And to thank me for the reward you may kiss my lips.

MONK. I may not kiss a woman.

WOMAN. Why could that be?

MONK. Because all philosophy and religion regard woman as a great distraction to accurate thought.

WOMAN. But what if the woman is beautiful?

MONK. Why then she ought to be especially feared and avoided.

WOMAN. And if she is ugly? Can you kiss her then?

MONK. Then the danger, I suppose, is less. But I am not sure, because our books seem to be concerned most of the time with beautiful women.

WOMAN. But if you may not kiss a beautiful woman, may you touch her with your hand?

MONK. By no means. We are much warned against it, except in greetings, like good morning or good evening.

WOMAN. Then good evening and good morning and forever good morning and good evening! I knew your books would find some way out of all that grumpiness. *(She takes his hands again)*

MONK. You are laughing at me a little.

WOMAN. They are the whitest hands I have ever seen. I will call them pilgrims, and me their shrine!

MONK. Pilgrims and shrines! You know something about the world after all!

WOMAN. I do? What curious things hands are. They have a thousand little private syllables — like balancing with the wrist to say "vaguely" — or tightening to say "I am afraid"; they serve; they are angry; they protest; and they are the paths by which lovers' hearts travel when the words don't dare as yet. Please don't frown! You are disappointed because my hands are not as white as yours. But my heart is as soft as your palm. *(The monk rises in great agitation)*

MONK. This is wrong. I have to be on my way. The peddler.

WOMAN. If I were a horrid leper you wouldn't go.

MONK. Now you are crying! What shall I do? All this is *so* unbecoming. We are strangers, after all.

WOMAN. Then sit down again and tell me who you are. I forgot to ask you. You are a monk, and you are looking for a peddler. Is that your profession?

MONK. I am a very young man not worth anybody's attention. I was weaned from the seminary a week ago to try the world and to make certain observations upon it which demand an absolutely clear mind. My biography, so far, would read, "He was born and raised."

WOMAN. That is so marvelously simple!

> Thank you for being born,
> For I was born as well, and so there's hope,
> Since I have seen the most eccentric birds
> Meet on a single thorn.

> Thank you for being raised,
> You might have died, and I too, on the way,
> We might have lain together grave by grave,
> And never faced.

And now we are getting to know each other. You have even met my family.

MONK. Why do you keep all these animals?

WOMAN. They come to me, and stay.

MONK. Is your father kind to you as far as he can be?

WOMAN. As kind as the moss: indifferent but soft.

MONK. Is your mother dead?

WOMAN. I don't know. What is this on your forehead? So deep a canal my little finger goes swimming in it!

MONK. Here? Why, I'm not sure. It feels like a furrow.

WOMAN. The first whipmark of time, and you didn't know it. Don't you gaze at yourself in the mirror?

MONK. No, of course not. Why should I?

WOMAN. Because your beauty would fill you with reverent pleasure.

MONK. My beauty! The abbot never mentioned such a thing to me. What an extraordinary idea! My beauty!

WOMAN. Yes, your beauty. I am bewitched by that little sluice between your nose and the middle of your upper lip. And bedeviled by your green eyes and the long lashes that make awnings over them. But now I want you to attend to me. Do you see this monstrous spot on my cheekbone? I would like to know whether it reminds you of a cockroach or some other ugly insect.

MONK. A pretty insect; a pretty ladybug dozing on a white leaf.

WOMAN. Is it? I will tolerate it from now on for your sake.

MONK. Sing for me.

WOMAN.   But I am singing all the while!
              How deaf you must be
              When all my nerves
              Sing in love's incalculable style.

              Why did you wait so many years,
              My unforgivable? I begged you
              To hurry, the wind heard,
              Only you covered your ears.

              So now at last let fingers clutch,
              Our limbs be neighborly,
              Breath dive into breath,
              Shoulder and shoulder touch.

(The monkey appears, and moans toward the woman, and tries to be cuddled) Naughty. I'll slap your muzzle! *(She chases the monkey)*

MONK.   There is something godless in the night
              When the summer brews honey double sweet
              And a girl's consonants chime as though
              Abstractions and lilies could meet. *(The woman returns)*

I want to be alone. I am far from calm. I need the critical sun. The best method is to sleep out of the moon's reach. I can sleep right here — I need nothing at all. And thank you so much. Give me your hand and let us say good night.

WOMAN. Your hand is trembling. Why are you afraid, when the very sparrows eat out of my palm?

MONK. Sparrows! Sparrows indeed! If I were a sparrow I too would nest in your hand. Who ever heard of a moral sparrow? I want to sleep. I've a long journey tomorrow, and I intend to dream of peddlers. Good night. Why don't you speak frankly and say good night?

WOMAN. But, dearest, do you go to bed without bathing?

MONK. Bathing! I have not enough philosophy left to turn a gnat from a spider web — I would kiss you if half a crumb less than God himself stood between us — and you talk of scrubbing backs and soaping faces!

WOMAN *(laughs)*. My strange lover!
                     I am not sure at all I know
                     What you say,
                     But neither do I know
                     Why the branches row
                     And why the squirrels don't pray
                     And why my love is rougher
                     Than the sudden undertow

> That pulls the swimmer in the bay
> And deep, beneath its cover,
> Makes his woebegone body play.

Come with me, monk, by the pool, where no one watches, neither above nor below. Come with me, let go your dusty fear. Come.

MONK. Take your bath! I want to be alone.

WOMAN. What a pity! I had such games in mind for the moon in the water and you and me.

MONK. What are you doing?

(The woman begins to undress among the shrubs)

WOMAN. Poor moon! he never says a word and acts quite cold,
> But at my touch he bursts into a hundred drops of gold,
> Yet though he's shattered the moment I come near,
> His higher self gives me a circular sneer —

MONK. You don't mean to undress completely before me?

WOMAN. I always undress here because I can hang my clothes on the twigs.
> You can go inside the house if you wish, my sweet.

MONK. Why should *I* go inside the house? Have *I* anything to be ashamed of?

WOMAN. Perhaps. Sweetest, won't you come with me?

MONK. Don't step nearer! I ask you.

WOMAN. Wait for me! *(Exit, singing)*

> My rose will endure,
> An angel is man,
> Kings will be poor
> And three shall be one.
> Then, then my mortal love will last.

MONK *(on his knees)*.

> My first night, my God, and I am slipping
> Out of my virginity glance by glance,
> Nothing by nothing. I should have been blind.
> And they needed a man to count the loaves
> And sell our garden's carrots; and the trade
> Was brisk. I might, by mere neglect of life,
> Have got myself a nook in Paradise
> To grow lilac and lilies. This girl
> And my first night — my first night, stupid
> With desire — I will be surely grasping her,
> And lust away my mind. And me, unpacked,
> The wrapping scarcely off — evil merchandise.
> I, study evil! The hunter was right —
> Corruption in its carcass pondering
> Corruption, is that science? And my mind,

The fragile egg it is, my poor offspring,
How will it fledge into the sky? Too hard
For me. Let me go home. The stillborn cell
For me, and the heart ticking as even
As the clock of the refectory. Up! *(He rises)*
This is much better. This solitude needs
Prosy neighbors to laugh at one's lechery.
If only the abbot were here suavely
To advise me. But oh won't it be rude
To leave without thank you, goodbye, a blessing
On her innocence, and several maxims
Recommending God in time of trouble?

(The monkey enters and dandles awhile in front of him)

Here, little fellow. If you could speak
You might say goodbye for me. Should I go?
Oh God, if this beauty were meant for taste —
Kiss unphilosophically, the way
This ape hugs another, the tingle, amusement
Of the skin, the friction, delirium — Lord!
I'm frightened, the flesh is too far from reason.
I want to stay. Who's that? The monkey
In a tree. I'll vanish before she comes.
The cunning of the white bodies of girls!
Dark pool, ignited by a water-lily.
Run, monk, take your mind in your hands and run!
Ah but the peddler, the peddler! I came
On business. I am sure he lost his way.
I came on worthy business. Let me leave
The handkerchief with her, then say goodbye,
Quickly depart, yet say goodbye; that way
She will not think that monks are harsh or clumsy.

(He pulls the golden handkerchief out of his sleeve) How the moon spanks these golden threads. Oh? *(The monkey, uttering a squeal, jumps up to the monk, and now tries to wrest the handkerchief from him)* No, it's not for you! Go away. Uah! Come back! *(The monkey snatches the handkerchief, and, gibbering with joy, runs away)* Come back! Where did he go? Come back; tk, tk, tk — I'll give you peanuts for it! Now he is probably high in a tree playing with it, or blowing his snout. How extraordinary — why should a monkey want a golden handkerchief? Well. No peddler, no handkerchief, no reason to stay. Except, of course, to tell her the monkey has stolen it. A good reason. Great heaven, there he is again! With the

peddler's bag! So! He is here after all! She lied! What does all this mean? *(The monkey opens the bag, leaping excitedly between it and the monk, and inserting the handkerchief where it belongs)* Yo ho, old peddler, are you there? What does the little beast want? I've heard stories of men murdered and faithful animals leading the law to their bodies. Yes, yes. What are you trying to tell me, poor squealer? Here is my hand. Yes, tell me all, or take me to the poor man. He seems to understand me! *(As though perplexed, the monkey returns to the pack and removes its contents methodically, laying all similar articles in separate piles)* Now he is sorting the peddler's merchandise as though he had seen the man do it. As though it were his own. As though — *(all the unseen animals suddenly make their noises)* My God, my God — can it be true? Are you the —? Oh God, and the other animals, are they —? A witch! God save me! Ah! Don't touch me! My umbrella!

(He runs away. The monkey dashes after him, then returns disconsolately and potters with the clothing. The animal noises die out, and all is silent when the woman returns)

WOMAN. He left. The peddler warned him, and he fled.
    And did you tell him how, for lust of me,
    While breathing rough, eyes shuttered, happy flesh
    Minutely bent on cavalcade between
    Indulgent thighs, you turned to what you were,
    All guzzle, tipple, lick and nuzzle?
    Turned, I say, to what you were, for though a witch,
    I never changed, I but confirmed a man.
    But you, poor monk, you should have held me fast,
    I was your health, your equilibrium!
    You needed my hilarities moistly infused
    Into your mind, green veins in sallow leaves.
    There was no sin in me if there is none
    In stars that drizzle from the face of night
    Like perspiration, or in the heaving wind.
    Denial such as yours, poor monk, belongs
    To rotting men two fingers from their grave,
    Bald craniums, sausage legs, and wattled chins.
    So be it. Hunter, I have done your bidding.
    Time, gallop, time, grizzle him! Old he came
    And old he goes. *(The monkey tugs at her)*
    Follow him and serve him.
    My work is done, now I can rest.
    Monk and monkey, go your ways and weep.
    When daylight comes, the witch must sleep.

Epilogue

(Same as Scene One. Next afternoon. The hunter sits bathing his feet in a large basin as the monk appears on a height, transformed into an old man)

MONK. Hunter! Hunter! *(He leaps off a boulder and almost falls)*

HUNTER. Slow and easy, granddad. Shake your head four times, say "the will of Somebody be done," and the dizziness will pass. At your age one doesn't go diving from a rock like a chamois.

MONK. "At my age?" Hunter, look at me — we met yesterday! I'm the innocent monk.

HUNTER. My word, so you are! Let me rub my feet dry. *(He slips into his boots and rises)* Oho, I understand. It's a disguise. Shrewd, sir monk! — a disguise to inquire into the evils of the wicked world without falling into temptations on the way.

MONK. I don't know what you mean. But I'm dreaming. I don't recognize my own voice, I have aches in my waist and in my legs — I walk doubled over — and you — *(frightened)* hunter, who are you? and who am I? Why did you pretend not to recognize me? Why do you babble about disguises?

HUNTER. How in the devil's name should I recognize you? This is no place for a costume party, you know. Here's a basin — pardon a few specks of muck in the water — look at yourself! *(The monk looks; there is a long pause)*

MONK. It's a dream. I am twenty years old. *(Shaking his head)* I have no wrinkles. I have no wrinkles at all. And my hands never tremble. *(Puts down the basin)*

HUNTER *(sententious)*. Live and change, change and live.

MONK. Now I begin to understand the truth.
> And I know you — a farcical spirit
> That fools between the first and fortieth wink
> Of God. Therefore before you rub your hands
> Or oil your mind for your next prank, let me
> Assure you that I am not frightened,
> And distinctly not tempted into anger.
> All I ask of God is to wake up;
> That is how sublimely simple it is.
> He will not let me creep at an angle
> Through the woods, and speak like sandpaper,
> My mouth between two corrugated cheeks,
> Laughed at by some minimal devil.

HUNTER. Minimal!

MONK.   Was I too slow hating the woman?
               Pardon me, pardon me. But I ran!
               I am not an animal. Sweet God,
               I need so many, many years to find
               Your face among the sins. This is
               Unjust. Wake up. Oh and with hurrah
               I broke the lasso of her arms, and cried
               "Me for the brambles, me for the needles!"
               Yet when I sang, after I had refused
               The girl, God I shall never forget it,
               I sang, and my voice splintered!

(*He becomes aware of the hunter once more*)

               As I stand
               And curse you, I never touched the girl.

HUNTER. I am not at all sure I understand your remarks, my venerable friend, or the strange name you called me. You monks are so superstitious. But what a pity you did not touch the girl! If I had been twenty ... Still, all things considered, you're not so badly off. Look here: one, no more anxiety about the world's carnivals, for no one will invite you; two, the help of little boys to cross the streets; and three, the end of all that unpleasant dissertation on evil you were going to bore the world with. I think we should celebrate your good luck.

MONK (*no longer hears the hunter*). Prayers, fasts, and abstinence will remind Him he has overlooked an item here. I will pray; I will wander and pray yard by yard until I wake up with my youth again. I have forty, fifty years to go. My health is superb! I could work another sixty years.

HUNTER. At your age?

MONK. You're an illusion! A warning! A trial! Devil, I exorcise you!
       (*He moves away*)

HUNTER (*half-aside*). It's been tried before.

MONK. God of mine, was I too slow hating the witch?
               But I ran! What more could I do? I ran!
               Me for the brambles! Me for the needles!
                       Total of sums,
                       Period of phrases,
                       King of ministers,
                       Truth of opinions,
                       Adorer of lovers,
       Save me, cleanse me, harbor me, cure me, praise me, hold me, remember me, remember me. (*Exit*)

HUNTER. What a lot of mumbling. (*He takes off his boots and starts to wash his feet again. The monkey crosses the stage in the monk's direction. The hunter laughs*)

> The sun warms his toes,
> The moon duly moons.
> Matters stand as matters should,
> And each thief has his spoons.
>
> The soldier has his horse,
> The sailor has his boat.
> Bird flies, fish dips, hare jumps,
> And gangsters vote.
>
> I like to do a touch of right,
> I like to touch a bit of wrong.
> The two together make a rhyme,
> With which, good souls, I end my song.

THE END

THE FATAL FRENCH DENTIST

CHARACTERS

BILL FOOT

MARY FOOT

BILL NETHERGOOD

MARY NETHERGOOD

BILL BILLIARD

MARY BILLIARD

SCENE ONE

(A room. Mr. Foot is working on a personality quiz in his newspaper; Mrs. Foot is doing nothing)

MR. FOOT. Newspapers are becoming more educational all the time. This quiz is called "Are You Socially Acceptable?"

MRS. FOOT. It seems a little insulting for them to doubt it, considering we're subscribers.

MR. FOOT. Nonsense. It's scientific. You mark four points if your answer is (a), three points for (b), two points for (c), one point for (d). Then, when you're finished you add up your points and check them against the table of social acceptability here at the bottom of the page. It's printed upside down so you're not tempted to cheat. Well, here goes. Question one: When you leave a party, do your hosts weep to see you go? (a) Torrents; (b) A little; (c) Not at all; (d) They grin. *(He makes a mark)*

MRS. FOOT. What are you answering?

MR. FOOT. This quiz is confidential, but so far I'm satisfied with myself. Two: How do you behave when an unwelcome guest rings your doorbell just as you are settling down for a quiet evening with your wife and/or TV? (a) You kill him.

MRS. FOOT. I'm sure I've never done that.

MR. FOOT. (b) You slam the door in his face; (c) You tell him to come in if he must, but to keep his mouth shut; (d) You make him feel he is the nicest thing that could have happened to you that evening. *(He makes a mark)*

MRS. FOOT. I would not answer the doorbell at all and pretend I wasn't home. It's the best solution, because it keeps you happy and doesn't offend your guest. I think killing him is simply too awfully brutal and unkind.

MR. FOOT. You do go on, don't you, my dear. Question three: What do you do when your hostess serves you a dish you do not like?

MRS. FOOT. *I* eat everything.

MR. FOOT. (a) You throw it on the floor; (b) You tell her you'll eat it but you wouldn't feed it to your hogs.

MRS. FOOT. Oh, that's a terrible thing to say.

MR. FOOT. Why?

MRS. FOOT. Well, I mean, throwing something on the floor isn't so bad; nobody need notice, especially if there's a low-hanging tablecloth, and maybe a cat or a dog under the table. But to say "I wouldn't give it to my hogs" is awfully rude.

MR. FOOT. I suppose it is, and yet when you look at it sympathetically it really isn't. Let's say the husband overhears me — "I wouldn't give these asparagus to my hogs," says I. He rises from the table, he's furious, "You've got a nerve telling my wife you wouldn't give these asparagus to your hogs!" "What," says I, "would *you?*" "Of course not," he hollers. "Well, that's precisely what I said," I reply, and he crumples.

MRS. FOOT. Well, fortunately there aren't any hogs in our dear little town, so why trouble our heads about them?

MR. FOOT. The hogs are metaphorical, my dear. Let me see, where was I? (c) You eat it but you sulk for the rest of the evening; (d) You wrench your mouth into a wonderful smile and you say —

(The doorbell rings)

MRS. FOOT. Oh, maybe it's somebody exciting at last!

MR. FOOT. Hope springs eternal.

(Mrs. Foot opens the door. Enter Mr. and Mrs. Nethergood)

MR. and MRS. NETHERGOOD. Hello hello hello hello.

MR. and MRS. FOOT. Hello hello hello hello hello.

MRS. FOOT. Wonderful to see you people! Those dear Nethergoods!

MRS. NETHERGOOD. So good to see you two again, plump and ruddy and all.

MR. NETHERGOOD. How *are* you, Bill?

MR. FOOT. How are *you*, Bill?

MRS. FOOT. Bill, get the Nethergoods a drink. Sit down, children, sit down, Mary.

MRS. NETHERGOOD. We absolutely can't, Mary dear. You stop those drinks, Bill.

MRS. FOOT. Why? What's the matter?

MRS. NETHERGOOD. We're on our way to a wedding. Bill Lumley and Mary Finkelberg, do you know them?

MRS. FOOT. I don't think so. Come on, tell us all about it, do sit down, both of you — five minutes, that's all, we'll set the alarm if you insist; I want to hear all about the wedding.

MRS. NETHERGOOD. All right, five minutes, but no drinks, not a thing. Sit down, Bill.

MR. FOOT. All right, but what's the rush? Just another wedding. And what's a wedding these days? A legal requirement for a divorce.

MRS. NETHERGOOD. But that's just it. This is *not* just another wedding. I'll tell you all about it if you swear to take the secret to the grave with you. Bill, you naughty, that goes for you too, you mustn't tell anybody —

MR. FOOT. I never tattle about people I don't know.

MRS. NETHERGOOD. Well — it's a dreadful story.

MRS. FOOT. Wonderful. Go on!

MRS. NETHERGOOD. The Lumleys and the Finkelbergs had agreed not to invite anybody on either side beyond uncles and aunts. Parents, grandparents, brothers, sisters, authentic uncles and genuine aunts, and that was to be all for the dinner. No cousins.

MR. NETHERGOOD. Mark this. No cousins.

MRS. NETHERGOOD. And that's where the roof fell in. It seems that Bill Lumley's cousin just came back from three years of mission work in darkest Boola-Boola. He's alone in the world, the natives ate his wife, he comes to New York penniless, all yellow with malaria and something shot off, an arm or leg, I don't know what —

MRS. FOOT. So?

MRS. NETHERGOOD. So, Bill Lumley decides to make an exception for the one cousin, in view of the special circumstances, you see. Well! The Finkelbergs go wild. *They've* got a cousin, it seems, who almost drowned while trying to leave a submarine before it reached the surface. A tragic case, half a lung taken out, a few medals on the sound side of the chest — so why the Boola-Boola cousin but not the submarine cousin? I assure you the marriage just about broke up. Mary's mother said that without the submarine cousin the marriage was off. Bill's folks answered that one exception was enough, because once you started adding exceptions you'd soon have the hall full of them.

MRS. FOOT. So?

MRS. NETHERGOOD. So, Mary said she surely wasn't going to give up Bill because of a cousin who didn't know enough to keep the door of a submarine closed when he was under water. And then she asked Bill to give up his missionary cousin. So Bill blew up and then Mary blew up and it was a mess.

MR. FOOT. But they patched it up?

MRS. NETHERGOOD. Yes, they decided to invite everybody. But nobody is talking to anybody; even the bride and groom aren't on speaking terms.

MR. FOOT. A quiet wedding, in short.

MRS. NETHERGOOD. Aren't people just too horribly stupid and cruel?

MR. FOOT. The trouble is, they're not socially acceptable.

MRS. FOOT. I always tell Bill, if only people were reasonable and did what's right, the world would be a better place to live in.

MR. NETHERGOOD. Bless you, those are almost exactly my words, aren't they, Mary?

MRS. NETHERGOOD. Be quiet, dear, and let me speak. What was I saying? Oh, yes, we absolutely must go. We only stopped in to bid you to a homely feast chez nous —

MR. NETHERGOOD. At Nethergood Manor —

MRS. NETHERGOOD. Next Saturday, dinner at eight; we want you to meet an exciting dentist visiting from Paris. He's looking into photodontic equipment in the States.

MR. NETHERGOOD. Dental surgery, actually. Top man in his field.

MR. FOOT. How drilling. (*He and Mr. Nethergood enjoy themselves*)

MRS. FOOT. You're an angel to ask us, Mary, and we'll be delighted to come. I simply adore Parisians. France wouldn't be the same without them.

MRS. NETHERGOOD. That's why we're asking only the two of you. We didn't want to scare him with too many strange people. Well — (*she embraces Mrs. Foot*) we've got to run.

MR. NETHERGOOD. Sorry we can't stay, old Billberry, but I'll hold you to a double scotch next time.

MR. FOOT. Great. Say, do you know the difference between a double scotch on the rocks and Siamese twins on gravel?

MRS. FOOT. Do stop, my dear, you're unbearable.

MRS. NETHERGOOD. Never mind, I think he's a love. Well, 'bye 'bye now.

MR. NETHERGOOD. 'Bye 'bye.

MRS. FOOT. 'Bye 'bye.

MR. FOOT. 'Bye 'bye.

(*The Nethergoods leave*)

MRS. FOOT. So here we are again. The excitement's over.

MR. FOOT. I hope they serve broccoli.

MRS. FOOT (*to herself*). Me, my husband, and the question why. Maybe something exciting will happen again before I pass on.

MR. FOOT. It says in the paper that according to the best thought of the day, people like you and I live the desperate lives of meaningless automata in a mass-organized society which has lost touch with the inner springs of a rich and fruitful existence.

MRS. FOOT. Well, the newspapers always make things sound more exciting than they are. It's true that you have your position in the company and we have our friends and our home and our birch tree in the backyard, but I don't think that the paper is right to point to people like us as models of anything.

MR. FOOT. I'd better get back to the quiz.

(*The doorbell rings*)

MRS. FOOT. More excitement I bet!

MR. FOOT. With this infernal doorbell going all day I'll never find out how socially acceptable I am.

(*Mrs. Foot opens the door. Enter Mr. and Mrs. Billiard*)

MR. and MRS. BILLIARD. Hello hello hello.

MR. and MRS. FOOT. Hello hello hello hello.

MRS. FOOT. Mary! How lovely to see you again! And dear old Bill with you for a change!

MR. FOOT. Dear old Bill and Mary.

MR. BILLIARD. Dear old Billberry and good old Mary.

MRS. FOOT. Come in and sit down. Fix the drinks, Bill.

MRS. BILLIARD. Don't make a move, either one of you. We're on our way to a funeral and we can't stay but a minute.

MRS. FOOT. What funeral? You scare me.

MRS. BILLIARD. Mary Spiffin's husband — don't you remember Mary Spiffin, at the Orphanage Circle?

MRS. FOOT. Of course I do.

MR. FOOT. You mean Bill Spiffin who was in gaskets?

MR. BILLIARD. That's right. Millions in the old sock, you know.

MRS. BILLIARD. Anyway, this is one funeral we don't want to miss.

MRS. FOOT. And yet you talk about running away without even telling us. No, I'll really be unhappy if you don't sit down for at least five minutes. We'll set the alarm if you insist.

MR. FOOT. Come on, be friendly with the natives.

MRS. BILLIARD. All right, but five minutes is all, I swear.

MRS. FOOT (to Mr. Billiard). Here, put this pillow behind your back.

MR. BILLIARD. Thanks. Go on, Mary, open the old valves and tell her about the funeral.

MRS. FOOT. Yes. You were saying —

MRS. BILLIARD. Well. About a year ago Mary Bartlett's husband died.

MR. BILLIARD. You knew Bill Bartlett, the piston man — left her holding the bag, but there were millions in it.

MR. FOOT. Sure I remember him. I wrote a policy for his outfit.

MRS. FOOT. So?

MRS. BILLIARD. So — the funeral that Mary Bartlett gave her husband positively turned Mary Spiffin's head. She was so jealous it was all she could do to bring out a decent condolence. There was Bill Bartlett lying on an adjustable mattress, satin and velvet and Venetian lace on the sides of the coffin, and looking ten years younger than what he'd been, and holding his pipe in his hand!

MR. FOOT. Bury me with a cigarette in my teeth, will you?

MRS. FOOT. Sssh.

MRS. BILLIARD. And when I say coffin, I should say triple casket: one of mahogany, the next of bronze, and the third a genuine Roman sarcophagus, flown over especially by an antique dealer in Italy. As for the guests, half of General Motors was there — with a floral piece by the Chairman of the Board himself — "For Bill Bartlett, whose pistons shall not be forgot." The eulogy was spoken by the archbishop, and while the organ played they had birds twittering I don't know where, it was deep and inspirational and we all cried. I counted fifteen boys in white standing around the caskets like so many cupids, you never saw anything so cute in your life. And in the midst of all, there was Mary Bartlett sobbing her heart out and saying "If only Bill were alive, he'd enjoy himself so much today."

MR. FOOT. Poor Bill.

MRS. BILLIARD. Well, you should have beheld Mary Spiffin. She was sitting there with her lips pressed together taking it all in, and swearing to herself she'd show that Mary Bartlett a funeral when the time came. But of course you can't just ask your husband to up and die so you can throw a big funeral — I don't think Spiffin would have gone in for that at all, because he wasn't the kind of man who approves of making a show, if you know what I mean, he was really a quiet sort of man. So all she could do was stare at him a great deal. And then suddenly he popped off after all — three days ago it was —

MR. BILLIARD. Keeled over while he was having a drink with the boys at the Gasket Association of America convention.

MRS. BILLIARD. Aren't men unpredictable? And that was that.

MRS. FOOT. What an opening for Mrs. Spiffin!

MRS. BILLIARD. Exactly. Naturally Mary Bartlett is at the top of her guest list, and I'm dying to see what she's rigged up. Well, we're sitting here chattering with you. Come on, Bill, we'd better be off.

MR. BILLIARD. My dear, you've forgotten what you came here for.

MRS. BILLIARD. Didn't I ask you over for Saturday?

MR. BILLIARD. No, you didn't ask them over for Saturday.

MRS. BILLIARD. I'm in a daze.

MRS. FOOT. Actually —

MRS. BILLIARD. You must join us next Saturday night — a simple get-together, maybe a couple of bridge tables.

MR. BILLIARD. Bridge at the Billiard Estates.

MRS. FOOT. We'd love to come, it sounds delightful, but I'm afraid we're taken next Saturday.

MR. FOOT. Broccoli and all the rest.

MRS. BILLIARD. What a pity.

MR. BILLIARD. A blow to the solar plexus, old Billberry.

MRS. BILLIARD. And I'd planned to ask the Nethergoods, too. Are you really sure?

MRS. FOOT. Positive. Oh my, I *am* sorry, though. It does sound like fun.

MRS. BILLIARD. I'll call the Nethergoods anyway and we'll catch you another time.

MRS. FOOT. Oh, but it's the Nethergoods we're going to! (*Mr. Foot coughs*)

MRS. BILLIARD (*miffed*). Oh, I see. That's odd.

MR. BILLIARD. Yes, that's odd. What's odd about it, dear?

MRS. BILLIARD. Nothing. Are the Nethergoods throwing a party?

MRS. FOOT. Oh no, nothing like that.

MRS. BILLIARD. They *usually* ask us.

MR. BILLIARD. How about our funeral, Mary?

MRS. FOOT. Couldn't you go a little later, and stay here a while?

MRS. BILLIARD. No, we really can't. Well, goodbye, my dear. *(She embraces Mrs. Foot)* 'Bye 'bye.

MR. BILLIARD. 'Bye 'bye.

MRS. FOOT. 'Bye 'bye.

MR. FOOT. 'Bye 'bye. We'll see you, Billberry old man.

(The Billiards leave)

MR. FOOT. Well, you've did it.

MRS. FOOT. Don't be funny. What was I to do?

MR. FOOT. Why did you have to tell the Billiards we were going to be at the Nethergoods? Wasn't it enough to say we weren't available on Saturday?

MRS. FOOT. I just saw a little deeper into the situation than you did, that's all, my dear. Mary Billiard was going to call the Nethergoods to ask *them* over. And what would have happened? Mary Nethergood would have answered that they couldn't because *we* — Oh, no, I guess not. *(She is appalled)*

MR. FOOT. You guess not! You see a little deeper into the situation than me! A nice puddle you've made of it. You didn't think the Nethergoods would have had enough sense just to say "Thank you but we're engaged"? What a woman! A social misfit.

MRS. FOOT. I made a mistake.

MR. FOOT. A whammer.

MRS. FOOT. I made a big mistake.

MR. FOOT. You've just caused an international incident between the Billiards and the Nethergoods. And they the best friends in the world. Adored each other, that's all. But the Billiards don't like to be left out.

MRS. FOOT. But why do you suppose the Nethergoods asked us without asking the Billiards?

MR. FOOT. Don't you remember anything? She didn't want to scare the French dentist with too many strange people. Very delicate, I think. Besides, do they *have* to ask everybody they know? The only trouble is that a French dentist would be a nice morsel for the Billiards, and they'd better not find out about him.

MRS. FOOT. Dear oh dear, what am I to do? How can I clean up this horrible mess? Wait. What time is it?

MR. FOOT. Let's see, let's see. *(He goes up to a grandfather clock and moves the hands)* It's eight o'clock.

MRS. FOOT. The funeral must be over by now. I've got an idea.

MR. FOOT. Tell me.

MRS. FOOT. Just let me do what I have to do. *(She dials the telephone)*

MR. FOOT. Hadn't you better tell me first?

MRS. FOOT. Quiet. *(Into the telephone)* Hello! Mary? This is Mary Foot. How are you, dear? How was the funeral? A smashing success? The Secretary of Commerce! And the Vienna Choir Boys! How simply lovely! Yes . . . yes . . . *(She gasps)* Bill! You have to hear this! Yes! . . . yes . . . Bill! Listen to this! They had a mausoleum ready for Spiffin, and they rolled him in lying inside his favorite Cadillac — they wheeled the Cadillac right into the mausoleum. Yes . . . yes . . . All they took out was the radio and the air conditioning . . .

MR. FOOT. This'll kill Bill Bartlett a second time.

MRS. FOOT. Yes? No! Well, why not? It's a thing you can do only once. That's right. That's right. You're so right. Listen, Mary, the reason I called — we got to thinking, after you left, Bill and me, it sounded a little funny, I mean about the Nethergoods — yes! — no! — I mean it — no no no! — of course! — I understand perfectly! — of course! — yes, yes, by all means! — I didn't — I didn't — anyway the point is that the Nethergoods are having a life insurance man over from India —

MR. FOOT. What's that?

MRS. FOOT. Yes, that's right — exactly — India — ha ha, cosmopolitan is the word — anyway, since Bill is in life insurance himself, they thought — that's it — naturally — right — awfully technical — indemnity tables and all that, frankly it's going to be a bore for me personally — but I thought — that's right — you're so right — *of course* — I'm so glad I talked it over with you. Are you lunching at Peewee's tomorrow? Wonderful. About twelve-thirty. 'Bye 'bye! *(She hangs up)* Satisfied? I'm a genius.

MR. FOOT. You're playing a dangerous game. You should have consulted me first.

MRS. FOOT. What would you have advised me to do?

MR. FOOT. To run away to Siberia.

MRS. FOOT. Very funny.

MR. FOOT. You'd better call the Nethergoods right away.

MRS. FOOT. What on earth for?

MR. FOOT. Don't you want to tell Mary Nethergood that you told Mary Billiard that she, that is to say Mary Nethergood, was having a life insurance man from India over for the soiree to which she didn't invite her, that is to say, Mary Billiard? I mean, they see a lot of each other. You'll be feeling pretty sick if Mary Billiard shakes her curls at Mary Nethergood at the beauty parlor next week and asks "How was your soiree with the life insurance man from India?"

"What life insurance man from India?" "Why, the life insurance man that Mary Foot told me about!" Bang.

MRS. FOOT. I'm going to have to take a chance on that.

MR. FOOT. Why?

MRS. FOOT. Very simple. You want me to call Mary Nethergood.

MR. FOOT. Right.

MRS. FOOT. But if I do, I'll have to admit to Mary Nethergood that I told Mary Billiard that she, that is to say Mary Nethergood, invited us for next Saturday. Insurance man or dentist, what's the difference? The point is that I'll be miserably exposed, and the Nethergoods will know that the Billiards know that they, that is to say the Nethergoods, did not invite them, and that it was me who told the Billiards. They'll never talk to us again.

MR. FOOT. Who?

MRS. FOOT. The Nethergoods, silly.

MR. FOOT. And if you don't call them?

MRS. FOOT. There's at least a chance. Mary Nethergood naturally won't tell Mary Billiard about the party. And maybe Mary Billiard will be tactful and proud enough not to let on she knows there *was* a party. And it'll all blow over. You'll see.

MR. FOOT. *Something* is bound to blow over. Oh, well, hand me the paper, will you?

MRS. FOOT. I'll sit down and do nothing for a while. It's the most restful thing when all's said and done.

MR. FOOT. Where did I leave off? Ah, here it is. "Why, in your personal opinion, is it incorrect to wear a necktie on the beach with your swim trunks?" (a) Because it is too conservative for our day and age. (b) Because it shows an exaggerated concern with your personal appearance. *(As the curtain comes down)* (c) Because the necktie would leave a white streak on your sun-bronzed chest. (d) Because you wish to avoid political and religious controversy.

SCENE TWO

(A bench in a park. Mr. and Mrs. Billiard are sitting on it)

MR. BILLIARD. Beautiful park. Come here, little robin. Look at the birds looping all over the air. Look at the grass growing like green hairdos on the earth's rump. Look at the wind tugging at the leaves. Look at the pretty people with sailboats or bicycles. Look at the romping butterflies. Love loveth the world.

MRS. BILLIARD. If the Nethergoods want to invite a life insurance man from India over to their house especially to meet Bill Foot because Bill is also a life insurance man, even though he is not from India, why make a secret of it? What is wrong with doing what they did? Was Mary Nethergood afraid I'd be offended just because she didn't invite *us*? Why *should* she invite us? You're not in life insurance, you're in preformed cardboard and you don't export to India. Why should we be offended? She must take us for a pair of fools if she thought we'd be small enough to resent her not asking us. Do *I* ask her over every time I have a guest, especially if he is in preformed cardboard? How stupid can a person be? Why didn't she talk to me honestly and say, "Mary, we're having a life insurance man from India over next Saturday for a few drinks. I'm asking the Foots, because Bill Foot is in life insurance, too. You don't mind, do you?" Instead she had to keep it a secret as though she'd been guilty of something, and when I met her on Thursday and asked her over to our house for Saturday, just to test her, mind you, just to test her, because I knew damn well that she was having her own party with the India man and the Foots, she just played innocent and pretended they were going out. I'm glad Mary Foot happened to tell me the truth. I like to know what goes on.

MR. BILLIARD. Look at the birds looping all over the air. Look at the grass growing like green hairdos on the earth's rump. Look at the wind tugging at the leaves. Look at the pretty people with sailboats and bicycles. Look at the romping butterflies. Come here, little sparrow.

MRS. BILLIARD. Hello hello hello hello.

MR. BILLIARD. Who's coming?

MRS. BILLIARD. Don't you see? It's the Nethergoods.

MR. BILLIARD. Well, I want you to be nice to them. Let's everybody be nice to everybody and everything will be nice.

MRS. BILLIARD. Be quiet. You talk as though I was a hyena. *(Enter the Nethergoods)* Hello hello.

MRS. NETHERGOOD. Hello hello.

MR. NETHERGOOD. Hello hello. Billberry old boy.

MR. BILLIARD. Glad to see you again.

MRS. BILLIARD. We haven't seen you in ages, Mary. Not since last Thursday.

MRS. NETHERGOOD. That's right. What an adorable purse you're carrying there. Just perfect for a spring day in the park. Is it new?

MRS. BILLIARD. It is. Bill gave it to me for my birthday. But where have the two of you been all these years?

MR. NETHERGOOD. In Nethergood Hall, where else? I always say I like to spend my time where I pay my rent.

MR. BILLIARD. Ha, ha, ha.

MRS. BILLIARD. By the way, we ran into the Foots the other day.

MRS. NETHERGOOD. Oh, how are they? I simply love that little purse. Look, Bill. It matches your outfit perfectly. But hasn't the weather been awful lately!

MRS. BILLIARD. They said they had a lovely time at your place last Saturday.

MRS. NETHERGOOD. Oh? I'm so glad.

MRS. BILLIARD. And they enjoyed meeting the life insurance man from India.

MR. NETHERGOOD. Life insurance man from India? There was only a French dentist.

MR. BILLIARD. A French dentist in life insurance in India?

MR. NETHERGOOD. What life insurance? Is everybody going crazy? He's a French dentist, I tell you, or a dental surgeon to be precise. Of course, Bill Foot talked to him a lot, and maybe he has a life insurance practice on the side, but that's more than I know.

MR. BILLIARD. Maybe he needs two jobs to make ends meet.

MR. NETHERGOOD. That's true. He might be divorced, and paying alimony.

MR. BILLIARD. Or he could be supporting an old mother or two.

MR. NETHERGOOD. Anyway, what with the rate of industrial growth having slowed down to 1.6% per annum in France, I wouldn't be surprised if a Frenchman actually had to have two jobs.

MR. BILLIARD. Well, that explains our little confusion, anyway.

MRS. BILLIARD. When are you two males going to stop chattering? Who cares how many jobs the man had? The main point is that the Foots had a very pleasant time.

MRS. NETHERGOOD. Well, I don't know where the life insurance story started, I'm sure he is a dentist and nothing else. We had a casual spur-of-the-moment thing at the house. He was going to show slides of French teeth and I know how your Bill gets those headaches whenever he's watching the slides of our World Tour. By the way, will you be free next Sunday afternoon? Could you stop by for cocktails? The Willoughbys will be there.

MR. BILLIARD. Old Bill Willoughby of the Metropolitan Federal Union Security Manufacturers Bank?

MR. NETHERGOOD. That's the one.

MR. BILLIARD. Fine. We'll be there.

MRS. BILLIARD (cold). You're forgetting we're engaged, dear.

MR. BILLIARD. We are?

MRS. BILLIARD (cold). I'm so sorry, Mary, but we can't this time. Our schedule is quite crowded. Come along, Bill. It's getting chilly. Goodbye, all.

MR. and MRS. NETHERGOOD. Goodbye.

MRS. NETHERGOOD. I'll call you.

MRS. BILLIARD. You do that. *(On the way out, to Mr. Billiard)* The liars, the simpering liars. *(They leave)*

MRS. NETHERGOOD. We goofed.

MR. NETHERGOOD. *You* goofed.

MRS. NETHERGOOD. *You* goofed.

MR. NETHERGOOD. We goofed.

MRS. NETHERGOOD. Why didn't you keep your mouth shut when she rattled on about the life insurance man from India? Why did you have to stick your stupid facts into the conversation?

MR. NETHERGOOD. What's the difference? She was mad already, that was as obvious as a pimple on an egg. "I hear the Foots had a lovely time at your house," she says with a snaky smile that would have poisoned you at fifty paces if you hadn't smiled right back. I told you you should have asked them to the house, too.

MRS. NETHERGOOD. Don't start on *that* again. It so happened that I didn't feel like asking them that time. Do I have to ask the Billiards every time I have anybody at the house? And I tell you that she wouldn't have objected if it hadn't looked suddenly as though we'd tried to keep the French dentist hidden from her for some evil reason or other.

MR. NETHERGOOD. Or if you hadn't told her last Thursday that we were engaged on Saturday when later she found out that we were engaged because we were having people at our place.

MRS. NETHERGOOD. Found out! But where in sweet heaven did she find out that we had asked the Foots, and where in all that's holy did she hear about the life insurance man from China? I can't figure it out.

MR. NETHERGOOD. India. Maybe somebody heard about the Foots meeting a life insurance man from India at another party.

MRS. NETHERGOOD. That's very odd. Mary Foot has never mentioned it to me. Why should Mary Foot make a secret of a life insurance man from India?

MR. NETHERGOOD. Well, then, suppose the Foots had this life insurance man from India at their own house along with some other people who happen to know the Billiards, and suppose they hadn't invited us. That would explain their not telling us about him.

MRS. NETHERGOOD. I suppose so. But behind our backs?

(Enter the Foots)

MRS. FOOT. Mary dear, oh, hello, Bill, there's something I'd better tell you.

MRS. NETHERGOOD. Oh, hello, Mary, hello, Bill.

MR. NETHERGOOD. Hello, both.

MR. FOOT. Hello, Bill and Mary. Nice day, pretty birds.

MRS. FOOT. There's something I want to tell you, Mary.

MRS. NETHERGOOD. As a matter of fact, there's something I want to ask *you*.

MRS. FOOT *(apprehensive)*. Oh. Why don't you ask first?

MRS. NETHERGOOD. No, you tell me first.

MRS. FOOT. Well, I couldn't get out of it, Mary. I won't go into details, but I had to tell the Billiards *something*, so I told them you had invited —

MR. and MRS. NETHERGOOD. A life insurance man from India.

MR. and MRS. FOOT. How did you know?

MRS. NETHERGOOD *(cold)*. We talked to the Billiards.

MRS. FOOT. Oh, no!

MRS. NETHERGOOD. We ran into the Billiards just now, and Mary said to me, "We heard you had a life insurance man from India over at your house last Saturday to meet the Foots," she said to me, and naturally Bill said, "What life insurance man? He was a dentist," and then it all came out. Now what I'd like to know, just for curiosity's sake, is why you made up that story about the life insurance man from India.

MR. FOOT. I told you.

MRS. FOOT. Oh, shut up. Mary, listen to me.

MRS. NETHERGOOD. You know how sensitive the Billiards are; you know one can't take a step without treading on one of their hundred toes. And yet you have to blab to them, and tell them a cock and bull story about a life insurance man from India. Excuse me for saying so, but it's plain stupid, that's all.

MR. NETHERGOOD. Besides, nobody in India lives more than thirty-five years. It's all thoroughly incredible.

MRS. FOOT. Mary, listen to me.

MRS. NETHERGOOD. I'm sure you had your reasons for inventing this idiotic figure, but you might have given a moment's thought to the impossible hole you were digging for me. You made me look like a liar, a plotter. Mary Billiard left here convinced *I* had told you to make up that story of the life insurance man from India. They gave us a frosty goodbye. Two of our dearest friends down the drain. Thank you very much.

MR. NETHERGOOD *(weeping)*. Bill Billiard, who was my buddy in the army, my chum at the Bowling League, my pal at the Lodge.

MR. FOOT. I told you.

MRS. FOOT. May I put a word in sideways one of these years? Is anybody going to listen to me? Thank you. I wish you'd realize, my dear, that I invented the life insurance man from India exclusively to save *your* face.

MRS. NETHERGOOD. Well, I never!

MRS. FOOT. I repeat — to save your face. I told the Billiards it was a kind of business affair — insurance shoptalk between the men — so that she wouldn't be offended at being left out.

MRS. NETHERGOOD. And how did she come to know I hadn't asked her in the first place? Answer that one, if you please.

MRS. FOOT. Well, why *didn't* you?

MRS. NETHERGOOD. I've heard too much.

MR. NETHERGOOD. Me too.

MRS. FOOT. And why were you fool enough to tell her "Oh no, it wasn't a life insurance man from India, it was a French dentist"? How naive can you get? A child would have guessed something, and would have confirmed my story.

MR. FOOT. My wife has a point there, you know.

MR. NETHERGOOD. I protest.

MRS. NETHERGOOD. Don't bother protesting. You can't argue with boors. Let's —

MRS. FOOT. Boors? Did you say boors?

MRS. NETHERGOOD. Boors. Without an ounce of breeding. You're a pair of public hazards, if you want an unbiased opinion. Come along, Bill, let the Foots enjoy the park by themselves.

MR. FOOT. We will, by Jove. Good riddance to the windbag.

MR. and MRS. NETHERGOOD. Boors. *(They leave)*

MR. FOOT. I guess they don't like us any more.

(Enter, from the other side, the Billiards)

MRS. BILLIARD. There you are.

MR. and MRS. FOOT. Oh my God.

MRS. BILLIARD. We heard all about your phony life insurance man from India.

MR. BILLIARD. Our eyes are unplugged and the scales have fallen from our ears.

MRS. BILLIARD. All of a sudden he's a dentist.

MR. BILLIARD. A French dentist.

MRS. BILLIARD. Who shows slides.

MR. BILLIARD. Which I can't look at because of my headaches.

MRS. BILLIARD. Next time, you and your friends had better get together on the fables you'll tell your stupid acquaintances. Come along, Bill. I just wanted to let her know we're wise to all of them.

MRS. FOOT. Will you —

MRS. BILLIARD. Don't worry — I'll put your copy of *Love in the Suburbs* in the mail for you at once.

MRS. FOOT *(weakly)*. You can finish it first.

MRS. BILLIARD. Come on, Bill. Let's leave the Foots and the Nethergoods to enjoy a good laugh at our expense. *(They leave)*

MR. FOOT. So here we are.

MRS. FOOT (*sitting on the bench and sniffling*). I'm sure I did my best.
  If you hadn't —

MR. FOOT. If *I* hadn't! I like that! If *I* hadn't! That takes the prize! I told
  you a thousand times —

MRS. FOOT. You told me! You're always telling me! You think you're
  Einstein, don't you? You're always telling me what I found out three
  weeks before.

MR. FOOT. Keep talking, and if it makes you happy to unload your guilt on
  me, go right ahead, it's cheaper than analysis, you can tear me to bits
  to relieve your subconscious frustrations. But in the meantime, don't
  forget you've ruined six beautiful friendships.

MRS. FOOT. So it's all my fault. You take their side. Everybody else's wife
  is a pure spotless angel, only your own is a monster. I should have
  known. (*Tears and moans*)

MR. FOOT. Oh, well, it's not as bad as all that.

MRS. FOOT. Nobody understands me, not even my husband.

MR. FOOT. Sure I understand you. God knows I understand you. Come on,
  Mary, don't cry in the middle of the park. There, there. (*He wipes
  her eyes with his handkerchief*)

MRS. FOOT. Do you love me?

MR. FOOT. Of course I love you. Who else should I love? Forget those
  Billiards and Nethergoods.

MRS. FOOT. We've plenty of other friends, haven't we?

MR. FOOT. I should say so. We've got so many wonderful friends that
  when a few of them get lost we don't even know they're gone. Look,
  Mary, we're in luck, look who's coming!

MRS. FOOT. Oh, Bill and Mary McGrue!

MR. FOOT. All right, make yourself presentable. We'll ask them over for
  drinks. Ready?

MRS. FOOT. Ready.

MR. FOOT. Forward!

(*They advance into the wings, smiling, arms stretched out*)

MR. and MRS. FOOT. Hello hello hello hello hello hello.

THE END

PROFESSOR SNAFFLE'S POLYPON

a burletta

Characters

Professor Lancelot Snaffle, *a fat physicist*

Hepsa Snaffle, *his wife*

Percy Loop, *his elderly assistant*

Pappendeck, *a young student of the physical sciences*

General Winston Culpepper, *a notable military figure,
though later reduced*

Mrs. Culpepper, *his wife, later* Mrs. Molassis

"Crusher" McBoodle, *Secretary of Defensive Expansion*

Mr. Nose, *a reporter*

A Spy, *whose actual name cannot be disclosed for security reasons*

An Interpreter

The Duke of Ostersund, *Chairman of the Dynamite Peace Prize
Selection Board*

Dr. P. P. Folpap, *a distinguished colleague of Professor Snaffle's*

Mr. Smith, *a Demonstrator*

Mr. Jones, *another Demonstrator*

An Elderly Couple, *in pantomime*

The tots: Miss Molecule
           Master Atom
           Master Proton
           Miss Electron
           Master Alpha Ray
           Miss Beta Ray
           Miss Isotope

Act 1.   Professor Snaffle Discovers the Polypon.

Act 2.   A Setback.

Act 3.   Professor Snaffle Harnesses the Polypon.

Act 4.   The Triumph of Professor Snaffle.

Act 5.   Showing that Man Stands at the Forefront of Creation.

ACT ONE

(The left side of the stage is occupied by a large, many-sided, colorful, odd-roofed structure: the Polypon. For its exact appearance, the spectator will rely upon the Stage Designer and the reader upon his imagination. The Polypon is equipped with certain apertures in the roof, several vents or crannies along the sides, and a substantial sliding door facing the audience. As the curtain rises, the sliding door opens, and we hear a heavenly tinkling music. We see the tots dancing gracefully about, all except Miss Isotope, who, being on the unstable side, has a little difficulty in keeping up. The interior itself consists in a rich garden which the Stage Designer will plant and water, be-rock and be-gravel as he pleases. As the tots dance, they sing both in chorus and separately.)

CHORUS. We jiggle and rattle
And scamper and prattle
And wiggle and prance
And retreat and advance.
We are the dancers, and we dance.

We trot, we scuttle, we skip,
We tipple, we putter, we flip,
We pirouette and trace
Quick curlicues in space,
We are the racers, and we race.

ATOM. We are the midgets
With the fidgets.

PROTON. We attract and we repel,
In orbit and in parallel.

ELECTRON. A snappy, happy phalanx,

ISOTOPE. Sometimes in, and sometimes out of balance.

ALPHA RAY. We burst, we fuse, we bump, we split,
Because we glow, the world is lit.

BETA RAY. The sounds which tinkle in our ears,
What can they be?

CHORUS. The music of the spheres!

MOLECULE. Zigzags, circles, dashes, spots,
Holes and angles, hooks and dots,
Crackles, thunders, motion, flight

From zone to zone and light to light,
Vast nothings between which we are
Now the dust, and now a star,
Oh, world of all that can forever be,
We are the law, the number and the harmony.

CHORUS.   Oh world of all that can forever be,
We are the law, the number and the loyalty.

(The dance continues for awhile, and as it does, the tots detach themselves one by one, introduce themselves, and then rejoin the dance.)

MOLECULE. I'm Miss Molecule, I'm big and basic, and I'm boss around here.

ATOM. I'm Master Atom, and confidentially, I'm even basicker than she, but of course I'm smaller as you can tell, and so I cooperate.

PROTON. And I'm Proton. Wherever Brother Atom goes, me too. Positively.

ELECTRON. As for me, I'm Miss Electron. I'm fast and charged and I can run circles around anybody. Take care!

ALPHA RAY. My name is Master Alpha Ray. I'm a big shot and I'm tough. I run out of breath easy but I do a lot of knocking down on the way.

BETA RAY. And I'm Beta Ray. I'm tiny, swift, and penetrating, and I'm unattached.

ISOTOPE. And I's little Isotope. I's unstable, you know, but it's a nice dopey life and I gets a lot of attention.

MOLECULE. Come back here, you!

ATOM. Dance!

CHORUS. Dance!

ALPHA RAY. Forward and forward!

ELECTRON. Round and round!

ISOTOPE. Stumble crumble!

MOLECULE. Organized, particles, always organized!

PROTON. Sanity and courtesy!

BETA RAY. Tra la la la tra la la!

ATOM. Always cool.

BETA RAY. Even when we sizzle!

MOLECULE. We are the law,

ALPHA RAY. The number,

ISOTOPE (quavering). And the harmony!

(The dance and music continue, but the front of the Polypon now closes, the order of the universe vanishes out of sight, and the music continues but faintly. Enter, on the other side of the stage, Professor Snaffle and Mr. Loop, engrossed in shop-talk which the profane are compelled to admire without understanding.)

SNAFFLE. We bring about, in due course, a hyperactive fusion of heavy hydrogen and liquid plutonium —

LOOP. Converting it to thorium 227.

SNAFFLE. We raise the temperature in obverse disrelation to the motion of rp over t, observing, of course, the rising deceleration and increasingly diminished reaction in the reinforced tank.

LOOP. At 50,000 atmospheres, Professor Snaffle?

SNAFFLE. At 50,000 atmospheres, Mr. Loop. The heated mixture concentrates, advances toward the critical point, velocity multiplies as frequency jumps, the radon particles are absorbed in the beryllium rods, quanta of energy enrage the nuclei, the critical point is reached, and —

LOOP (modestly). Pop!

SNAFFLE. Precisely.

LOOP. The world splits —

SNAFFLE. Mountains disintegrate —

LOOP. Rivers boil —

SNAFFLE. Monkeys and birds diffuse into space —

LOOP. Mankind dissolves —

SNAFFLE. And I prove, beyond the vestige of a doubt, that the center of the earth is a drum of compressed cooking gas extremely useful to the American housewife.

LOOP. The only possible objection —

SNAFFLE (dangerous). An objection, Mr. Loop, before you have completed your thesis for me?

LOOP. No, nothing — only a thought — nothing at all.

SNAFFLE (still more dangerous). Speak up, Loop, my boy. We scientists thrive on free discussion.

LOOP. Well — I was only going to ask — a detail — namely, who will use the cooking gas.

SNAFFLE. Who will use the cooking gas? What kind of an eccentric question is that?

LOOP. Well, sir, what with the annihilation of housewives —

SNAFFLE. I'm amazed! Does the pure scientist concern himself with who uses what and why?

LOOP. Oh no, I realize that, Professor Snaffle. I was only thinking —

SNAFFLE. What you were thinking is sociology, Mr. Loop.

LOOP. Goodness! Is this what I —

SNAFFLE. Furthermore, the scientist solves one problem at a time, Mr. Loop.

LOOP. Of course, Professor Snaffle, and yet —

SNAFFLE. He isolates the irrelevant and the variable —

LOOP. Of course, Professor Snaffle, but —

SNAFFLE. But nothing. The survival of housewives is simply not in my field of specialization. I state my hypothesis: cooking gas. And those who love me agree with me, Mr. Loop.

LOOP. I hope, sir, you have always found in me an ardent supporter of that hypothesis. Cooking gas — with, possibly, a few traces of iron.

SNAFFLE. Oh? Really? What makes you say iron?

LOOP. I was reading P. P. Folpap's analysis —

SNAFFLE (*terrible*). Percy Loop!

LOOP (*frightened*). Yes, Professor Snaffle?

SNAFFLE. Folpap is a clyster.

LOOP. Sir — I didn't know — I —

SNAFFLE. I have confuted him fifty times!

LOOP. I didn't — I had no —

SNAFFLE. I do not require his analyses!

LOOP. Indeed not, Professor Snaffle, indeed not. I — may I say, sir, that I, for one, in the thesis I will be presenting for your approval — in due time — I will attempt —

SNAFFLE. Oh?

LOOP. In a modest way —

SNAFFLE. Very good.

LOOP. To show that the presence of iron posited by — eh — posited elsewhere is not capable of experimental verification through any known method of — of — verification.

SNAFFLE. Which Folpap tried to deny.

LOOP. Overlooking the fact, I remember now, that the thiocyamate test yielded not a speck of iron.

SNAFFLE. And what about his amateurish attempt to precipitate it by using ammonium chloride?

LOOP. When did he do *that*?

SNAFFLE. The time he brought up his so-called sample.

LOOP. And he used ammonium chloride? Oh no! (*He laughs*)

SNAFFLE. Before even getting his filtrate! (*He laughs louder*)

LOOP. Before getting his filtrate? Oh no no no!

(*Here Loop laughs so hard that he loses his equilibrium, collides with the Polypon and thereby discovers it, although this fact will not be known to posterity. The music stops at the moment of impact*)

SNAFFLE. What's that?

LOOP. An object in experience. It struck my nose.

SNAFFLE. Measure it! Calibrate it! Tabulate it!

LOOP. Calm yourself, sir.

SNAFFLE. Here's something I may have been looking for all my life without knowing it. And now I've found it. It's all mine, mine, mine! Pappendeck, my instruments!

(*Enter Pappendeck, carrying a profusion of enormous tools, for which the imagination of the Stage Designer, tempered this time by prolonged studies, will range freely once more. At the same time, a large computer*) *descends from the flies)*

PAPPENDECK. Here is your equipment, Professor Snaffle.

SNAFFLE. Ah, and my computer, standing at my side, ready as always to multiply my genius.

PAPPENDECK *(patting the computer).* I don't know, sir. Poor Bessy was complaining a little this morning.

SNAFFLE. Why?

PAPPENDECK. She calculated that you hadn't fed her in two days.

SNAFFLE *(delighted).* Did she for a fact?

PAPPENDECK. I have the coded signals here, Professor Snaffle. I figured you'd like to see them. She clicked shyly when she delivered the tape, and heaved a sentimental clank. But I gave her a proper lubrication.

SNAFFLE *(tenderly reading the tape).* 011/0110/1011/00. Oh Bessy! *(He embraces the computer)* Here I am. That parting oo! So like a tender reproach! Do you hear the dying cadence? oo! But don't be melancholy, Bessy, let me see your indicators flash again! There! And wait till you see the new program I'll be feeding you!

LOOP *(wiping a tear; to Pappendeck).* He knows her dynamic pulse unit so well!

PAPPENDECK *(weeping).* Every crystal diode of hers is dear to him.

SNAFFLE. Come, gentlemen, let us address ourselves calmly to our problem. Give me a research tool.

LOOP. I suggest this kinetic thrust agent. *(He offers a hammer)*

(Meanwhile the Polypon's door has opened again. Now the tots are sitting around a table, looking uneasy. While they speak, Snaffle cautiously examines the Polypon)

BETA RAY. I still say something's wrong. There was a collision.

PROTON. The cosmos is full of collisions, Beta Ray.

ATOM. But the music stopped for this one.

ELECTRON. I think we made a mistake when we left Interstellar D Major to come here.

ALPHA RAY. We came by accident, remember? Laws of probability and all that.

ATOM. The place is crawling with proteins.

ISOTOPE *(timidly).* Why don't we try dancing again?

ATOM. I don't know.

SNAFFLE. Let's take a sample.

(He gives the Polypon a great blow and a piece falls off. The tots cry out and scurry. Snaffle, Loop and Pappendeck surround the chunk at a respectful distance)

MOLECULE. Stop, stop! It's only a jostle!

ELECTRON. No, it's something more. I feel it, I know it!

ATOM. Maybe it's anti-matter. Puff, we're gone.

MOLECULE. Silence. Let's wait and listen.

BETA RAY. If it's an enemy, I'll flash.

ISOTOPE. What's a enemy? I's scared.

(The door of the Polypon closes. Snaffle, after trying in vain to get Loop or Pappendeck to pick up the chunk of matter, picks it up himself)

SNAFFLE *(tossing the chunk from one hand to another).* It sizzles! Ergs and joules! What's going on? It's burning a hole through my hand! Catch it!

(He tosses it to Loop)

LOOP. Fascinating, sir. *(Hastily tosses it to Pappendeck)*

PAPPENDECK. Sensational. *(Tosses it back to Snaffle, who has put on a pair of gloves)*

SNAFFLE. It sizzles, and yet it was cold! *(Sniffs it)* There are things imbedded here — some devil of a new element. I can smell the pi-mesons frying in it. Give me that Geiger counter. The polarimeter too. And the velocity selector. And all the rest of it!

(The chunk disappears in a mass of instruments)

SNAFFLE *(excited).* Gentlemen — feed Bessy. Bombarding energy 1.85 Mev, flight path 150 centimeters, channel width 0.594 times 10^{-9} seconds. Detector bias in plastic scintillator 800 kev, 10,000,000,000 negative pions per millisteradian in the forward direction for a $6^0/0$ momentum interval at $2.8^0/0$ Bev per c! Apply Thompson's formula to the whole bezazzle.

LOOP. I've got it, Professor Snaffle.

SNAFFLE. I said 0.594, not counting leftovers.

LOOP. Right. Bessy is humming.

SNAFFLE. Have her shuffle time intervals, distribution, speed, pulse height, angular momentum, frequency, acceleration, and resistance.

LOOP. Right away, sir.

SNAFFLE *(rising from the instruments).* But my mind leaps ahead even of Bessy. And what I see — ah!

PAPPENDECK. Professor Snaffle! What do you see? Tell us for God's sake!

SNAFFLE. Nothing less than a revolution. A flat contradiction to received notions of radiation. In short: spontaneous frigoradiant emissions!

LOOP and PAPPENDECK. Spontaneous frigoradiant emissions!

SNAFFLE. One millimicrosecond ago, gentlemen, we stood in the smelly old ordinary world, and the next — frigoradiant emissions . . .

LOOP *(confidentially).* Sir, may I — a word on the side —?

SNAFFLE. What is it?

LOOP. Only a thought, sir. Hm. The unusual nature of the — hm.

SNAFFLE. Yes; go on, Loop.

LOOP. Perhaps a word to the press — a newsleak so to speak —

SNAFFLE *(whisper).* At once. *(Loud)* No, my loyal colleague, for science works without publicity. Above all, no fanfares! *(To Pappendeck)* You, boy, call my wife and tell her to report to me. And don't snoop, or I'll ionize and discharge you.

PAPPENDECK. Yes, sir. No, sir. *(Leaves)*

SNAFFLE. And you, attend to what you know.

LOOP. On the wings of duty, sir. *(Leaves)*

SNAFFLE. All mine! All mine! Folpap will burst. I shall control this object. It will yield. I will squeeze my profit out of it. A fallout of riches and renown. Ah, the future comes to me in a vision! I accept decorations, honors and contracts. At last I take the Dynamite Peace Prize. No! I turn it down. Better yet! I accept it so I can publicly bestow the money on the Interracial Institute for Unwed Orphans. And when I am dead — if I can die — a building at Harvard is named after me. If necessary I pay for it myself. Students in days to come will report for lectures not to Physics 207, but to 207 Snaffle Hall!

(Enter Loop with Mr. Nose, the journalist)

LOOP. Professor Snaffle, I happened to run into Mr. Nose here, the journalist. A chance encounter. And I couldn't forbear —

NOSE. Professor Snaffle, let me shake your hand. My nose for news and my hunger for scoops has led me straight to you; and sure enough Mr. Loop tells me you've dug something up that's going to remake the future before it's even happened. Will you tell the world what it is?

SNAFFLE. Only if silence becomes impossible. It's a new structure in space.

NOSE. A structure?

SNAFFLE. Yes. We predicted its appearance, and it appeared according to our calculations. It is too early yet to announce practical bearings, and please, Mr. Nose, let your publication be cautious with its claims. However, I am free to report that my laboratory, directed by myself, is conducting a series of experiments — under my direction — which may revolutionize our concepts of the universe, explain the beginning and the end, leave the Russians far behind as usual, and put an end to human melancholy. My purpose is to open new vistas to mankind, and to share the fruits of our research with all men, the enemy always excepted. Let the spirit of free inquiry prevail!

NOSE *(who has been taking furious notes)*. Exclamation mark! End quotes. Have you given your discovery a name, Professor Snaffle?

SNAFFLE. I have. It is provisionally called the Snaffle Polypon, one *el*.

NOSE. "The Snaffle Polypon." And now, if I may ask —

SNAFFLE. Of course, of course! I am a happily married ex-bachelor, the father of two children, a boy of 14 and a girl of, needless to say, 9. We live in a pleasant and unostentatious house on Elm Street, near the Institute, and my greatest pleasure is to help my children with their homework in mathematics. Our little joke is to call it "math." In spite of my international reputation, I am shy. My attractive wife is devoted to gardening and grows the best begonias in the neighborhood. She is also an active non-sectarian church member who bakes chocolate cakes. I am myself a familiar figure on the tennis courts. Popular with my students, who call me Old Snaffle-bags — unbeknownst to me — I take a personal interest in their intellectual development, and it is touching to report that many of them write to me long after they have left the Institute. My only ambition is to continue, as long as health permits, in my unswerving and selfless devotion to the Spirit of Science.

NOSE. "Spirit of Science." I'll capitalize these, if I may. Thank you, Professor Snaffle, for taking this forthright stand. The public appreciates fearless men. Excuse me. My deadline is at hand. (He shakes hands with Snaffle and Loop, and leaves)

SNAFFLE. And now, friend and inferior, back to work. Folpap will burst! (Snaffle starts to poke about the Polypon. He takes a stool or ladder to climb to its roof, tapping, taking measurements, etc. etc. Meanwhile the door opens again, revealing the apprehensive tots around the table)

ATOM. I feel a scraping and a crawling.

PROTON. A thumping and a tapping.

MOLECULE (feebly). Courage, friends. Stand by your principles.

ISOTOPE. I's scared.

BETA RAY. None of us is feeling too chipper, so be still.

ALPHA RAY. What's this? A branch?

(Snaffle's arm has gone through a hole in the roof)

SNAFFLE. Victory!

LOOP. Professor Snaffle, where is your arm?

SNAFFLE. I've found an aperture! I'm groping in a vacuum!

(Molecule has picked up a pebble)

ELECTRON. What are you going to do, Molecule?

MOLECULE. I'm going to react. That's our business, isn't it?

ISOTOPE. I's scared.

(Molecule flings the pebble at Snaffle's hand)

SNAFFLE. Ouch!

ATOM. Impact! (He throws a pebble too)

SNAFFLE. Ouch squared! Look here! (He tries to get his arm out)

LOOP. Professor Snaffle! Are you in danger?

SNAFFLE. Stop Snaffling me and help me out, you fool. (All the tots are tossing pebbles now) Ouch! Ouch! (He frees his arm with many a heave and groan) Well!

ATOM. The extension in space is gone!

ELECTRON. The Denominator be thanked!

ALPHA RAY. It's spoiled my day anyway.

BETA RAY. Shouldn't we dance again, just to try?

MOLECULE. We'd better keep a lookout. (*They all sit again, watching the ceiling*)

SNAFFLE (*who has been exercising his arm, helped by Loop, and now examines his hand*) Extraordinary. My hand is mauled. Shot through and stinging.

LOOP (*hopeful*). Perhaps you will die of radiation exposure, Professor Snaffle.

SNAFFLE. Possibly. But the scientist is always ready to be the martyr of his own experiments. Forward. Plug Bessy in again. More data coming. March! I'll plunge a beam of photons into the Polypon. Hand me the camera, but first clamp it to a pole. (*Loop attaches a camera equipped with a flash bulb to a pole*) I know there's an untapped source of energy here that will make all the cooking gas at the core of the earth look like a midget's burp. Here, give it to me. (*He carefully inserts the pole with its camera into the hole. The tots all stand up aghast, with one "Oh!" and stare into the camera*) Smile! (*He triggers the camera. The flash bulb goes off, the tots scream and fall down*) Ah, Loop, this is a great moment. The silent universe and I, Lancelot Snaffle, asking my question of it. (*He has retrieved the camera*) Remove the plate and let me examine the emulsion. Into the amidol it goes. So. And now, Snaffle probes.

(*Both engage in research*)

ISOTOPE (*blubbering*). I want leave to go away.

MOLECULE. That horrible flash reminded me of the time Nova 3011 went off. I almost changed from tungsten to hydrogen, I was that startled.

ELECTRON. What's going to happen to us?

ALPHA RAY (*gloomy*). Maybe we're being harnessed, mates.

PROTON. By the ambulant protein complexes?

ALPHA RAY. Maybe.

ATOM. How about fighting back? I like the place just as it is; insofar, of course, as I'm capable of liking.

BETA RAY. We're not supposed to have any feelings, you know.

ISOTOPE (*still blubbering*). I want permish to go away.

MOLECULE. Let's try the dance again.

SEVERAL (*without enthusiasm*). All right, let's try.

(*They form once more; the sweet tinkling music starts again, but more hesitantly, and with a few false, disharmonic chords*)

SNAFFLE. Loop! Take a look! Here, here — do you see the distortion? In the upper right. There, a frumpy proton, 50 microns off course!

LOOP. I see it, sir. Does it mean —?

SNAFFLE. Beyond a doubt! I *know* we're dealing with frigoradiant emissions. But this is just the beginning.

LOOP. We must follow up.

SNAFFLE. With a massive assault on the unknown. Loop, is everything wired up?

LOOP. Yes, sir.

SNAFFLE. First, then, I bombard the Polypon with particles of infra-matter at various angles of incidence, rates of dispersion, and curves of alacrity. You'll check the responses and feed them to Bessy. Next I dig in with thermocouples. Keep a sharp lookout on the potentiometer. And I might as well stick in a hydrometer or two. Finally I spray the Polypon with positive ions — don't worry about the noise — and wind things up in a blaze of mass spectroscopy. Ready, Mr. Loop?

LOOP. Ready!

SNAFFLE. All right, Loop, my boy, here I go.

(Now events speed up so much that the scribe can no longer keep abreast of them. Snaffle throws balls into the Polypon. The music and the dance stop. The tots scramble for cover. Exclamations ad libitum. Isotope still wants to go away. Atom and Molecule encourage the others to fight back. They pick up the balls and vigorously return them. The balls bounce around. Table and chairs turn over, the garden is trampled down. Molecule cries "Save our garden!" while from Snaffle we hear "A reaction is setting in!" etc. Loop takes readings and feeds them to Bessy in a frenzy. Next Snaffle grasps a long pole and pokes about the Polypon, uprooting shrubs, striking the tots, etc. Cries of "I'm bleeding! I'm scratched! I'm torn! I'm beheaded!" Atom catches the pole and a tug-of-war begins)

SNAFFLE. A resistance! The curve is isotropic! Heat up the cathode! Switch back the photomultiplier! (Atom pushes the pole out completely and Snaffle falls down)

SNAFFLE. Tremendous energies are concentrated in this thing, Loop! (He rushes back with an enormous syringe and starts spraying the Polypon with a black liquid. The tots scurry about; the scene is a shambles, Isotope is howling, Snaffle is pumping, Loop is reading and feeding, Bessy is crackling. Finally Snaffle, crying "A multiple experiment," manages to set going simultaneously inside the Polypon a mighty wind, a violently blinking light, a penetrating smoke, and a peevish high-voltage whine. The tots are driven by the wind to the far side of the Polypon. Cries and exclamations, coughing and stumbling)

PROTON. It's the end of the universe!

ATOM. Never! Energy is indestructible!

ISOTOPE. Alas! (And the door of the Polypon closes upon this scene of *cosmic terror)*

SNAFFLE *(descending and wiping his face).* Woof! That was a job of a job.

LOOP. I too feel exhausted, Professor Snaffle. Considering my age . . . But Bessy is doing her business. Look at the gleam in her dials!

SNAFFLE *(patting the computer).* We've got to give her time, though. Never overexert a woman or a machine. Go get some dinner, Loop, but first cover Bessy up so she won't catch any dust. My lord, this has been a busy devil of a day.

LOOP *(placing a cover over the computer).* Keeps out stray cosmic rays, too. Shall I bring you a sandwich, Professor Snaffle?

SNAFFLE. No, my boy, I need a clear stomach tonight.

LOOP. Very well, sir. I'll be going home to mother. *(Leaves)*

(Snaffle is alone. He contemplates the Polypon, while the computer hums contentedly under its sheet, and soliloquizes)

SNAFFLE. Folpap will burst. This is my king of days; let every alley-cat dine on broiled fish tonight. After the mule came steam, after steam, petroleum, after petroleum, electricity, after electricity, atomic energy, after atomic energy, my polyponal impulses. Benefits to mankind. Benefits to Snaffle. Polypon stations on the moon. Cucumbers five feet long and a cure for hay fever. Universal happiness. Snaffle's happiness. But of course the data must be analysed. Another series of experiments. Grants from the government. Let me see. Why not an anthracene scintillator? Then a trip to Hawaii what with the grants. Naked girls. And be sure to check the silver chloride crystals.

(Enter Mrs. Snaffle, thin, enthusiastic, far from the opposite of unhandsome, and inclined to giggling)

MRS. SNAFFLE. Lancelot, dear.

SNAFFLE *(sunk in contemplation).* Why not a Total Shower Absorption Counter?

MRS. SNAFFLE. Goosypie.

SNAFFLE *(still sunk).* Yes, Duckypuddle.

MRS. SNAFFLE. It's long past dinner-time, dear. Mr. Pappendeck told me I could find you here.

SNAFFLE *(still sunk).* I'll shoot the beam into a magnetizing coil. What did you say?

MRS. SNAFFLE. The children ate two lamb chops each, extra rare, and drank their milk without spilling.

SNAFFLE *(still sunk).* A collimator will do it.

MRS. SNAFFLE. But Timmy — that's our son, dear — Timmy is fretting about his math assignment, and he'd like you to help him.

SNAFFLE *(still sunk).* But what's the impedance?

MRS. SNAFFLE. Are you listening to me, Lancelot?

SNAFFLE. Of course. Let's hear the silly problem.

MRS. SNAFFLE. Three men are digging a hole in a garden, while 12 faucets are filling $8\frac{1}{4}$ bathtubs at the rate of 15 gallons of water every 60 seconds. The faucets are set at 3 mile intervals from New York City and the hole is speeding at 54 miles per hour toward the oncoming bus. What is A's hourly wage?

SNAFFLE. One dollar and twenty-five cents.

MRS. SNAFFLE. One dollar and twenty-five cents?

SNAFFLE. Right.

MRS. SNAFFLE. But — you figured it so quickly, dear — are you sure?

SNAFFLE. Show me where I'm wrong.

MRS. SNAFFLE. Well, I'd never —

SNAFFLE. Is there an error in the division?

MRS. SNAFFLE. I'm sure —

SNAFFLE. Come on, tell me *your* answer if you know so much!

MRS. SNAFFLE. *My* answer!

SNAFFLE. Did I misplace a decimal point?

MRS SNAFFLE *(breaking down)*. Oh Topsituttle, please, I'm sure you didn't. How could you? I'll tell Timmy right away, one dollar twenty-five cents and let him hush up. And don't you be too long, naughty Lancelot.

SNAFFLE. Go your way, woman, but kiss me first. Mmmm.

MRS. SNAFFLE *(giggles)*. Dear me!

SNAFFLE. Send those brats to bed, and pillow yourself in the dark till I come. We'll mutilate the mattress! We'll joggle the chandelier! I'll add my Unit to your Nought till dawn!

MRS. SNAFFLE. I'm always ready. *(Snaffle is escorting his wife out. Suddenly Mrs. Snaffle, though occupied with thoughts of love, notices the computer)* What's that?

SNAFFLE. You mean the High Speed Electronic Digital Automatic Universal Computer? Never you mind.

MRS. SNAFFLE *(outraged)*. I thought so! *(She tears away the cover)* There she is! Hiding! *(To Snaffle)* Oh you horrible man! Making love to me with all your weight in order to distract me from *that!* That *machine!* Look at her! Winking and giggling! She's enjoying herself! But I'll show her. *(She slaps the computer, which burps and tosses out a punched tape. Mrs. Snaffle picks it up)* What's this?

SNAFFLE. Hepsa, my angel —

MRS. SNAFFLE. What does she say? oo/oooo/ooo1/oo. Barefaced hussy! All right, Lancelot Snaffle, you tell me what this means, and no formulas.

SNAFFLE. But Hepsa, my angel —

MRS. SNAFFLE. Read it, or I'm going home to mother.

SNAFFLE. Well . . .

MRS. SNAFFLE. And you'll cook your own meals and the children's too.

SNAFFLE (*hastily*). I'll read it, dear. oo/oooo/ooo1/oo. It's rather technical. I'd have to —

MRS. SNAFFLE. I'm going. You know where you can find the stove.

SNAFFLE. Wait! I'll read it. It means — well — "eliminate interference." But only in the accumulator, dearest, only in the accumulator. I swear it!

MRS. SNAFFLE. Eliminate interference! That's all I wanted to hear. I know who the interference is, let me tell you, Professor Snaffle, and I'm not going to impose my presence any longer. Good-bye.

SNAFFLE. But dear — poopynippy —

MRS. SNAFFLE. Do you dare call me poopynippy? I'm Hepsa Snaffle, née Wilkins, and I am sick and tired of scrubbing dishes and underwear for you and looking after your unbearable brats while you play around with a computer that everybody shines and makes eyes at all day just because you went to college while we poor married women get wrinkles in our faces polishing the forks and mending the socks and cleaning the windows and then having to pretend we're beautiful ravishing mistresses on top of the laundry baskets while you're wearing us out and with children besides and you all that time what else have you got to do except playing around with a computer's buttons and tickling its switches, they never do any honest work, they just sit and compute, you don't grow old doing that and then what happens they tell you to eliminate interferences even though you're married to them! (*She bawls*)

SNAFFLE. But my dear — how can you — my connection with Bess — with the computer — is strictly business — scientific research — cold and calculating — ha ha ha ha — calculating! Did you hear the little joke?

MRS. SNAFFLE (*bawls louder*). Jokes! Jokes!

SNAFFLE. You're my love — my only love — my beauty — my companion — my human being — ever young, captivating, admired by every man — that's it! Admired by every man!

MRS. SNAFFLE (*comes out under the sobs*). What do you mean by that?

SNAFFLE. Why, wasn't it last week you picked me up at the Institute?

MRS. SNAFFLE. Yes.

SNAFFLE. That was when Loop looked out of the window and called everybody from the electroscope when he saw you. "Look at that virginal beauty!" he cried out, and the rest were open-mouthed! And then Pippleheim, the vacuum-tube washer, turned around and said," That's not a virginal beauty! That's Mrs. Snaffle!" And so it was.

MRS. SNAFFLE. You didn't tell me.

SNAFFLE. Loop only told me this morning. Come here. (*He kisses her*)

MRS. SNAFFLE. Oh Lancelot, I shouldn't forgive you. But will you take me to Tahiti this winter and forget that miserable computer?

SNAFFLE. I will.

MRS. SNAFFLE. All right then. Here's a peck for you. I have to run now. Don't be too late, do you hear?

SNAFFLE. I won't, my love.

(*As Mrs. Snaffle leaves, the computer blips*)

MRS. SNAFFLE. What's that?

SNAFFLE. Nothing, dear. I dropped my pencil. Bye bye.

MRS. SNAFFLE. Bye bye. (*She leaves*)

SNAFFLE. Impeccable woman. Ergs and joules, what charming lips, what seductive fire in those eyes! I *will* take her to Tahiti, poor dear, scraping the dishes all day long for my sake. How insanely passionate she is about me! Ah woman! But down, flesh, and back, Lancelot Snaffle, back to stringency.

ACT TWO

(*The Polypon, still standing where it will remain throughout these conjunctures, is closed and quiet. The computer is in its place. Installed in front of it are a few chairs, on which are sitting, or near which are standing the following: Mr. Nose, General and Mrs. Culpepper, Mrs. Snaffle, and Mr. McBoodle. While they chat, Mr. Loop enters, dressed in his whitest*)

LOOP. It's four o'clock, ladies and gentlemen, and I'd like to announce that Professor Snaffle will be joining us very soon.

NOSE. A truly historic occasion.

CULPEPPER. All of us in the military entertain the highest hopes for Professor Snaffle's Polypon. Of course, as a fighting man I speak bluntly.

MRS. CULPEPPER. Yes, dear.

MCBOODLE. A mysterious frigonuclear reaction! Another breakthrough for us. And once more we are on the right side of the gap, so to speak. Let the enemy take note. I won't name him because I'm here in my official capacity; but his capital is Moscow. Let the informed read between my lines.

NOSE. May I quote you, Secretary McBoodle?

MCBOODLE. Go right ahead. As Secretary of Defensive Expansion, I feel that Professor Snaffle's investigations will stiffen our defensive

posture. Another defensive punch, in short. Perhaps the Polypon
will encourage other nations to eliminate their costly military
burdens and to entrust these burdens exclusively to us.

NOSE. What are *your* feelings, General Culpepper?

CULPEPPER. To speak bluntly — I agree with everything.

LOOP. Would anyone care to take a closer look at the Polypon before
Professor Snaffle arrives?

MRS. CULPEPPER. Oh, we'd better not, Mrs. Snaffle. These scientific gew-
gaws are usually so greasy!

MRS. SNAFFLE. You're perfectly right, Mrs. Culpepper. Gentlemen, leave
the delicate ladies behind!

LOOP. This way, please.

(The men inspect the Polypon, guided by Mr. Loop)

MRS. SNAFFLE. Dear Mrs. Culpepper, I declare it to the world, your dress
is a haze of radiance. Nothing, but nothing compares with shantung
for a fragile femininity like yours! And how serenely it nibbles the
waist, with more than a hint of the woman within! And so demure
as it folds here, billow upon shimmering billow. You scintillate,
Mrs. Culpepper! Your eyes, your teeth, your zipper, your diamond
necklace! But I won't even talk about that necklace! Fancy dear
General Culpepper fetching in enough money to pay for it, because
I'm simply *convinced* it's real! It thrills one with dreams of fabulous
Taj Mahal. But stop! What fragrance is this? In the crook of your
elbow! *(She flings herself upon the crook of Mrs. Culpepper's elbow
and takes a mighty whiff)* I knew it, I recognized it at once: *Défense
d'Afficher!* It brings out in you the elemental woman who dwells
eternally in man's desire, where her every golden silence whispers
yes. And what darling shoes! They take away my breath. Garbanzos
from Florence, aren't they? May I? *(She takes off one of Mrs.
Culpepper's shoes)* I was right! Garbanzos they are! Allow me.
How beautifully they match your alligator purse. Do let me run my
fingers on it! It almost bites! I love fierce things, don't you? Alligator
bags, leopard jackets, tiger's milk, bear skins. But may I peek into
your bra? "Formfitted natural uplift custom-cupped by Le Gros."
My dear, your bosom is a superb creation! A work of art! And your
corset? *(She lifts Mrs. Culpepper's dress)* No corset! Your very own
genuine shape! And a lace slip — I who just *rave* about lace. And
lace undies to match! The very very same little lace forget-me-nots
on slip and undies. Forget-me-nots! What a hint for a delicate man!
Oh Mrs. Culpepper, I pronounce your taste exquisite from top to
— bottom.

MRS. CULPEPPER. Have you noticed my ring? My dear Winston liberated
it from the finger of a Congolese chief he disemboweled in the

recent African difficulties.

MRS. SNAFFLE. How quaint! I *knew* he couldn't have found it in this country. A disemboweled chief! One must simply *struggle* to dress properly these days.

MRS. CULPEPPER. I am glad you admire me as you do, dear Mrs. Snaffle. One does like to have one's tastes confirmed by others.

MRS. SNAFFLE. Oh if only my Lancelot were a general. The conquests, the medals, the travel opportunities, the fresh air —

LOOP. Professor Snaffle!

(Snaffle briskly steps forward. General greetings)

SNAFFLE. Excuse me for being late, ladies and gentlemen. Last minute adjustments in the Expulsator. The countdown a trifle off. But we're ready now.

(He blows a whistle. Pappendeck comes in with a large instrument looking rather like a bellows that has undergone reformation in an Aerospace Laboratory. He and Loop busy themselves attaching the Expulsator, as it is called, to the underside of the Polypon by means of an enormous plug, and performing "routine checks" of the apparatus, while Snaffle addresses a few choice words to the company)

SNAFFLE. As you all know, I have worked on the Polypon for an extended period of time, verifying the amazing new potentialities through an elaborate series of experiments, and relying of course on our magnificent computer — affectionately known as Bessy — which we owe to the generous foresight of our Secretary of Defensive Expansion.

(Applause)

SNAFFLE. It has required time and effort — sweat and tears and even blood *(Loop brandishes a bandaged finger; an awed murmur is heard from the company)* — in short, untold hours of selfless devotion — to work out the optimum military applications for the Frigoradiant Polyponal Emissions, or FPE, as they are popularly known by now. My close friend and esteemed colleague, Dr. P. P. Folpap, has speculated that the Polyponal Emissions cannot be adapted to warfare. His opinion must be weighed with the greatest respect, and for myself, I refuse to regard Dr. Folpap's five successive failures with the directional system of our Goliath missile as casting any doubt on his judgment. Fortunately, scientific hypotheses are capable of verification, and I am at this moment in a position to perform before you an experiment, the results of which are likely to revolutionize our concepts of warfare. What I am contributing, ladies and gentlemen, is a foolproof means of neutralizing any Russian attempts to infiltrate our country with agents, spies, or saboteurs, plus a means of paralyzing their combat troops in the heat of action.

(Applause and exclamations)

CULPEPPER. Bravo, Snaffle — I speak bluntly, but I say: Bravo!

NOSE. We're deeply impressed, Professor Snaffle. The art of war will yet reach perfection if we keep men like yourself busy and satisfied.

MCBOODLE. Tell everybody how this new miracle of science works, Professor Snaffle.

SNAFFLE. Miracle of science indeed, Mr. McBoodle. Are we ready, Mr. Loop?

LOOP. Yes, Professor Snaffle. Eh — May I? *(He pulls Snaffle aside)* We need a few minutes; the transducer is belching again.

SNAFFLE *(low)*. All right, but get on with it, or I'll transduce every bone in your body. Of all times — *(loud)* Ahem. I am asking my assistant to give me another few minutes, my friends, because, eh, Mr. McBoodle's affecting remarks about "miracles of science" — if he will let me repeat his elegant phrase — have, eh, deeply affected me. Miracles of science! Let us look about us, my friends, and what do we see? Our mighty factories adorning our countrysides, our power lines arching their graceful nets over our metropolitan streets, our steel and glass homes, so snug and so hygienic, the melodious roar of jets in the skies and of trucks and automobiles in our very neighborhoods, our telephones, radios and televisions communicating ever more rapidly our noblest thoughts, the hot water in our houses sparing us the degrading work of heating it, our automatic stoves saving us from the agonizing work of striking matches; miracles and miracles! how can a man speak without choking, when he allows his fancy to range from the lowliest can-opener to our penetration of the moon! At this moment a flock of satellites is circling round this earth of ours, capable not only of launching our finest bombs over any chosen site with an accuracy which fills us with pride and adoration, but also of bringing to the humblest household of this world the live image of our great comedian, Spiffy Pumpkin, as he places his five toes in his mouth, all the while wiggling his ears. Calcutta sees him, Buenos Aires sees him, and — Peking sees him! Think of the promise of universal peace and brotherhood contained in that little fact! Spiffy Pumpkin's wiggling ears spreading laughter in every Communist home! And speaking of universal peace and brotherhood, let me point with ill-concealed emotion to our magnificent arsenal of supersonic fighters, our flame-throwers, machine guns, cannons, aircraft carriers, submarines, hydrogen bombs, poison gases, mortars, radar equipment, missiles and anti-missiles, and even — you will smile — the homely rifle with its everyday bullet — these too are making their patriotic contributions! What, you will say, these dangerous weapons? Is it possible, dear Professor Snaffle? Yes, my friends. These weapons, which on first appearance seem almost unfriendly, keep the enemy's teeth out of our sirloin steaks; these weapons mean butter on the bread of our working men, duties for our public servants, maneuvers for our generals, swimming-pools for our industrialists, grants, Mr. McBoodle, for our men of science, excitement for our radicals, debates for our intellectuals, sermons for our clergymen, and hope for our undertakers. Oh my contemporaries, compare yourselves with your wretched ancestors, compare your smiles, your good health, your high spirits with their gruesome medieval dejections and their dark age bank accounts, and you will join me, I know, in praising and repeating the story of Human Progress, the story of a spreading springtime of blossoms over the created land, to which, if I may conclude on a personal note, I hope I will have contributed a daisy of my own.

(*Applause*)

NOSE. And we newspapermen — you forgot to mention us, Professor Snaffle — who faithfully report the news of our progress.

MCBOODLE. And the government which makes progress the law of the land.

MRS. SNAFFLE. And we women who pass progress on to our children.

MRS. CULPEPPER. And husbands.

CULPEPPER. And the Armed Forces, which impose progress on the world, goddamit.

(*A ghastly electronic music begins, and everybody except Loop and Pappendeck, who are busy with the Expulsator, dance to it in a ring. Each one steps out of the ring to speak his verse, then rejoins the dance. Before it opens, however, Snaffle has a quick word with his invaluable assistants*)

SNAFFLE. How about that transducer?

LOOP. Almost, Professor Snaffle.

PAPPENDECK. We've almost got it, sir.

SNAFFLE. All right, all right, get on with it, you boobs.

(*Here the divertissement begins*)

CULPEPPER.	Stone Age life, in one blunt word, was crude,
	The men were mostly in a filthy mood.
	They glared and growled and took great whacks
	With club and hatchet, spear and axe.
ALL (*singing*).	But we have remedied all that.
	We wash our laundry at the laundromat.
	No Stone Age, God forbid, for me.
	We've got science, progress, and democracy.
NOSE.	In ancient Egypt who could life endure?
	For some were rich, but most were poor.
	The poor ate grass, the rich licked honey,
	And holidays abroad cost money.

ALL (*singing*).   But we have remedied all that.
We rinse our saucers in the dishomat.
No ancient Egypt, if you please, for me.
We've got science, progress, and democracy.

MRS. SNAFFLE.   And who can talk of Periclean Greece
Without a shudder in her knees?
Girl liked boy, but boy liked boy,
Even when a girl was far from coy.

ALL (*singing*).   But we have remedied all that.
We wash our laundry at the laundromat.
No Periclean Greece, no sir, for me.
We've got science, progress, and democracy.

MCBOODLE.   The Roman Age was never long at peace.
Nations, in those days, had enemies.
Between diplomacy and slaughter
They impolitely robbed each other.

ALL (*singing*).   But we have remedied all that.
We rinse our saucers in the dishomat.
No Roman Empire, my friend, for me.
We've got science, progress, and democracy.

MRS. CULPEPPER.   In Chaucer's England, horrible to tell,
Marriage was, from time to time, sheer hell.
A drunken husband and a nagging wife
Were not uncommon in pre-modern life.

ALL (*singing*).   But we have remedied all that.
The line forms at the automat.
No Middle Ages, above all, for me.
We've got science, progress, and democracy.

SNAFFLE.   Rule who ruled, Cromwell or Pope Gregory,
Ivan, Plantagenet, or Medici,
Existence was no ring of posies
But a sack of hardships and neuroses.
People coughed, and cursed, and cried,
And somehow everybody died.

ALL (*singing*).   But we have remedied all that.
One nickel in the automat.
The past is dead, our tale ends cheerfully
With science, progress, and democracy.

(*Here the divertissement ends, as Mr. Loop recalls us to the serious business of life*)

LOOP. The Expulsator is ready!

(*General satisfaction*)

NOSE. "A subdued excitement could be plainly felt in the audience."

SNAFFLE. Take your places, if you please, and let me explain the operation of the Frigoradiant Polyponal Emissions. Briefly: when the FPE are trained through the Expulsator on the coeliac ganglion of the adult Soviet male or female, they trigger the sympathetic trunk nerve, the superior laryngeal nerve, and the entire glossopharyngeal system east of Brest-Litovsk. This in turn sets up vibrations in the *plica vocalis,* known to the vulgar as the vocal cord, and these vibrations emerge as involuntary sound, to wit, the strains of *God Bless America,* in high-fidelity at less than $1/4\%$ harmonic distortion.

MRS. CULPEPPER. This is divine!

SNAFFLE. Certainly an unusual effect.

NOSE. Incredible!

SNAFFLE. That is, of course, what they told Columbus, Galileo, and Darwin. For the moment, I admit, we are able to direct these emissions only at individual subjects; but I want to paint for you a picture of what will be possible when full use is made of the Polyponal Emissions, and a whole division of enemy infantrymen is stopped in its tracks, singing *God Bless America,* while we mow them down. But these are future benefits. Let us return to the present, and begin our experiment. This is where we are all obligated once more to our Secretary of Defensive Expansion, who — but will you take it from here, Secretary McBoodle?

MCBOODLE. Well, all we've done is to contribute a live Russian spy we happened to catch the other day. Come on, let's bring him in.

(McBoodle claps his hands, and the interpreter brings in the spy by a rope affixed to a thick collar. The spy is very bushy, and his hands are tied)

MRS. SNAFFLE. I just *adore* dangerous spies.

MRS. CULPEPPER. And I am attracted to beards. It's my one secret. Yes, even enemy beards.

MCBOODLE. The man's name is Tipoff. Step forward, Tipoff, and stop muttering. Curious case. He was betrayed to the Secret Service by his own gang, who felt he'd become a liability to them. Doublecrossed by his own comrades, in short.

NOSE. Why didn't they want him any more, Mr. McBoodle?

MCBOODLE. The poor chump made the kind of blunder the Soviets don't forgive. Stole one of our top-secret designs for a retrojet unit. Passed it on to his contact. Contact passed it on to his. Bang! The design was a Russian design to begin with! — *we'd* stolen it from *them,* and now Tipoff had stolen it back from us! *(General guffawing)* Come on, Tipoff, is that the truth or isn't it? He's blushing into his beard. What's the good of being faithful to your bosses now?

SPY. Vernosts kak syr; chem starshe, tsem silneye!

MRS. CULPEPPER. Good heavens, what was that? It sounded so foreign.

INTERPRETER. He says in the dialect of the Malozemelskaya Tundra: "Loyalty is like cheese. The older, the stronger."

CULPEPPER. He must be a military man. On with the experiment, Professor Snaffle. We're all anxious to see this.

SNAFFLE. Roger, general, roger. Mr. Loop, the Expulsator, please.

MRS. CULPEPPER. Is it quite safe, Professor Snaffle? I am very sensitive.

SNAFFLE. Perfectly safe. Except for the subject, of course. (He takes hold of the Expulsator) Ready?

EVERYBODY. We are go!

SNAFFLE. Do you all know the strains of God Bless America?

EVERYBODY. Yes!

SPY. No! (With a thick Russian accent) Stop the experiment or I swear you'll be sorry!

CULPEPPER. Silence, dog! Or ten extra years in the pen.

SPY. You'll be sorry!

CULPEPPER. Shut your muzzle! (To the ladies) I apologize, dear ladies, but sometimes a soldier must talk rough. On with the experiment, Snaffle. (The spy tries to speak again) Boo!

NOSE. "An air of expectancy hung in the air."

(Snaffle gives a signal. The lights go down. The Polypon begins to crackle, rays flash from the Expulsator)

MRS. SNAFFLE. Oh, I think I'm going to faint.

MRS. CULPEPPER. Come, Mrs. Snaffle, take my hand.

(Sounds begin to come out of the spy)

MCBOODLE. Listen! He's beginning to sing. And look, he's as rigid as a flagpole!

CULPEPPER. Good work, Snaffle!

SPY (suddenly bawls out).

> Arise ye prisoners of starvation,
> Arise ye wretched of the earth!
> For justice thunders condemnation,
> A better world's in birth!

SEVERAL. What's he singing, Professor Snaffle? — This isn't God Bless America! Maybe it's a new version! — Devil's work afoot!

SNAFFLE. Mr. Loop!

LOOP. Yes, sir?

SNAFFLE. What was the man singing? I am holding you personally responsible.

LOOP. I don't know what he was singing, sir.

INTERPRETER (gloomily). He was singing the Communist Internationale.

(Sensation. The lights go on again)

CULPEPPER. An insult to my uniform!

MCBOODLE. Snaffle! We've poured twelve million into this! You've got a winter home in Florida and an expense account!

SPY. I told you you'd be sorry. Better send me back to jail.

SNAFFLE *(flings himself at the spy with a cry of rage)*. He's not a Russian spy! He's masquerading! *(He tears at the spy's beard and hair, not without meeting with strong protest, and as a matter of fact the beard and hair do come off, revealing a nice Midwestern face and a crewcut. Another sensation. The ladies scream. Snaffle is as surprised as the rest)* Holy megaton!

CULPEPPER *(thunderously)*. Agent PX-91767!

SPY. Reporting, sir.

CULPEPPER. What are you doing here?

SNAFFLE. I knew it! I knew it! The Frigoradiant Polyponal Emissions do not lie. Let me shake your hand, sir, and I hope somebody will untie it soon. You are a fine American. The experiment has been a complete success.

MRS. SNAFFLE *(embraces Snaffle)*. A chaste and wifely kiss.

MCBOODLE. You mean he's one of *your* boys, Culpepper?

CULPEPPER. Well — to speak bluntly — I —

SPY. The pipe is leaking, General. Drip drip.

CULPEPPER. Isn't he one of yours, too, McBoodle?

MCBOODLE *(indignant)*. Certainly not! The PX spy series is yours, General. I know the old Pentagon jazz but I'm not jazzing with you. I never saw the man.

NOSE *(who has been busy taking notes)*. "Thunderclap Breaks Up Experiment." What's the story, General Culpepper? Where's the slip-up?

CULPEPPER. Well — I'd have to refer to my files — I can't be expected — but the gist of it is that PX 97616 here —

SPY. 91767, General. I don't like my name mispronounced.

CULPEPPER. Agent PX 91767, as I was saying, was assigned to investigate — eh — to obtain — in short, he was on a secret mission. Right, Chuck?

SPY. How about untying me a little bit.

CULPEPPER. Oh, of course. *(The interpreter unties the spy, who bows to the ladies and sits down. Nose offers him a cigaret)*

MRS. CULPEPPER. He has excellent manners.

SNAFFLE. The main point is that the Polypon doesn't lie.

MCBOODLE. All right, PX 91767, out with it. How did you land into this mess, and how the hell did you manage to drop into our own jails disguised as a Russian?

SPY. I don't think you want to know.

MCBOODLE *(exploding)*. You don't have to think! You're in government service! Just talk, and talk good if you don't want to live on dry bread for the next twenty years.

SPY. OK. You asked for it. I was a double agent.

(*The ladies gasp*)

SNAFFLE. The Polypon knew it.

MCBOODLE. Shoot the details.

SPY. Don't rush me, Mac. OK. I'm one of your boys. That's the basic fact. OK. The Russians think I'm one of theirs, name of Tipoff. They arrange to turn me over to you. A fake double-cross. Plan is for me to give out to you like I'm sick of the Commies and I'll spy on them for you. OK. You fall for this gag, they think, and you let me make a break out of the clink so I can slip back into Russia. OK. I'm in Russia. I send you phony information to gum up the military peace effort here. Mission for the Russians accomplished. OK. But all the time I'm not really Tipoff, I'm Agent PX 91767. You people know the whole set-up —

CULPEPPER. Now I remember! I can see before my eyes the file-cabinet where I've got you!

SPY. OK. You play along. You give me the trick trial and you let me off because of the phony deal to spy for you, when I'm *really* gonna spy for you! and then you sneak me off to Russia, but let on you feel sick and crappy about it. And sure enough I send you a lot of fake secrets to please the Commies, but I mark it fake with a secret signal and send you the 24-carat stuff on the side. And that's the ticket. Pretty neat, too. But now you let that silly-ass professor experiment on me, Culpepper, the champagne is down the drain and bubbles to you.

SNAFFLE. He called me a nasty name.

MRS. SNAFFLE. Poke him, dear.

MRS. CULPEPPER. I didn't understand a word of his story, not a word, and the beard is gone too.

MCBOODLE. Please, ladies. Well, General, what have you got to say for yourself?

CULPEPPER. Well now, I just didn't — I couldn't — God frizzle it, McBoodle, am I supposed to carry my 17,000 file-cabinets all in my head, and with the budgetary squeeze we're in — 46 bleeding percent of the national revenue? The hell with it! Question the colonels. Besides, I'm a paratrooper, not a typist.

MCBOODLE (*voice of thunder*). General Culpepper!

CULPEPPER. Yes, sir.

MCBOODLE. Come here.

CULPEPPER. Yes, sir.

(*McBoodle tears off the General's stars and decorations as a token of official displeasure over his shortcomings*)

MCBOODLE. There. There. There. So much for you. I demote you to the rank of corporal and assign you to kitchen police in the Pentagon.

MRS. CULPEPPER. But that's unjust, Secretary McBoodle! Winston and I are invited to a garden party at the General Trollopes' next Sunday!

MCBOODLE. Your husband will serve drinks with a towel over his arm.

CULPEPPER. I'm bearing it like a soldier. I've broken the dishes and I've got to pay for the damage.

MCBOODLE. Fine. You're adapting to your new station in life, Corporal Culpepper. You are excused.

INTERPRETER. I could tell there was something wrong by the way he pronounced the s's.

MCBOODLE. You are excused too. (*The interpreter leaves, dangling the rope and collar*)

MRS. SNAFFLE (*very kind*). I will let you do my sewing, dearie.

MRS. CULPEPPER (*grateful*). Thank you, Mrs. Snaffle, thank you in the name of our five or six little ones. Come, Winston, I will remain at your side. Remember the Culpepper motto!

CULPEPPER. Yes, dear. "Our Wives Fight With Us Forever."

(*The Culpeppers leave*)

NOSE. A gripping scene. (*Aside to the spy*) The *Morning Pest* will offer you 25,000 for exclusive confessions.

SPY. 50,000.

NOSE. Sorry.

MCBOODLE (*to the spy*). As for you, my boy, none of this may be your fault, but your usefulness to the nation is at an end and we'll have to place you on half-pay with a good character.

SPY. Excuse me, sir. I am bound to be a nuisance to my country and a burden to the taxpayer. A secret agent, and especially a double one, knows his duty when his mission fails.

NOSE. What do you plan to do?

SPY. This. (*He produces a pistol and shoots himself*)

MRS. SNAFFLE. How tragic, and yet how inspiring.

MCBOODLE. One of our most popular spies.

NOSE (*aside*). Oh remorses! I wouldn't give him the 50,000 and he blew his brains out! (*Leaves, clutching his brow*)

SNAFFLE. Nothing Slavic about him. The Emissions are infallible, and so am I. (*To Loop and Pappendeck, indicating the body*) Would you mind?

LOOP. Not at all.

PAPPENDECK. A pleasure, sir.

SNAFFLE. Besides, I want a few words in private with the Secretary.

(*Loop and Pappendeck carry out the spy. As they do so, however, the spy hoists a small American flag*)

MCBOODLE. Patriotic even beyond the verge of life.

MRS. SNAFFLE. His mother will be so pleased.

SNAFFLE. Now then, McBoodle, I'm glad everything turned out so well. Nothing stands in the way of a contract now. Six or seven million will do for the first fiscal year, plus the usual complement of assistants, equipment, office help, nightclubs, official automobiles, and a per diem for inci —

MCBOODLE *(voice of retribution)*. Professor Snaffle!

SNAFFLE. Yes?

MCBOODLE. Your Polypon pooped.

MRS. SNAFFLE. Secretary!

MCBOODLE. Pooped I said, and pooped I mean. What, Professor Snaffle, do you propose we do with a secret weapon which causes our own mothers' boys to break out singing the Internationale at the moment of crisis? Your Polypon, sir, is a limp banana. Work on it, tinker as much as you like and come to us with results; but use your own funds! Your own funds, Snaffle! *(He leaves)*

SNAFFLE *(destroyed)*. My own funds!

MRS. SNAFFLE *(weeping)*. What's to become of us?

SNAFFLE. Hepsa Snaffle! Run full-steam after McBoodle, throw yourself against his shins! Remind him of our affection for him with madness in your eyes and delirium in your voice! Run!

MRS. SNAFFLE. I'll try, dear. *(She runs after the secretary, her arm pathetically stretched out, and crying "McBoodle!")*

SNAFFLE. What can have gone wrong? Where did I miscalculate? And you, Bessy, cold creature, is it possible? Are you willing to crush poor me like a butterfly? Do you want to see Folpap grinning from east to west? Oh, I hate you now, yes I hate you. No! What am I saying? Bessy! I meant Folpap! *(He kneels)* Hail Computer, full of cogs; the Datum is with thee; blessed art thou among devices, and blessed is the fruit of thy output terminals, Data. Holy Computer, Mother of Data, work for us physicists, now and at the hour of our miscalculations. Amen. Dear Bessy, how could I get along without you?

(Enter a folding screen, which, opened, reveals the spy dressed as a coolie. Snaffle does not notice him)

SPY. Recognize me? *(He giggles in a Chinese manner)* Me little Chink coolie now — and so forth. Now that I'm legally dead, I can be useful again in this stunning disguise. I will continue to serve what has always been my true and only fatherland: Bolivia! Yes! I am a *triple* agent! *(As the curtain falls)* Viva Bolivia! Muerte a los extranjeros! Bonitas mujeres! Frijoles refritos! *(The curtain is already down, and the applause from the audience is over, when the spy emerges again)* It's a miserable life, I tell you, but the work is steady.

ACT THREE

(Professor Snaffle sits snoring in a chair, his arms hanging down. It is a few hours after the regrettable events of the second act)

SNAFFLE *(punctuating his snores)*. Input. Output. Input. Output. My own funds! *(Enter Mr. Loop. He busies himself with the Polypon, makes sure that Snaffle is asleep, dusts off the computer, arranges the chairs, pulls his tongue at Snaffle, tinkers with the Expulsator, finally drops the Expulsator or turns over a chair. Snaffle wakes up with a start)*

SNAFFLE. Ergs and joules! Oh, it's you, Loop.

LOOP. Yes, sir. I thought I'd clean up a bit, after these fearful events.

SNAFFLE. I'd better set sail again too. Especially now. Grmph.

LOOP. I lament the disgrace that has fallen on you, Professor Snaffle.

SNAFFLE. Thank you, Loop.

LOOP. And I am very sorry that Mrs. Snaffle was not admitted to see Secretary McBoodle, and that his receptionist chased her away.

SNAFFLE. Very good of you, Loop.

LOOP. I deplore, too, that you will be cut off without a penny, sir. I feel it deeply.

SNAFFLE. I appreciate your sympathy, Loop.

LOOP. But I fervently hope that Dr. Folpap can be kept ignorant —

SNAFFLE. Blast your eyeballs, Loop, another kind word from you and I'll slap five more years on your thesis. Get out of here, I've got work to do.

LOOP. Yes, sir. *(He leaves)*

SNAFFLE. The impudence of these assistants. You use them day in and day out for sixteen years and they're not even grateful. Grateful! And who, I ask you, *is* grateful these years? The nation maybe? Ha! "Use your own funds!" Men have lost their human warmth, and we scientists are abused and exploited by the cold machine of government. Monday, as you are sharpening a pencil, an official stands before you. "Snaffle, teach us a trick to lay a dozen enemy cities flat." So we do. Tuesday, same official, "Snaffle, what's the best way to pull those cities up again? Remember them? They've become our allies." We tell them the way, and never a grumble, mind you; selfless. Wednesday, another official; the last one's in jail for selling his own chickens to the government. "Look here, Snaffle, can you make beer bottles grow on trees?" "Full or empty, sir?" "Don't waste our money with gags, Snaffle. The natives of Zanzibar want beer bottles on trees and if we don't do it for them the Russians will." I scratch my head and say, "It's an unusual problem; give me five minutes to read *Chemical Abstracts,* will you?" "Five minutes? Take five years! But there's twenty like yourself in line for this juicy contract that aren't asking for five minutes. Good-bye and use your own funds!" And that, in a word, is official gratitude. All right, gentlemen, have it your way. Secretary McBoodle, I propose to devote my efforts henceforth — or henceforward, sounds even nastier — exclusively to the non-military uses of my Polyponal Emissions. That'll show them. Peaceful applications. They'll crawl to me for a way to pulverize a population or two and I'll shout, "Nothing but peaceful applications, you gangsters!" I'll apply peaceful applications to their behinds and send them flying out of my office. Snaffle will have his revenge. Bless my goggles, what is that? Holy megaton, the Polypon is discharging!

(And, in fact, Miss Isotope is squeezing herself out of the Polypon through the rooflight. Shaken by her experience with man, she manages to climb down and to wobble about, looking hopefully for a moment of stability, or the equilibrium to which all matter aspires, including mankind. Snaffle is hiding and watching)

ISOTOPE. I's scared and I's going to break down.

(Snaffle makes a mighty pounce, catches Isotope, and waves her aloft, practically throttling her)

SNAFFLE. Ha!

ISOTOPE. Eek!

SNAFFLE. I've got you, you little weasel. The greatest discoveries are made by accident. Talk! Unzip the facts! Where do you come from? And don't deny it!

ISOTOPE *(choking).* Ggggg.

SNAFFLE *(relaxing his grip a little).* What's your name and what's your atomic weight? Out with it!

ISOTOPE. My name is Isotope.

SNAFFLE. U-238?

ISOTOPE. No, I's only seven and a half. I decay awful fast.

SNAFFLE. Listen to me, you particle. You're about to tell me precisely what's going on in the Polypon.

ISOTOPE. The whatsipon?

SNAFFLE. The Polypon — that's the scientific name of the place you've just come from, but then I don't suppose you particles know anything about science. You're going to tell me what it looks like and how it ticks.

ISOTOPE. And what if I don't?

SNAFFLE. I'll convert your bloody mass into bloody energy until there isn't any you left.

ISOTOPE. Don't do that, lord and master. I gets dizzy when I's a burst of energy. That's why I slowed down enough to be me in the first place.

SNAFFLE. Sentimentality won't help you. Get on with it. What's it look like in there? What are the laws?

ISOTOPE. I got a few snapshots, lord and master of creation. Here they be.

SNAFFLE. I'll keep them.

ISOTOPE. May I get back to the floor?

SNAFFLE. All right, but I'm holding on to your arm. What gives in the Polypon?

ISOTOPE. We dance. The bunch of us we dance all the time.

SNAFFLE. All right. I'm sitting and watching. Show me and don't try to escape.

(Isotope does her part of the dance and sings the tinkling tune of the heavens as best she can. Snaffle takes notes and makes diagrams, with an occasional "oho," "I thought so," and "the pieces fit." Suddenly Isotope stops)

ISOTOPE. That's the music of the spheres sort of, but I don't carry a tune too good.

SNAFFLE. Keep vibrating and don't change the frequency.

(Isotope resumes, but after awhile she stops again)

ISOTOPE. It just ain't right, sir lord. I mean, without the trillions of us. You don't get the — what d'you calls it? —

SNAFFLE. The configuration?

ISOTOPE. Thass right.

SNAFFLE. I'll tell you what. You volunteer to show me the way back into the Polypon so I can take in the scenery myself. That's an order.

ISOTOPE. But I don't want to go back. I's scared, and you scared up everybody else too. Everybody's spinning around.

SNAFFLE *(pulling a pistol)*. Do you see this?

ISOTOPE. Yes. It's nice.

SNAFFLE. If I let it pop, it will smash you into smudgeons. Does that appeal to you?

ISOTOPE. No.

SNAFFLE. I knew we'd agree. Back to the Polypon.

ISOTOPE. Back to the Polypon.

(She clambers up the Polypon, with Snaffle puffing after her)

SNAFFLE. Give me a hand. I'm slipping.

(They get to the top)

ISOTOPE. I's got to slip through here again but it's too tight for you.

SNAFFLE. I'll look through the hole.

ISOTOPE. You won't see much from that there angle, lord and master. But here's a place with a cork.

SNAFFLE. Sure enough. Eureka. Fancy my not noticing before. The ingenuity of Nature! *(He pulls the enormous cork and peers inside, thus*

*becoming the first man in history to obtain a direct view of the
Polypon)* There they are! Kind of battered, sure enough. All right
you. In you go.

ISOTOPE. Do you promise, lord of tissue, not to mix us up no more?

SNAFFLE. I promise —

ISOTOPE. Down I goes. *(She vanishes)*

SNAFFLE. — nothing. *(Pulls out a telescope)* I can see them all together.
Ergs and joules, they don't even look happy to see her again. Nature
is indifferent. *(We hear faintly the music of the spheres)* The little
bastards are dancing! So . . . Hmm . . . So that's it. Random motion?
We'll fix that. Look at the little positrons stuck fast to each other!
Amazing spin angular momentum. *(He takes out a stopwatch and
mumbles some calculations)* Unbelievable, but of course quite
predictable. If ever I strain the graphite out of this, God of Gods,
what a bang. Now they're starting all over. But I've seen enough.
(He produces a megaphone and applies it to the large orifice) Stop!
Stop all of you! Here is Professor Lancelot Snaffle, well known to
Nature. This is an ultimatum. I demand that you open the Polypon
to me, and to me only; and that you keep it sealed to all my enemies,
especially my friends. You are to serve me, and me only and only me.
I am imposing these conditions in the name of mankind. I am man
and without me your existence has no reason. If you refuse to open
and to surrender within ten seconds, and with smiles on your faces,
I intend to resume my deadly experiments: to shoot you full of
masers and lasers; to bring you to the heat of a billion suns; to
decompress and unhinge you; to dissolve you in horrifuric acid; and
to freeze you forever at absolute zero, or less. I am waiting. *(Silence.
To himself)* Matter is sometimes refractory. *(He brings out a hand
grenade)* We'll see. *(He tosses the grenade into the Polypon.
Explosion. Smoke appears through the vents)* Sure enough. I thought
so. *(A white flag emerges)* A white flag! And a note attached! "Walk
to the front of our Temporal Structure, knock four times, and recite
slowly: I am what I do, and I do what I know, therefore I am what
I know, yet I know not what I am." So then Snaffle, you've
conquered once more. Down you go to take possession. Folpap
is through.

*(The spy has emerged with the deepest secrecy. He is keeping a motion
picture camera trained on Snaffle, and laughs diabolically)*

SPY. No he isn't.

(Snaffle stands in front of the Polypon and knocks four times)

SNAFFLE. "I am what I do, and I do what I know, therefore I am what I
know, yet I know not what I am."

(The door of the Polypon opens. The tots, their faces smudged with

smoke, are prostrating themselves)

SNAFFLE *(royally)*. How beautiful! My children! My children! I am here for peaceful applications only.

(The spy is peeping in)

MOLECULE. Organic lord of the inorganic. We submit to you.

(Snaffle enters to the sound of triumphant trumpets, and the door closes)

SPY. I too have seen enough. It's all written down inside a sham peppermint I keep behind my second molar. If Dr. Folpap agrees to work for Bolivia, the information is his. *(He slinks out with extreme caution, but not without uttering a spine-chilling chuckle)*

ACT FOUR

(The Polypon is still in place, but the door is chained and locked. The computer is gone. Instead, we see a platform with a speaker's stand, adorned with a bright cloth showing the picture of a rocket in launching position, but half-metamorphosed into the trunk of a tree, from which leafy branches are issuing. Over the nose of the rocket hovers a dove. A placard descends from the flies. It bears the words "This is Sweden," and vanishes. Chairs have been placed in front of the platform, but for the moment a pleasant group of people is standing about and chatting vivaciously. We recognize the following: Mr. Nose, Mr. McBoodle, Mrs. Snaffle, Mr. Loop, the young Pappendeck, Mrs. Molassis — formerly Mrs. Culpepper — and the former General Culpepper, now a waiter with a moustache and a French accent who is handing cocktails and digestible dainties around)

MRS. MOLASSIS *(to Mrs. Snaffle)*. Ten minutes after I met my dear Molassis on his yacht, he declared he simply could not exist without me. I am told he dropped three lady-friends on the spot. This made quite a noise, of course. One of them was a soprano. But nothing could quench his desire for me. It was caviar and pheasant all the way. But I told him, "Bathing in Chateau Lafite is very well for your sopranos and your Spanish duchesses, but I am a simple American girl and with me you'll have to come by your raptures legally."

MRS. SNAFFLE. Bravo! And what did he say to that?

MRS. MOLASSIS. He was ever so understanding. And I could see that I had won his respect. What a high C could not accomplish, a moral stand did.

MRS. SNAFFLE. But what happened next, dear Mrs. Molassis?

MRS. MOLASSIS. I divorced Culpepper on grounds of extreme cruelty, namely his reduced income, and I married dear, dear Triandaphilos — that's his little name — on board his yacht between one Cyclad and another. It was marvelously thrilling. Princess Grace was with us, of course. She plays such a divine roulette!

MRS. SNAFFLE. I'm so sorry dear Mr. Molassis couldn't be among us this afternoon.

MRS. MOLASSIS. He simply can't stir from our yacht, my dear. He becomes landsick.

CULPEPPER *(with a tray)*. Cocktelles, ladies?

MRS. MOLASSIS. French waiters have such — such Savor Fair! Ah, there's our dear McBoodle!

MCBOODLE *(kissing hands)*. Delighted, delighted.

MRS. MOLASSIS. Naughty! He only kisses a lady's hand when he is abroad. Are you in Sweden just for the ceremony, Mr. McBoodle?

MCBOODLE. And the usual small-talk about rocket bases, Mrs. Molassis. But where is dear Mr. Molassis? Whipping the galley-slaves, eh? *(Laughs)*

MRS. MOLASSIS. Oh — such an idea — Mr. McBoodle — these are wicked, wicked rumors. Molassis is ever so democratic. He calls the whole crew "his boys" and he dunks his bread in the gravy. Oh, Dr. Loop, so delighted!

LOOP. Alas, still old Mr. Loop, dear Mrs. Molassis, but at your service as always.

MRS. MOLASSIS. Dear me, what Europe does to people! *(She takes Loop by the arm)* I am simply fascinated by thermodynamics, and you and I are going to gossip about retarded potentials. *(They walk away)*

MCBOODLE. My dear Mrs. Snaffle, this must be the greatest moment of your life. And such an honor to our country! Ever since Dr. Folpap defected to Bolivia, we have been afraid of losing our keenest brains.

MRS. SNAFFLE. Oh no, Mr. McBoodle! Lancelot would *never* defect. Wintering in Florida is simply his addiction.

MCBOODLE. A great man, Mrs. Snaffle. When I see a person of his calibre getting the Dynamite Peace Prize, I realize there is a Justice in the world, an Eye that watches us all.

MRS. SNAFFLE. The dear works hard enough, I'll say that for him.

MCBOODLE. Why, his Polyponal Pedilift has brought relief and comfort to untold millions. At last a substitute for walking!

NOSE *(joining in)*. "Untold millions" is newspaper talk, Mr. McBoodle, and I take this pretext by the horns to butt in.

MRS. SNAFFLE. Do, dear Mr. Nose.

NOSE. My ravishing lady, I covered your husband for my paper from the moment he laid hands on the Polypon. But how I wish that I could cover you!

MRS. SNAFFLE. What *does* Europe do to people?

NOSE. Waiter!

CULPEPPER. Monsieur.

NOSE *(with a new drink)*. I propose a toast to Professor Snaffle, whom the world honors today with the most coveted award in Christendom. For the record or off the record, McBoodle?

MCBOODLE. One for and one off.

NOSE. A toast!

(The others join and all raise their glasses to toast Professor Snaffle. Mrs. Molassis, Loop and Pappendeck are now in the foreground)

LOOP. You have met my young assistant, Pappendeck.

MRS. MOLASSIS. Yes. And here you are, the two of you who have labored at the side of the great Lancelot Snaffle, the disciples who followed with him the shining star of knowledge. It's simply thrilling.

PAPPENDECK. I am more thrilled to be standing so close to you at last, Mrs. Molassis.

MRS. MOLASSIS. Your young man is a graduate in compliments as well, Dr. Loop. Charming!

LOOP. Europe . . .

PAPPENDECK *(pressingly)*. I have always longed for a middle-aged woman to teach me the wild caresses she knows only too well.

MRS. MOLASSIS. Middle-aged! Excuse me, but —

PAPPENDECK *(languorously)*. Let me place my monograph on "Excitation of Magnetic Susceptibility" at your feet. I broke through every equation to reach a proposition which might find favor in your eyes.

MRS. MOLASSIS. A proposition! Already! Excuse me, but the ceremony is about to start and I *must* do my hair. *(She leaves)*

LOOP. You've done it, Pappendeck, you frightened her with the wild caresses and all that. Now she's gone off to comb her hair.

PAPPENDECK. No, I could see that my adolescent fires troubled and aroused her. Disheveled is not her hair but her soul.

MCBOODLE *(joining them)*. Your assistant has a long antenna out for Mrs. Molassis, if I'm not mistaken.

LOOP. The lab is such a poor outlet for a young man's tempestuous cravings, Secretary McBoodle.

MCBOODLE. If he wants to visit a broad that bad, let him join the Navy and travel. *(Roars with laughter)*

CULPEPPER. Un cocktelle, messieurs?

MCBOODLE. Sure. Say, I'll bet my diapers I've seen you somewhere before.

CULPEPPER. That is not impossible, monsieur.

MCBOODLE *(takes him aside)*. Fact is, you're as like General Culpepper as two jiggers of scotch, except for the moustache and the voulezvous stuff.

CULPEPPER *(dropping the accent).* I *was* General Culpepper, McBoodle.

MCBOODLE. I never forget a man, especially when I've done him in. But I bear no grudge against you, Culpepper. How's life been treating you?

CULPEPPER. You assigned me to kitchen police in the Pentagon.

MCBOODLE. I remember.

CULPEPPER. They made me wait on tables, and I got to enjoy the life. So I decided to quit the army and go professional. Nobody can take orders like an ex-general.

MCBOODLE. Leave it to McBoodle. He knows where a man belongs.

CULPEPPER *(French accent again).* Pardon, here is Madame Molassis who enters without a drink. *(To Mrs. Molassis)* Un p'tit cocktelle, madame? *(Confidentially)* I am your humble adorateur, Madame Molassis.

MRS. MOLASSIS. What? *(Culpepper is gone again)* I'm positively persecuted today! A boy who shaved for the first time a week ago, and a faded French waiter, not to mention the knuckle-smooching of McBoodle. Well, it does prove I appeal to all kinds.

MRS. SNAFFLE. Dear Mrs. Molassis, do join our little circle.

NOSE. We are toasting Professor Snaffle once more, as much, it must be confessed, for the sake of the excellent liquid as for that of the matchless Professor.

MRS. MOLASSIS. A toast!

(Culpepper presents her with a glass. Professor Snaffle is toasted. And at that moment he himself enters, preceded by the Duke of Ostersund. Spontaneous applause. The Duke directs Snaffle to one of the chairs by the speaker's stand. Snaffle is holding a small box, which he carefully places on the chair next to his, and which he will be stroking amiably now and then. He and all present, it goes without saying, are dressed with the greatest formality and elegance. The Duke is kissing Mrs. Snaffle's hand)

DUKE. Dear Mrs. Snaffle!

MRS. SNAFFLE. Dear your Grace!

DUKE. My friends, please possess your places. The ceremony is about to incipiate and I must be deliver my speech. *(He mounts the platform and takes the speaker's stand)* Ladies and gentlemen, as Chairman of the Selection Board of the Dynamite Peace Prize, I am deeply afflicted to give the prize this year to the renownable American physicist and mathematician, Professor Lancelot Snaffle. *(Ovation)* The Dynamite Peace Prize, I am glad to reminisce you, was funded by Sigurd Loftung, who did give the world so much explosive without he kept it from any nation that wished to have it, he was so generous. How happy Sigurd Loftung would be if he is with us today, when we honor and do give money to Professor Snaffle for the Polyponal Pedilift! Let me bepaint the human's condition before the Pedilift exploded in the scene. The humans had maked missiles who fly to the Moon and to Mars. Good. They fabricate airplanes who fly from one ending of the globe to the other. Good. They invent steamships who run over the ocean and submarines who are giggling under the water. Good. They make railroads and autobuses and scooters. It is the miracle! The human man makes more and more effort to make less and less effort. And this, ladies and gentlemen, is the aiming of science and technology, is to make the life easy. Relax, as you Americans say.

MCBOODLE. Such a brilliant diplomat.

DUKE. But evermore and yet, the man and the woman must use and articulate his muscles of the leg: the *sartorius*, the *quadriceps femoris*, the *biceps femoris*, the *adductor magnus*, and much others, all in Latin. Because not all the distances are formidably enormious. Professor Snaffle has magnificently calculated that 65% of humane trajections is of the order of 2 km or under. Imaginate! The terrible sap of energy, the attrition of lymph, the unendless output of heat, the debiliting of the heart, the decay of the tissue — all this, and it is a malicious picture — means that our life is extremely shorter as it has the necessary to be. We relax when we do travel from New York to Stockholm, but we do not relax when we do walk to the grocery storage to purchase a bottle of milk, if I may be let loose a filthy image. 65% of our trajections are using non-necessary animal energies. And also it is using non-necessary spiritual attentions, because we see a dog in the way and we say "excuse me," and we notify a piddle in the street and we are worried not to bestep it. In one word, we are watching our muscles when we can be thinking over noble and great thinkings. And that is why the Pedilift is a liberator! It releases to the liberty new energies hitherbefore by mankind expended into the mechanical ambulating locomotion. One day it is perhaps that walking can be annihilated completely. Not perhaps! I beforecast certainly! Man shall be conquering the painful walking! But until that glorible day, we shall proudly step into the earth with Professor Lancelot Snaffle's Pedilift. (*Ovation*) And now, I present Professor Lancelot Snaffle himself!

(*Snaffle acknowledges the applause, shakes the Duke's hand, and takes the speaker's stand, blowing his nose and wiping a tear*)

SNAFFLE. I am overcome . . . So many friendly faces . . . The tear must fall. My friends, pardon this weakness. Your Grace, Duke of Ostersund, before I accept the modest yet nutritious check awarded to me for my peaceful application, I want to offer you all a little surprise: the Pedilift itself!

(*Applause*)

DUKE. Delicious!

(*Snaffle blows his whistle, and Mr. Smith the demonstrator enters equipped with the Pedilift. The Pedilift, speaking roughly, consists of an extremely heavy kind of metal knapsack, containing the machinery. From this piece, which burdens the demonstrator to a perspiration, emerges a system of rods, shafts, cams and gears which culminate in a pair of braces for the legs and feet. The Pedilift also has a conspicuous opening for the insertion of the Frigoradiant Capsule, and levers for starting, stopping, speed, direction, etc. The demonstrator walks like a very noisy robot*)

SNAFFLE. The demonstrator is still using his own energy, ladies and gentlemen; energy which, as his Grace pointed out a moment ago, should be put to higher uses than getting from one place to another. I am not the first Benefactor of Mankind to have attempted to relieve man of the primitive need of using his own feet; but I *am* the first to have given the problem its final solution. This solution, ladies and gentlemen, is due to my Polypon, whose Frigoradiant Emissions I have succeeded in concentrating in capsule form. Here is a typical pellet. It will be sold in attractive packages at every supermarket in the country. Mr. Smith, will you kindly introduce it into the Injector? Observe, ladies and gentlemen, that this tiny capsule, which I am holding in my ungloved hand, has such a lengthy half-life that it hardly needs a full life. It will last Mr. Smith 300,000 years! (*Murmur of amazement among the laymen*) Remains only the project of making Mr. Smith last 300,000 years. Here, Mr. Smith. (*He gives Smith the capsule*) Watch him if you can. He sets the Directional Pointer and the Path Computer. Now he sets the required speed, which he can change midcourse at will, or pre-change through the built-in electronic brain. Now he switches on the Angular Release, which enables him to ascend or descend steps, and to kick impediments away. Are you ready, Mr. Smith? Have you chosen your destination?

SMITH. Yes sir.

SNAFFLE. Contact!

(*The demonstrator walks with a great noise. Exclamations of admiration. He walks up and down the steps of the platform*)

DUKE (*beaming and applauding*). Disgraceful!

MCBOODLE. Ouch! My foot!

SMITH (*passing by*). Sorry, Mr. McBoodle.

SNAFFLE. Please observe, all his energies are now available to him for intellectual functions.

NOSE. Where is he going?

(*Mr. Smith walks straight to Mrs. Molassis, kisses her passionately, and picks her up under his arm*)

MRS. MOLASSIS. How unusual!

SNAFFLE. Mr. Smith!

PAPPENDECK. Mrs. Molassis!

NOSE. "The Romance of Science!"

MRS. MOLASSIS (*as she is carried away*). My worst enemy is my beauty. Thank God. (*Smith vanishes with her*)

DUKE (*still applauding*). Most disgraceful and delightly!

PAPPENDECK. What a wink she gave me as she left!

MCBOODLE (*to Culpepper*). Aren't you going to stop them?

CULPEPPER. Why? Madame left her glass behind, didn't she?

SNAFFLE. Well! This ought to remove any doubt as to the efficiency of my Pedilift. Your Grace, I am ready to be honored.

DUKE. An expiring spectacle, Professor Snaffle. Another applause? To the Pedilift, and the happiness of Mrs. Molassis. And now, in the name of the King, the Cabinetry, and the Dynamite Peace Prize Selection Board, I present to you, Lancelot Snaffle, the Sigurd Loftung Award of the year. (*He produces a large shopping bag, extracts from it some groceries, and finally a large tin whose label, "Laurel Crowns, imported from Greece," he reads aloud. He opens the tin, extracts the crown, remarking that it is very fresh, and places it on Snaffle's head. Applause. Then he produces a check from a wallet*) In Swedish kronor, Professor Snaffle, at 5.18 to the dollar.

(*Snaffle has his hand out for it, when Dr. P. P. Folpap makes a dramatic and most unwelcome entrance. He sports a villain's mustachio.*)

FOLPAP. Stop! The award is mine!

SNAFFLE. Folpap!

(*Sensation*)

DUKE. Dr. Folpap, the great Bolivian theoretician!

MCBOODLE. Deserter!

FOLPAP. Silence! I come forward to challenge Lancelot Snaffle! He has forfeited his right to the Dynamite Peace Prize!

ALL. Why?

FOLPAP. Because he stole *my* idea!

SNAFFLE. Stole? Stole your idea?

MRS. SNAFFLE. Your Grace —

DUKE. Stole, Dr. Folpap? That is an illegitimate word.

FOLPAP. I withdraw it. But I contend that Professor Snaffle has been less than original in his invention, for his Pedilift shows an unmistakable debt to my own Footomat, a debt which candor would have compelled him to admit in public.

DUKE. That is better.

SNAFFLE. Better, your Grace, you call this better? I'm dreaming! Who discovered the Polypon? Who created Frigoradiant Emissions? Who published the results in the *Physics Quarterly*?

FOLPAP. And who miscarried in his experiments so wretchedly that he caused an American spy to intone the *Internationale*?

SNAFFLE. And who flubbed the Goliath missile five times?

FOLPAP. And who lost his government contract?

SNAFFLE. It's a lie!

FOLPAP. A lie? A lie? You say this to a member of the Institute for Advanced Brooding?

DUKE. A lie, Professor Snaffle . . .

MCBOODLE. No international incidents, Snaffle. Bolivia is touchy.

SNAFFLE. I apologize. But I affirm under oath that my esteemed colleague has drawn a hasty inference, and that his conclusions are not, perhaps, convincingly buttressed by the available evidence, nor marked by the forthrightness we have come to expect of him.

MCBOODLE. That's very handsome, Snaffle, old man.

NOSE. "Scholarly Debate Enlivens Peace Prize Giveaway."

PAPPENDECK. We're with you all the way, Professor Snaffle.

CULPEPPER. I will refuse to serve him, Monsieur le Professeur.

MRS. SNAFFLE. Oh, thank you, thank you. This is such a trial for me. (*She breaks down*)

DUKE. Is it peaceful among us again? Sigurd Loftung —

FOLPAP. Your Grace! It is *not* peaceful! I am indignant! But I intend to maintain my case by visible fact. Allow me.

(*He too blows a whistle, and Mr. Jones, the second demonstrator, comes in, wearing a hat. He is carrying pretty much the same apparatus as Mr. Smith — though in a different color — but his has an additional contraption, namely an articulated claw which clasps his hat*)

NOSE. Another Pedilift!

FOLPAP. Not a Pedilift, sir. A Footomat.

DUKE. This is a real disturbement.

SNAFFLE. A miserable copy of the Pedilift.

FOLPAP. I scorn to reply. Your Grace, if you will kindly stay where you are, I will ask Mr. Jones to walk in front of you while reading a newspaper. Mr. Jones?

JONES (*producing a newspaper*). The Ogallalla Daily Gazette. I am reading it and paying no attention to anything.

(*He starts the levers and walks with his nose in the newspaper. As he passes before the Duke the respectful machinery lifts his hat and sets it back on his head*)

MCBOODLE. Say!

NOSE. It lifted the hat!

CULPEPPER. Very French.

LOOP (*rushing to his doom*). Excellent! Excellent! Excellent! (*He claps*)

SNAFFLE. Mr. Loop!

LOOP. Bravo, I repeat. It lifts the hat. Dr. Folpap, I wish to congratulate you on this brilliant invention.

FOLPAP. Thank you, *Dr.* Loop.

SNAFFLE. Loop, you cockroach, you scumbum, he doctors you, but you just wait.

LOOP. Piffle.

SNAFFLE. I'm dreaming! Hepsa!

MRS. SNAFFLE. Oh Lancelot!

FOLPAP. Please observe, your Grace, that my Footomat affords its user an amazing new convenience; to wit, it allows a mechanism to take over the burdensome and distracting duties of everyday courtesy. The benefits which will accrue to mankind through the automation of politeness can hardly be overestimated. And note that my Footomat will doff the hat of the most backward jungle native as easily as yours and mine, thus promoting the cause of world understanding. It will also shake hands through an elaborate system of cranks and shafts at a small additional cost.

NOSE. This is front page meat. "Jet Age Comes to Good Manners."

DUKE. Professor Snaffle, what do you please to say to this more refined achievement?

SNAFFLE. Very impressive, of course.

DUKE. Aha. Excuse me — (*He removes Snaffle's crown*) Dr. Folpap —

FOLPAP. Thank you. The money too.

SNAFFLE. Eh. One moment. May we see the demonstration again, my dear Folpap?

FOLPAP. Gladly. Mr. Jones, the Gazette. Go!

(*Snaffle pretends to come in for a close observation, but instead he places a chair in Jones' path while everybody is exclaiming over the hat. Jones falls over the chair with an homeric clatter*)

FOLPAP. Jones!

EVERYBODY. Oh!

JONES. Who's the idiot? Help me up, you fools. Goddam shaft in my rib.

SNAFFLE. Poor man. Take my hand.

MCBOODLE. Up you go. Watch out for my foot.

MRS. SNAFFLE. Serves him right.

FOLPAP. I suggest that this chair did not travel fortuitously to the locus of intersection with Mr. Jones!

JONES. Stuffed hokum! Somebody put the chair in my way and I'm gonna make him eat it!

DUKE. But this is beyond belief, Dr. Folpap.

SNAFFLE (*nobly*). No. Dr. Folpap is right. It was I who placed the chair in Mr. Jones' way.

FOLPAP. He admits it!

JONES. Why you — wait till I get rid of this junk —

MCBOODLE. Snaffle! Our prestige —

SNAFFLE. One moment! Mr. Jones, I apologize to you and Mrs. Snaffle will tip you at the exit. For the rest, my friends, I only intended to show you the shortcomings of my brilliant colleague's imitation of the original Pedilift. No, Dr. Folpap, *I* am speaking now.

(*He blows his whistle again. Smith reappears, still carrying Mrs. Molassis, though she is now in a state of minor disarray which discretion must overlook*)

MCBOODLE. Welcome back!

PAPPENDECK. She found me again!

MRS. MOLASSIS. Do set me down in a chair, Jimmy sweet. (*She tousles Mr. Smith's hair*) Dear friends, have I been missed?

CULPEPPER. Another cocktelle, madame?

MRS. MOLASSIS. Thank you. Mrs. Snaffle! (*They embrace*)

MRS. SNAFFLE. Dear Mrs. Molassis! I have gone through so much!

SNAFFLE. Delighted, Mrs. Molassis. Come here, Smith, and let me equip you. (*Aside to him*) Damn it, you took off the machinery. What for?

DUKE (*to Mrs. Molassis*). I will tend over you in the tingling of an eye. (*He kisses her hand*) What are you doing, Professor Snaffle?

SNAFFLE (*taking the secret device out of the box*). I am equipping the Pedilift with radar.

SEVERAL. Radar!

FOLPAP (*aside*). Lost!

LOOP (*aside*). My doctorate is dead!

MRS. MOLASSIS. Jimmy, do be careful!

SMITH. No danger, lassie. I've been vaccinated.

SNAFFLE. Gather round, ladies and gentlemen, gather round and watch. The Frigoradiant Capsule, Smith?

SMITH. Here it is, sir.

MRS. MOLASSIS (*to Mrs. Snaffle*). Isn't he darling? My own Tirian — Tridalph — Trinian — oh dear, these exotic names! But what's in a name, as Desdemona says? I simply mean my own Molassis; he is rich but he is practically an Ancient Greek.

PAPPENDECK (*who has nuzzled in*). And I am poor but young, Mrs. Molassis.

MRS. MOLASSIS. Naughty! (*To Mrs. Snaffle, in strict confidence*) Between us, these capsules have a marvelous effect on — in short, a marvelous side-effect.

SNAFFLE. Ready! Dr. Folpap, may I trouble you for the Ogallalla Gazette? Now, Mr. Smith, leave the room for a moment while I allow the audience to scatter in a random dispersion. *(Smith leaves with the Gazette)* All right, everybody, take up any position you like, sitting or standing. Dr. Folpap, will you monitor the experiment? And my excellent Mr. Loop, and Mr. Jones, may we have your cooperation as well, in the interest of science?

JONES. I'm game.

LOOP. Delighted, Dr. Snaffle. A brilliant experiment.

MRS. MOLASSIS. I'm so glad I didn't miss this!

PAPPENDECK. I will disperse myself at random beside you.

MRS. MOLASSIS *(coquette)*. I really don't think I should let you, Mr. Pappendeck.

MCBOODLE. I'll take up a chance position near the martinis.

SNAFFLE. Everybody ready?

EVERYBODY. Ready!

(Snaffle blows his whistle. Enter Smith, arduously reading the Gazette)

SNAFFLE. Not a word, not a whisper from anybody. Take a casual walk, my boy.

(Smith circulates with a ghastly clanking among the spectators in the room, neatly avoiding them all. Whenever he comes near a person, there is a toot from a horn, and he veers away. Gurgles of suppressed amazement. Folpap tries in vain to make him collide with himself; Smith avoids him every time)

SNAFFLE. Test him, test him, worthy colleague. Still plunged in the Gazette, mind you. An interesting publication from the provinces.

(Smith finally arrives before Mrs. Molassis, who prepares herself for another abduction. But the horn toots, Smith clanks on and vanishes from the scene)

MRS. MOLASSIS. Jimmy!

(The others applaud and cry Bravo)

MRS. SNAFFLE. My hero! *(Embraces Snaffle)*

LOOP. A magnificent achievement! A Pedilift with radar and 100% accurate!

DUKE. Professor Snaffle, the prize is yours! Not another word!

CULPEPPER. Champagne!

(General enthusiasm)

MRS. MOLASSIS. Jimmy . . .

FOLPAP *(in a corner)*. I am disgraced forever. History books will caricature me as a spiteful failure. And yet I too was a gifted man. *(He flees)*

JONES. Hey, my wages! *(He clanks after Folpap as best he can)* Damn this contraption! *(Exit)*

(Everybody except Pappendeck and Mrs. Molassis is crowding around

Snaffle)
DUKE. The laurel crown.
SNAFFLE. And the check.
(Much hand-shaking, compliment-making, champagne-bibbing)
PAPPENDECK. Mrs. Molassis, I am still here.
LOOP. Professor Snaffle, it is with a feeling as deep as the abyss —
SNAFFLE. Sir, you are dust.
LOOP. Yes, Professor Snaffle.
SNAFFLE. You will take your dingy person and your limp degree elsewhere.
LOOP. Yes, Professor Snaffle.
SNAFFLE. You will pick up your pipettes at the lab, and bestow your absence on me. I know you no longer.
LOOP. I deserved this. Let oblivion snuff me out. *(Stumbles off)*
DUKE. Morality has winned, as always.
NOSE. "Traitor Meets With Just Deserts."
MRS. SNAFFLE. The ungrateful man! After twenty years of service to my husband.
CULPEPPER. More champagne!
DUKE. Music! Let the fanfares jubilate!
(Music. Procession. Clanking of Pedilift and tooting of horn. Brandishing of champagne glasses. General hilarity)
SNAFFLE *(drinking)*. Next step: an atom smasher in every backyard!
EVERYBODY. Hurrah!
(The procession is on its way out)
PAPPENDECK *(to Mrs. Molassis)*. Dearest Ursula . . . tonight, in my private cloud chamber . . .
MRS. MOLASSIS. Rudolph, my good name!
DUKE. Let the trombones festivate!
(Pappendeck roots a passionate kiss on Mrs. Molassis' hand as the procession leaves the stage)

ACT FIVE

(The Polypon as before. From the flies a placard bearing the inscription "U.S.A." appears for a moment, followed soon after by the spy. He is dressed as a British agent — mackintosh and all — and speaks accordingly. He lights a cigarette, glances right and left in a professionally inconspicuous manner and starts to make calculations on a pad)

SPY. Smashing. Fitz-Gordon, you've done it again. Sold Snaffle to Folpap, and then sold Folpap to Snaffle. Might have shuttled two or three times more — sold Snaffle's secret information about Folpap's secret

information about Snaffle back to Folpap, and then forward again
to Snaffle — but that kind of beauty's beyond these science chaps.
What ho, here's the old blighter at last.

*(He tucks his pad away. Enter Snaffle, with extreme but less professional
caution, walking on tiptoes, his collar turned up, his head anxiously
wagging to and fro. He sheers toward the spy)*

SNAFFLE. Pardon me, have you got a light?

SPY. You bet. But where's your cigarette?

SNAFFLE. Damn. *(He fumbles in his pockets)* Have you got a cigarette too?

SPY. Never mind, gov'nor. Let's push on with it. Where's the 3,000 quid?

SNAFFLE. It wasn't easy, Fitz-Gordon. I borrowed —

SPY. Borrowed my mother's navel! You're making millions with your
bloody capsules. Come on, Snaffle, pop out the three thousand.

SNAFFLE. All right, all right. *(He counts out a bundle of banknotes to
the spy)*

SPY. Right. Well, good luck to you, Yank. *(Leaves)*

SNAFFLE. Now I am master at last! I have bestowed the Pedilift on
humanity and given bunions their death-blow. Astute in my bene-
factions, I leased the Pedilift patent for an outrageously businesslike
sum of money, while I retained full and exclusive rights over the
capsules which make it move. I am now not only extremely
intelligent and extremely foul-minded, but extremely rich into the
bargain. I am so important that I will not go to the john without
my lawyer's advice. I have also become modest, and why not?
The world sees through my modesty. Women adore me for my well-
publicized secret charities. And, to sum it all up, I am a man to whom
headwaiters bring telephones in the middle of dinner with urgent
calls from Paris or Damascus. But come along, I am going to inspect
my Capsule Corporation.

*(Snaffle unlocks the Polypon, whose doors slide open again. Factory
scene with fluorescent light and assembly belt. An office desk at one side.
The tots in a grey platoon are turning out capsules. Appropriate back-
ground noise)*

SNAFFLE. Look at them. Fully automated!

TOTS *(performing a Factory Dance)*.

> When long ago, without much explanation,
> The Primal Blast put tiny us in operation,
> Some say what set us fussing was Creation;
> We, however, call it automation.
>
> And since we started, sad to tell, we've carried on
> Planting suns and moons on the celestial lawn.
> We make the waves carouse, the robins peep,
>   the salmon spawn;

We are the sonnet and the cyclotron.

And now we labor for mankind and bend
To turn out capsules to your hearts' content.
Mankind will pass, of course (we don't mean to offend),
But we march forward, automated to the end.

(Snaffle blows his whistle. The tots lay down their tools, advance in regimental order, and salute. Molecule steps forward)

MOLECULE. Molecule reporting, sir. All Tots accounted for. Machinery at 35% capacity to prevent overproduction and buttress prices. Quota for today 76% filled.

SNAFFLE. At ease. All right, you brats, back to work and no coffee break. Let me see today's orders and the mail. *(He sits at his desk)*

MOLECULE. Here you are, sir.

SNAFFLE *(to Atom, using a long whip-handle to reach him)* You.

ATOM. Yes, sir.

SNAFFLE. Drop that oil can and let me see some of these capsules. *(Tapping Isotope)* And you. Light me a cigar and make an ashtray. *(Atom and Isotope obey. While Atom returns to work, Isotope stands by the desk holding her hand open for ashes. Snaffle examines a few capsules)* Not bad. Not bad. Good quality control. The petroleum interests are yelling guff and murder. Wells closing down from Oklahoma to Yemen. *(To Molecule)* All right, you. Take these capsules back and don't dawdle. Your time is my money.

MOLECULE. Yes, sir.

SNAFFLE. Let's look at the orders. Hm. Manchester wants 22,300 capsules, delivery in three months. Liège: 20,000. Düsseldorf: 14,500. What's this? Five! Oh, Lichtenstein. Ha ha, the usual from Smolensk: 30,000 for this month, but must be labelled Made in Smolensk. *(To Isotope, as he flicks an ash)* Are you staring at me?

ISOTOPE. No, lord and master of albumen.

SNAFFLE. I know you're as willing to work for the enemy as for us. Damned particles! Get rid of these ashes and scratch behind my left ear. A little lower. A little higher. Enough. Get back to the production line . . . Hm . . . Where's the mail . . . Ergs and joules! Pink envelope and rose-blossom perfume. Yum-yum! *(He is about to open the letter when the intercom buzzes)* Miss Growley? *(Aside)* Miss Growley is my secretary's secretary. Yes? So what? I know he's been waiting for three hours. Muttering! Who does he think he is? I'm busy. What's that? . . . Oh, all right, have him come in but tell him I'm busy. *(Aside)* That'll show him. *(Enter McBoodle)*

SNAFFLE. So, it's you, McBoodle.

MCBOODLE. Yes, Professor Snaffle. *(Meekly)* I hope I haven't disturbed you by waiting in your reception room a tiny half-hour.

SNAFFLE. No, that's all right. Sit down if you want to and tell me what's on your mind. I'm in a hurry.

MCBOODLE. Thank you; I'm most grateful. I hope that Mrs. Snaffle —

SNAFFLE. To the point, man, this is a business office, not a drawing-room.

MCBOODLE. Quite so. Amazing efficiency. Admiration of the world. I'm here, Professor Snaffle, on behalf of the government — specifically, of course, the Department of Defensive Expansion —

SNAFFLE. Which awarded me a handsome kick in the rear not long ago.

MCBOODLE. We are extremely interested in renewing contact with your enterprise. The Pedilift might be adapted for jungle and mountain warfare — places where the conventional foot-soldier is still needed. You see the picture, Professor Snaffle.

SNAFFLE. Sure. But I'm dedicated to peaceful applications, thank you.

MCBOODLE. I might secure a contract for you — may I lean forward? — this is an approximate figure — *(He whispers a figure to Snaffle)*

SNAFFLE. I see. Of course, jungle and mountain warfare are a kind of peaceful application too. Peace of mind for the Army.

MCBOODLE. Exactly.

SNAFFLE. I hope nobody has ever questioned my patriotism, in spite of my devotion to peace.

MCBOODLE. Questioned your patriotism! Professor Snaffle, the very thought is shocking.

SNAFFLE. The contract you were talking about —

MCBOODLE. Is only a beginning. That's understood. A period of extensive testing . . . Of course, certain congressional committees must be sold on the idea.

SNAFFLE. Sold . . .

MCBOODLE. And I'm prepared to use my influence.

SNAFFLE. Sit over here, McBoodle, you'll be more comfortable. Put your feet up; here, that's better. I think I've got a bottle of something in the cabinet. Wait. *(He pours drinks)*

MCBOODLE. Here's to you, Snaffle old man.

SNAFFLE. And to you. Hey! it's good to see an old friend again. How's Mrs. McBoodle these days?

MCBOODLE. I'm not married, but I bet she'd be fine if I were.

SNAFFLE. Let me fill you up again.

MCBOODLE. Thanks.

SNAFFLE. What's the deal, old man? You know me; cards on the table.

MCBOODLE. Snaffle, this is the time to strike. The sky's the limit. But you need an inside man, and that's where I come in. If there's one guy in town who can tell you where the switches are located, it's Crusher McBoodle.

SNAFFLE. I always knew it. Many's the time I've wished I could work something out with you. But cards on the table, McBoodle. What's in this for you?

MCBOODLE. Nothing at all, Snaffle.

SNAFFLE. That's going to be more than I can afford. But if you're willing to be reasonable, I'll listen to your proposition.

MCBOODLE. All I want you to do is take on a man — I'll name him — take him on as — I don't care what — vice-president in charge of procurement — and put him on a ten-year contract — at a hundred thousand a year.

SNAFFLE. Seventy-five.

MCBOODLE. Ninety.

SNAFFLE. Eighty.

MCBOODLE. Eighty-seven.

SNAFFLE. Eighty-five.

MCBOODLE. Shake.

SNAFFLE. Shake.

MCBOODLE. We're in business, pal.

SNAFFLE. There's only one more thing I want from you, McBoodle.

MCBOODLE. What's that?

SNAFFLE. I want you to use your credit to get me —

MCBOODLE. Get you what?

SNAFFLE. I'm blushing.

MCBOODLE. Go on, you rascal.

SNAFFLE. No, I really am blushing.

MCBOODLE. Go on, drink up — one, two — and tell all to old Crusher.

SNAFFLE. Well, I'd like — I've always wanted — it's nothing, actually —

MCBOODLE. Out with it!

SNAFFLE. A few — statues to Lancelot Snaffle — in squares and parks — here and there — now I've said it.

MCBOODLE. You've got a sensational idea there. Snaffle, you're one of the finest promotion men in the country. What a stunt! Statues! "A great public servant!" I'll get it done, Snaffle, it's gonna rain statues, leave it to me. "In recognition for his" etc. etc. What a stunt! Okay, Snaffle, I'm off. Remember I came here to talk to my old pal about tennis and golf.

SNAFFLE. Right. (He switches on the intercom) Miss Growley, will you see Secretary McBoodle out? Thank you. So long, old friend.

MCBOODLE. Nice to see you again, and say hello to the Misses for me. (He leaves)

TOTS.   And now we labor for mankind and bend
               To turn out capsules to your hearts' content.
               Mankind will pass, of course, (we don't mean to offend),
               But we march forward, automated to the end.

SNAFFLE. Cut out that doomsday wail or I'll crack you, by thunder. Let's hear you sing a verse from the Employee's Song of Joy instead.

MOLECULE. Must we, lord of amino acids?

SNAFFLE. Where's my whip?

MOLECULE. We'll sing.

SNAFFLE. Everybody's happy in this organization.

TOTS.   I like the company I'm working for,
     It's been my dad and mom and nurse!
     That's why I'm pushing it from shore to shore,
     And putting dollars in its purse!

SNAFFLE. All right. This is in lieu of your lunch break. Back to the production line.

MOLECULE. Yes, sir.

SNAFFLE. So much for that. I've got McBoodle in my pocket, a government contract, a slice of defensive expansion, and still more money. But where was I before he came in? Oh, the pink envelope! Here it is again. Ho ho ho, very promising. (*He opens the letter*) Stradella Nussbaum. "Dearest and yes, beloved Professor Snaffle, I adore you." Another one! Blessings on my aging flesh!

MRS. SNAFFLE (*off-stage*). Lancelot!

SNAFFLE. Yes, dear? (*Conceals the letter*)

MRS. SNAFFLE (*appears in her apron*). Are you coming home, dear? Dinner is almost ready.

SNAFFLE (*standing*). Yes, bunnybottom. I'm checking out a few defective capsules, but I'll be with you très très soon!

MRS. SNAFFLE. All right, dear. (*Leaves*)

SNAFFLE. Damn it, I want to read that letter! "I adore you." This kind of language gives me a punch. "Oh, do not be frightened. My love is pure and spiritual, being only a silent admirer of yours, beheld from afar. I am nineteen years old and they say I am beautiful. But what is beauty to me? Beauty is such a transitory thing. It dies as the flower dies. I long for a deeper beauty of the soul which does not drown like the common dust. I hate the mediocrity of life! But something mystical that has flowed from your spirit to mine tells me you have felt this thing too, for you have sacrificed your comfort to enthrone a ray of hope in the hearts of mankind which is so unhappy. I know that you are a man who would understand the poetry that is so ready to blossom within me. To you I can write,
     I lifted up mine eye that is aye mortal,
     And lo, an angel smiléd from his portal!
But you will shake your head and take umbrage with my boldness. Oh do not scold your Stradella! You see, I already call myself *your* Stradella. Oh, do with your slave whatsoever you please. What care

I for conventions? Let the world talk! I fling my throbbing heart at your foot which longs for love and understanding and the ideal. Do, do respond, for otherwise I shall not, will not, live." Signed, "Your Stradella Nussbaum, 2136 Olive Street," etc. etc. etc. *(He places the letter in his wallet)* Number four, Lolita, Daisy, Sue Ellen, and Stradella. Snaffle, the time has come for a decision.

ISOTOPE. Can we dance a little for ourselves now, Sir Human?

SNAFFLE *(snatches up his whip and cracks it)*. Silence! The master is thinking. *(To himself)* Now, Lancelot Snaffle, you listen to me. Does a man in your position drive an old model of a car? No. Does he show himself with an old model of a wife? Even less. People are beginning to say you're behind the times. And look at you! *(He pulls out a mirror)* A rosy skin, boyish lip, a jest in the eye, but with all this a nose as proud as a fortress. Arise, you fool, the charming flesh of impatient virgins is imploring you for spiritual communion! Snaffle, take hold of yourself. Divorce your Hepsa, make her demand an alimony that will enhance your reputation, and clasp glamour to your bosom. Would you board Molassis' yacht with a wife you haven't changed in thirty years? Are you impotent? Too poor for a handful of new weddings? Unacquainted with good society? No, enough is enough. Hepsa, my love!

MRS. SNAFFLE *(rushes in at this very moment and wildly embraces her startled husband)*. Lancelot, listen to the wonderful news! We're going to get divorced!

SNAFFLE. Ha! *(He tries to speak)*

MRS. SNAFFLE. No, I have to talk first! Shush! It's my turn, it's my turn!

SNAFFLE. All right, but ye gods!

MRS. SNAFFLE. Listen to me! I was sitting in the kitchen with my finger in the pudding when who do you think calls on the telephone? Dear Ursula!

SNAFFLE. Ursula?

MRS. SNAFFLE. Ursula, you dumb duck, Ursula Molassis.

SNAFFLE. Oh.

MRS. SNAFFLE. "Dear Mrs. Snaffle," she says, "Molassis and I are planning the wildest craziest cruise of the century and you *must* join us!" "What cruise?" says I, "but it sounds like a million champagne bubbles already." "Well," she says, "you'll pop your belly-button laughing when you hear about it. We're calling it the Gay Divorcee Tour of the Mediterranean. Our boat will be simply stacked with the most amusing people, males and females of all sexes who've achieved the state of being single!"

SNAFFLE. Achieved?

MRS. SNAFFLE. That's what I said after I got my voice back from laughing. "Achieved?" I said. "But of course," says she, "everybody's *born* single, you know, but we don't want that kind! Well," she said, "are you or aren't you coming?" So of course I said of course!

SNAFFLE. Superb! What a coincidence! Just imagine, me too! I was going to tell you we're getting divorced!

MRS. SNAFFLE *(hilarious)*. When I came in?

SNAFFLE. When you came in! *(Innocent merriment)* And I was going to make you sue me for an enormous separate maintenance. My position, you know.

MRS. SNAFFLE. Isn't life a miracle? I'll take basketfuls of money and live in Teheran in a palatial mosque.

SNAFFLE. In Teheran?

MRS. SNAFFLE. Yes. Ursula told me one of the guests is Yamshidi Shams, a Persian with violent black hair, a whiplash in every glance and three thousand slaves on his estates. Oh Lancelot, I'm delirious! Now listen to me. The only problems are the children and the pudding.

SNAFFLE. I'll eat the pudding.

MRS. SNAFFLE. And I'll store the children with the maid. Teheran, here I come, ripping the veil off my face! *(She pulls out a handkerchief and waves it to Snaffle)* Farewell, farewell, dear ex!

SNAFFLE *(waves his handkerchief too)*. Farewell, dear ex-ess! *(Mrs. Snaffle whirls off)* Impeccable woman. Yes, life *is* a miracle. Can a luckier combination of events be imagined? The only disappointment is that Hepsa and not I will be boarding the Molassis caravelle, but what of it? There are other vessels and other seas. What's this? *(A letter is fluttering down from the sky. Snaffle picks it up)* No perfume. "The City of New York." *(Opens it)* "Esteemed Professor Snaffle. In consideration of your unique contribution to the welfare of mankind, the City of New York," etc. etc. etc. "At the suggestion of Secretary McBoodle . . ." Ha! The dog has kept his word. "Our fair city has erected an impressive statue of yourself in the garb of a Roman legislator distributing benefits to the nation. The statue has been placed in a beautiful grove in Central Park, where it has already become one of the city's major tourist attractions. We are indeed proud" etc. etc.

(While Professor Snaffle was reading this flattering letter, the statue itself — all in white — descended from the flies, along with a chaise longue and a quantity of autumn leaves)

SNAFFLE. I must say, this gesture gives me real satisfaction. Come on, you particles, it'll cost me money but today's a holiday. We are going to pay a visit to my statue. *(He blows his whistle and the tots fall in line)* Forward. One, two, one, two, one two, one two. Halt! *(They are all outside the Polypon. Snaffle closes its door, locks up, and affixes a large sign: KEEP OUT. MAD DOG AND DANGEROUS RADIATION)* Forward. One, two, one, two . . . *(The squad meanders off-stage, reappears, always to the sound of Snaffle's counting)* Stop! There's the statue. An excellent likeness. Such humility in my chiselled countenance! Let me see the inscription. "Lancelot Snaffle: *Amplificator Imperii Humani.*" Or, in honest language, Enlarger of the Human Empire. How many men, not counting South American generals, have lived to look on their own monument? *(He walks around the statue)* A little piece chipped off my behind. And another inscription: *"Homo Fronte Creationis Stat."* That is to say, Man Stands at the Forefront of Creation. With a caterpillar inside the F! And the autumn leaves under my feet. Ah, gentle melancholy. *(He sits on the chaise longue, the tots in grey array behind him)* What dignity! What benevolence! But look who's coming! Folpap and Loop, fallen from their high estate and become park custodians! I'd better disguise myself. *(He puts on a false beard)* *(Enter Dr. Folpap and Mr. Loop, reduced indeed to the honest and yet unenvied rank of park custodians, with rake, broom, pick and bag. They push the leaves around without eroding the park)*

FOLPAP. Here's a corner of Central Park I cordially dislike.

LOOP. It fills me with thoughts of blood-baths.

FOLPAP. Have you got the hammer?

LOOP. Here it is.

FOLPAP. Is anybody looking?

LOOP. I see a man with a false beard, but he's asleep and snoring.

FOLPAP. Good. *(He chips a little more from the statue's behind)*

SNAFFLE *(one eye open)*. Pimple-bottomed louse.

FOLPAP. What did you say?

LOOP. Nothing. I'm just raking the melancholy autumn leaves.

FOLPAP. Well, I did it. Bit by bit. One chip at a time.

LOOP. I don't know. I made water over the inscription yesterday, but what can you do against Latin?

FOLPAP. One chip at a time will do it.

LOOP. Oh Dr. Folpap, private action is so useless. Why don't you join our cell? Mother is a wonderful organizer. United, we can overthrow the state, secure justice for all men, shoot our enemies, and liquidate Snaffle.

SNAFFLE. Grrr.

FOLPAP. No, that's not the way for me. I believe in revenge through private enterprise. I'm going to take my hammer and chisel to every Snaffle statue in the country.

LOOP *(plaintively)*. If only I were in my old lab again. This fresh air is bad for my yellow complexion.

(Snaffle saunters up and admires the statue again)

SNAFFLE. New statue, isn't it?

LOOP. Yes, sir.

SNAFFLE. "Lancelot Snaffle: *Amplificator Imperii Humani.*"

(Folpap and Loop exchange a significant wink)

FOLPAP. We'd be glad to give you the official tour. We are both — ahem — licensed guides.

SNAFFLE. Go ahead.

LOOP *(voice of the official guide)*. The statue of Lancelot Snaffle is made in its entirety of red porphyry, a 20-ton block of which was hand-carried from Karelia to New York. Its style is late flamboyant Gothic, although obvious traces of the neo-Byzantine workshops of Siena appear in it as well, particularly in the superb arching of the upper lip.

FOLPAP *(same)*. The noble figure of the physicist, clad in an ample robe symbolizing Purity, has been called by one critic "the last breath of the Hellenic spirit in a world of welded steel." The left hand, whose index finger deserves special attention for its plastic vigor, holds the scroll of the Dynamite Peace Prize, symbolizing Chastity, while the right, outstretched to the people in a gesture full of simple grace, symbolizes the Four Cardinal Virtues.

LOOP *(same)*. The statue adorns a secluded yet popular corner of Central Park. It is open to visitors on weekdays. Entrance — ahem — 25 cents.

(Folpap and Loop stretch out a hand)

SNAFFLE. Oh, a pleasure. *(He tips them)* It might interest you, though, that I'm personally acquainted with the man Snaffle.

LOOP. Really, sir? A noble figure.

SNAFFLE. Densest mass of vices this side of the bubonic plague. I should know. I'm his accountant.

FOLPAP *(changes his tone)*. Well! Confidentially, we've heard the same judgment from many experts.

SNAFFLE. You have, have you? Tell me more.

FOLPAP. We know what we know. It's a fact that he stole the Pedilift from a brother scientist. I don't know if you ever heard the name. Folpap, I think it was.

SNAFFLE. Yes, I *have* heard something about that episode. And didn't he also sack a faithful old assistant of his?

LOOP. He did, and for no reason at all. He drove the poor lad to a premature grave.

SNAFFLE. Oh, he's dead, is he?

LOOP. To peace and comfort.

FOLPAP. So we're told.

LOOP. Yes, so we're told.

SNAFFLE. Well, he's a tough old custard. He'd steal the crutch from under his grandmother's armpit and beat her with it.

FOLPAP. Oh no, sir, he wouldn't do that.

SNAFFLE. No?

FOLPAP. A crutch costs money. He'd use a plain stick from a tree and sell the crutch.

SNAFFLE. A garish beast of a man.

LOOP. Bribed the mayor to have this very statue made. We know it for a lugubrious fact.

FOLPAP. And stole the idea for the Pedilift, don't forget that. It's his only really unforgivable crime.

LOOP. Along with the sacking of the assistant.

SNAFFLE. You're right.

FOLPAP. Who deserved the statue? Folpap, I tell you. This Folpap was worth ten Snaffles.

SNAFFLE. Twenty! I told him so myself.

FOLPAP. Let me shake your hand! You really know that barrel of dung.

SNAFFLE (*holding Folpap's hand*). Know that barrel of dung? That's nothing! Shall I tell you something more?

FOLPAP and LOOP (*eagerly*). Yes!

SNAFFLE. I *am* that barrel of dung! (*Tears off his beard*) What now!

FOLPAP. Snaffle!

LOOP. Misery!

SNAFFLE. You wait, you lapses of nature! Malformations! Dead-ends! (*He blows his whistle*) Battle stations! Load! Fire! Fire again! Puncture their hides and let the air fizz out.

(*The tots are puffing blowguns at the slanderers, who have proved themselves worthy of the severest treament*)

FOLPAP and LOOP. Ouch! Ouch! Murder! Mercy! (*The tots prevent their escape*)

SNAFFLE. Fire! Who bribed the mayor? Fire! Who stole the Pedilift? Fire! Dribble them! Pepper them! Pox them! I'll hound the last tatters off their skins and naked they shall go to the flophouse!

FOLPAP. Robber! We'll unmask you —

SNAFFLE. Fire!

LOOP. Some other time! Ouch! (*They run away*)

SNAFFLE. Hold it, men. That will show the world who steals his grandmother's crutch. What a rout! At ease, particles. Any casualties in the ranks?

MOLECULE. None, sir. We are ready to go into action again.

ISOTOPE. Me too.

SNAFFLE. Good. Take five. Let this be a lesson to all men, and to the elements as well. He who holds the key to nature holds the key to power, and he who holds the key to power can lay flat any Folpap or Loop that pollutes his lemonade. *(He returns to the chaise longue and amorously releases his weight to it)* I've earned what I've got, I think. Whew! *(He sits up suddenly)* Particles! The works this time! Make me see the glory!

TOTS. Yes, sir!

(To the sound of a blood-curdling electronic music, the dancing tots stick a cigar in Snaffle's mouth, dust his clothes, bring him a refreshment, fan him, blow his nose, perfume him, shine his shoes. And here culminates Professor Snaffle's distinguished success in harnessing for mankind some of the weltering energies of the cosmos)

TOTS.   Alert — unquestioning — obedient —
               Rapid — reliable — convenient —
               What shall the universal forces do?
               (Fortissimo) Shine man's shoe!

(In the foreground, while Snaffle lounges and purrs, an elegant elderly couple appear, taking their afternoon stroll in the park, and enjoying the leaves, the birds, and the butterflies. He is probably a retired investment banker, she the widow of an important corporation. They are strolling arm in arm, equipped with the Pedilift, for which the clank or "music" is heard once more. When they arrive center-stage, a minor mishap occurs: the lady's Pedilift jams and her leg refuses to move forward. Snaffle becomes aware of them. Gleefully he rises, glass in hand, and observes them from the vantage point of the statue, against which he fondly leans. The gentleman gallantly produces a few charming tools, and, kneeling, betakes himself to work, she lifting her skirt with coquettish giggles and roguish reluctant delay. The Pedilift starts again, the gentleman is proud but modest, the lady grateful, and both pass off the stage)

SNAFFLE *(triumphantly)*. What shall the universal forces do?

TOTS *(fortissimo)*. Worship you!

SNAFFLE *(journeying to the chaise longue once more)*. For man stands indeed, as the inscription says, at the forefront of creation. However, some men stand at the forefront of creation — help me down again — stretched out full length on pillows — aah! — and some do not. What an alarming thought that is! But only the afflicted need to think, and I, Lancelot Snaffle — loosen my necktie, you — I am — what is the old word? — happy.

THE END

THE SENSIBLE MAN OF JERUSALEM

And they compelled a passer-by,
Simon of Cyrene ... the father of
Alexander . . . to carry his cross.
Mark 15:21

CHARACTERS

SIMON

ALEXANDER, *his son*

RUTH, *his wife*

SERON
BACCHIDES } *Phoenician merchants*

PETER

JOHN

CHRIST

GABINIUS
MARCELLUS } *Roman centurions*

MATHIAS
ZADOK } *Young Hebrews*

TWO PHARISEES

TWO SERVANTS

SOLDIERS

(Before Simon's house on a street in Jerusalem. Enter Seron and Bacchides)

BACCHIDES. Here then is Simon's house. I recognized it after all.

SERON. It looks very quiet. Do you suppose he is gone with the crowd to watch?

BACCHIDES. He is not the man to watch an execution. But it must be a sad day for him, when he hears the clamors of a cruel city disturbing the gardens.

SERON. Are men cruel, Bacchides?

BACCHIDES. Yes, Seron.

SERON. But are men cruel?

BACCHIDES. No.

SERON. Old business friends like us will cheer him up. But will he recognize us after so many years?

BACCHIDES. Wait.

(Enter Mathias and Zadok)

MATHIAS. I wonder if he's still at home. Or did his bleach-blooded father lock the door today?

ZADOK. Alexander!

MATHIAS. Alexander!

(Alexander appears on the roof or at a window)

ALEXANDER. I'm still here. Wait in the street for me.

MATHIAS. All right, but let's try to hurry, shall we?

BACCHIDES. That was Simon's son. I recognize the name. I remember when he was born, and Simon was deciding what to call him. "I'll call him Alexander," he said, "not to commemorate that arch-criminal of a conqueror, but to perpetuate the name of Helen of Troy's lover." Or similar words. Those two don't like the looks of us, I think.

SERON. They slouch with a kind of insolence and swagger.

BACCHIDES. Sons of rich fathers, I'm sure; namely the most disreputable people on earth. Shall we be casual and walk through them?

SERON. I'd rather wait till they go away with their Alexander.

(Enter two dignified Pharisees)

FIRST PHARISEE. My own view is simple. *(Sneezes)* Seven false Messiahs — seven, you'll recall, is the number of apocalyptic scourges — and then the true and final Redeemer appears and delivers us. Delivers us metaphysically, of course. I don't meddle in politics.

SECOND PHARISEE. But how will he do it? Isn't that the more important question? Will he destroy the world, God forbid, and then establish the heavenly kingdom? Or — what seems more humane to me —

will he establish the heavenly kingdom on earth? "By these three trumpets the third part of the nation was killed," says the text; but what does it really mean?

FIRST PHARISEE (*plaintively*). It means a crowd: that's certain. Wherever you look, in a text or in a street, there's sure to be a crowd, and when there's a crowd, *I* catch a cold. Like today. Oh God, I sweat when I think of that crucifixion. Nothing but rabble. (*Sneezes*) You see!

SECOND PHARISEE. "My wrath is upon all the multitudes." Ezekiel, seventh chapter.

SERON. Watch this.

ZADOK (*to the Pharisees, in an unpleasant manner*). Citizens.

FIRST PHARISEE (*a little frightened*). Are you talking to us?

ZADOK. Yes, to you. Are you on your way to the execution?

(*The two Pharisees stare at each other. They do not know what the right answer is.*)

SECOND PHARISEE. What business is that of yours?

BACCHIDES (*to Seron*). A knife!

SECOND PHARISEE. We —

FIRST PHARISEE. We hadn't decided as yet. What do you want with us? We're standing peacefully in front of Simon's house.

ZADOK. Your business is to be at the execution. Aren't you Hebrews?

FIRST PHARISEE (*thoroughly alarmed*). What else?

ZADOK. On what side? Rome? Jesus Christ? or Liberty?

FIRST PHARISEE. Good grief! On what side? I —

SECOND PHARISEE (*has an idea*). How dare you ask us on what side? On what side are you? I challenge you to tell me in the open.

ZADOK. I'll tell you what side we're against, yellow Pharisee; against you, against Rome, against Jesus; and for our people!

SECOND PHARISEE. And what do you think *we're* for and against? Are you going to start beating up your friends? Freedom for the Hebrews! Down with the appeasers! (*In a lower voice*) Down with Rome.

FIRST PHARISEE (*not too loud*). Freedom for the Hebrews!

(*He carries his friend away*)

MATHIAS. You're taking risks.

ZADOK. I hate the sight of them. Temporizers. They'd lick the devil's dung — like Simon. And who are those two skulking over there?

(*Enter Alexander from the house*)

MATHIAS. At last. We thought you might not be able to come.

ALEXANDER. Of course I'm coming. You don't imagine I'd miss that carnival, do you? Only I can't right away. I'm — I must talk to my father.

MATHIAS. You make me laugh.

ALEXANDER. Besides, the whole procession is going to pass in front of my house, isn't it? But I tell you I *am* coming along! Meantime take my knife and slip it into one of your sleeves. I don't want it found on me.

MATHIAS. I'll take it.

SERON. Do they all carry weapons here?

ALEXANDER. Now listen carefully, both of you. Three men the Group want us to find in the crowd. The first is Jonas. Show him the point of your dagger and tell him we know that he dines and drinks at the house of Caius Lutetius, and Caius Lutetius is a Roman, a Roman Roman. Next, find Daniel.

ZADOK. Which Daniel?

ALEXANDER. The son of Menelaus. Show him the point of your dagger and tell him we know that he has got in his possession a Spanish sword with the carved image of Mars on the hilt. Tell him also that he went to the bathhouse on the Sabbath, which things we account insults to the Law. And thirdly, find Eleazar. Show him the point of your dagger and tell him we know on the one hand he inclines toward the appeaser Christ and on the other he spoke the following words last Tuesday in the open market: "We Hebrews will find a way of living with Rome."

MATHIAS. Living with Rome? Good.

ZADOK. Jonas, Daniel, Eleazar.

ALEXANDER. I will join you as soon as I can. Death to the appeasers.

MATHIAS. Freedom.

ZADOK. Under the Law.

ALEXANDER. Go quietly.

(*He returns to the house*)

BACCHIDES. Could you make out what they said?

SERON. No. But I could feel the texture, so to speak. They're coming this way.

BACCHIDES. Let's quietly cross them.

MATHIAS. Who are you and why might you be staring at us from your corner?

SERON. Who might you be to ask us, my boy?

MATHIAS. Don't boy me, foreigner. And answer straight. Crooked answerers don't live long in Judaea.

SERON. We are two Sidonian merchants. We deal with Simon, the Jew from Cyrene, who is an old customer of ours.

BACCHIDES (*calling*). Simon! Simon!

ZADOK (*with contempt*). Phoenician merchants! Money-clinkers! Come along. (*Zadok and Mathias leave*)

SERON. Knives in the open street!

BACCHIDES. Simon!

SIMON *(in the house)*. I'm coming! *(Enter Simon, at the door of his house)* No!

BACCHIDES. Yes indeed! Old Simon!

SERON. Let me embrace you!

SIMON. Seron! Bacchides! Old pirates! Alive and in front of my house! Let me kiss you! Let me look at you! Unbelievable! My Phoenician seagulls! Wait! Don't say a word! Here's plenty of shade. You shall not come into the house without a libation to the gods. Ruth! Ruth! Where is the woman? Ruth!

BACCHIDES. Don't worry about the libation! Let's look at you and talk to you! And don't go upsetting your household for us.

SIMON. Upsetting! You'll be upsetting my miseries, aren't you ashamed? Ruth! Seron, you've grown stout! *(Enter Alexander from the house)* Where are you going?

ALEXANDER. To the execution; where else?

SIMON. Just one moment. I said just one moment! *(Embarrassed)* Friends, will you find — of all times — wait — *(to Alexander)* Don't move. Ruth! *(Enter Ruth)* Here are Seron and Bacchides after two hundred years and you're off dawdling in the cellar.

RUTH. I am so pleased to see you again. Welcome to our house.

BACCHIDES. The blessings of God on you and yours.

SERON. And a kind afternoon as well.

SIMON *(to Ruth)*. Let the servants bring a table, chairs, and wine at once! Seron — Bacchides — will you —? Let me embrace you again. I am rude. But do excuse me while I say two words to my son. I must.

BACCHIDES. It's the two of us who need to be excused. Come; Seron and I will go into the house. *(To Ruth)* Will you lead the way?

RUTH. With pleasure. *(Aside to Simon, in a whisper)* Please don't lose your temper.

SIMON. A few minutes, gentlemen, a few seconds. The servants will wash your feet. The Safed wine, Ruth.

(Exeunt Ruth, Bacchides, Seron. During what follows, table, chairs, etc. are brought out)

ALEXANDER. All right, here I am. You can let go my sleeve. Are you about to lecture me in Greek? I don't seem to be respectable enough to be introduced to your friends.

SIMON. I want you to stay in the house this afternoon.

ALEXANDER. What? Ha! There's a joke. Goodbye.

SIMON. Wait. Alexander, I said wait. Don't come back gleeful with the poor man's blood. He hasn't done you any harm.

ALEXANDER. I could spit when I hear you talk. In my lifetime God will send his Messiah, Judaea will smite Rome, and we shall stand in judgment over mankind; and there you lounge, loafing over your Epicurus and your Aristippus! God will tear them leaf by leaf out of your hands.

SIMON. Why do you talk so much nonsense?

ALEXANDER. "Cursed is the man who breeds swine and twice cursed the man who teaches his son Greek science." But no, you must always be smiling. Weren't you smiling when that counterfeit Messiah stood up — when he had the stomach to stand up, that blaspheming Nazarene peasant, and tell us "I am able to destroy your Temple and to rebuild it in three days." Weren't you smiling then too?

SIMON. Of course I was smiling.

ALEXANDER. I'm ashamed for you in front of my friends. I can't repeat what they say about you. But every time you talk about peace and every time you open your God-confounded Aristotle —

SIMON. Enough! The puppy is lecturing me! Stay home today, your father is speaking.

ALEXANDER. I am going to see that peasant put to death.

SIMON. What in God's name has that man done to you?

ALEXANDER. How in God's name can you stand there my own father and ask me? Didn't he come raging into the Temple — straight out of his Tiberian hamlet — and didn't he announce like one of *us* the coming of the Son of Man? "I come with a sword," he was shouting. And so do we, we told him: the sword, we told him, is in our fists and the blades are sniffing Roman blood. I leaped up beside him and made my speech about the sword and death to the Romans — the crowd was applauding — and I thought thunder would strike me but he walked away and off the rostrum in the middle of my speech without a fare-you-well; and later outside the Temple he took me by the collar in front of my friends and said, "The sword I spoke of will smite you as well as the Romans, for it is the sword of peace." "It is the sword of peace!" I didn't say anything. But I waited. I knew he wouldn't live long. Now one of his own lads has sold him and no one's going to keep me from laughing till I shake when they hang the cross on his shoulders like the peasant he is. But that's enough. I'll be late. You've seen it my way, haven't you? Now, father, be glad you've got a son who's not too lazy to fight. (*Good-humored suddenly, he embraces Simon and leaves. Simon remains motionless for a moment, then follows a few steps. Enter Seron and Bacchides*)

BACCHIDES. His son has left him to go toward the blood.

SERON. It might not be tactful to transact business now.

BACCHIDES. I don't know. We might amuse him. Business was always a game to him. Simon! Don't try to conceal your heaviness. We know what has happened.

SERON. Perhaps we shouldn't have come today. But the thought occurred to us that precisely today —

SIMON. And you were right. Precisely today. I'm glad that you know something, and that you've guessed the rest. Sit down. Here; in the deep of the shade. *(He pours wine)* My friends, you have aged a little. So have I. I didn't remember you so stout, Seron. And I have been anxious about your traveling too much in your old age.

BACCHIDES. We are bachelors, alas, without sons who can travel for us.

SIMON. Yes, a man ought to have sons; but to travel for him? No. He ought to be free of his sons. Let a man travel by himself.

SERON. Are you going to sit by while we drink up your wine? Come on, your turn. Here's to sound currency.

SIMON. And to all sweet casual traffic. I'll send servants to guide your men to the house. We'll dine, and then I will exhaust you with questions.

BACCHIDES. It will be an imposition on you.

SIMON. You are a comfort to me, won't you believe it? Only — I should warn you — an unpleasantness in Jerusalem — but you say you've heard something about it.

SERON. Yes, we have. Please forgive an old dolphin for being tactless — but is this poor crucified man a relation of yours?

SIMON. Is that what you see in my face? No, he's only another prophet, and I've seen more than a dozen Messiahs come and go in my own lifetime. The last one promised to cleave the Jordan and make a dry path for his disciples. And he would have succeeded if he hadn't drowned.

BACCHIDES. You Hebrews never cease to astound us with your antics. But what about this latest wizard? Why are you upset about him?

SIMON. A mob murders a simple man. The government winks for higher political reasons. The people and my own son pant after living blood. There's your whole story.

SERON. Maybe the man preached against the law.

SIMON. Oh, of course! Here is what he preached: the world is wicked, and the world ought to be good. Be kind and happy and innocent, he cries, and then you will be kind and happy and innocent. Oh, I smiled too. But then he looks through you with his large eyes, as though he were asking, "Why do you not believe that I am the son of God? It is perfectly evident to myself, and you know I am honest!" Until, at last, I myself became weak and helped him.

BACCHIDES. Ah! You're involved.

SIMON. Don't misunderstand me. Helped him with a trifle of money and with a little protection. I have some influence here, not much.

SERON. With the procurator?

SIMON. Yes. Our fifth since they removed Herod. He trusts me, because I am not an angle in our geometry of hate. I told him several times, the man is a north-country villager; leave him alone; he eats meat with his hands, and the first time he saw a woman with cosmetics on her face, he thought she was being treated for an illness. But when he began to call himself King of the Jews, Pontius became alarmed. How does it sound in Rome, he asks me, to have a man in one of our — well, our colonies — going about calling himself King?

SERON. King of what? You Hebrews don't want him, I gather, precisely because he won't fight the Romans like a king.

SIMON. True. He is a peaceful king.

SERON. But that's absurd!

SIMON. It is. Are you surprised? Anyway, he stood before Pontius and like an idiot he refused to take it back. His father wouldn't let him!

BACCHIDES. His father? His father travels about with him?

SIMON. Not exactly. I told you: his father is God.

BACCHIDES (softly). Well, then, I agree with you, the man is an idiot.

(Long pause. Simon stares at Bacchides and Seron)

SIMON. He is not. Or say he is. Marvelous if mankind believed his idiocy and fell down before him! He speaks in a soft dialect; you know the strange pathos of dialects — the little brave words with homely juices — and my pen stops over a figure as he babbles — "six thousand two hundred, payable at maturity" — and I see the awesome and laughable picture of a universe of grave, courteous persons, forever affable, agreeable, mild-mannered, reverent to children, horses, trees, neighbors, angels and God — the preposterous vision of being washed clean, all of us, of this daily fatigue of bickering, improving ourselves, keeping up appearances, making an impression, consolidating our gains, taking advantage, making the best of a bad deal, oh God, all the fatigue of it; and instead, the universal courtesy; dear friends (he nods here), dear friends (he nods there); the world is singing; come to my arms! And so forth. Can you acquaint me with a truth sweeter than this rubbish?

SERON. Not I.

SIMON. He says to the astonished Tax Commissioner, a man who has supported a three percent levy on cement for twelve years, Be as a child again; and to the dumbfounded Public Works Inspector, in the middle of an unfinished aqueduct, Love human beings. He says this, mind you, not to old snuffling women at religious camp meetings, but to perfectly serious men. You understand what I mean by serious men.

SERON. We understand.

SIMON. Well, let's for heaven's sake talk like serious men about ledgers and invoices. Invoices are soothing on a day like this. By the way, may I pour again?

BACCHIDES. Enough to fill a thimble.

SERON. For a thick finger.

SIMON. I have found your agents honest of course but hesitant. Your coming in person at last will expedite our traffic. I can place orders almost immediately, and put them in writing by tomorrow. Did you hear something? *(He stands up and peers)*

SERON. I didn't.

SIMON *(sitting again)*. I feel noises in the distance. Not far enough away. As I was saying —

BACCHIDES. If you want nothing unusual, we can promise delivery within three months, with God's help and quiet seas.

SERON. Will you be ordering a shipment of linen ware?

(Simon seems to be listening to something else. Bacchides and Seron exchange glances)

BACCHIDES. Will you be ordering linen ware?

SIMON. Linen ware?

BACCHIDES. We'll show you —

VOICE OF PETER *(off-stage)*. Simon! Simon!

SIMON *(rising, almost frightened)*. Who is calling my name?

VOICE OF PETER. Simon! Don't run away!

SIMON *(to Seron and Bacchides)*. Please stay here. They are men of Christ. *(Peter and John appear)*

SERON. Don't be afraid.

SIMON *(to Peter and John)*. I can't save him.

PETER. You must. Simon: you must. They have rammed the cross on his shoulders that two men couldn't carry. They are beating him with rods. They are tearing his skull with thorns. He's bleeding. John, speak to him. Simon, will you stand there like a pillar while they're killing him? You are a power here. Use the money that makes you so ugly. Give it to Pontius Pilate.

SIMON. Peter! It's no use; let him go; he's dead. Pontius is helpless; *I'm* helpless; I'll be murdered if I lift a finger.

PETER. God oh God, he's making speeches. Simon, Christ is dying. Think of your eternal soul. Save him. What does it matter if *you* die? He is your master I tell you.

SIMON. Let me go, Peter; we're too old for these games; let's keep —

PETER *(on his knees)*. Simon, save him. Bribe them. You loved him. Save him, and me too, oh God, while there's a little time. *(Weeps)*

SIMON. You too? I don't understand. Who is harming you? Get up, for

God's sake!

JOHN. Come away, Peter. *(To Simon)* I didn't want to stop here; my master needs no help; he chooses his time to go.

PETER *(rising)*. Look at me. I will tell you something so hideous —

JOHN. All is forgiven, Peter, let's go away.

(Gabinius has appeared in the street. He watches the scene, half-concealed, and tries to catch the words)

PETER. I betrayed him! As you see me here I renounced him! *(Simon shrugs his shoulders)* They took him before Pontius and then somebody looked at me in the light. "There he is," he said, and then the soldiers clutched me under the arms and said, "Are you the man who drew a sword when we arrested Jesus?" and I said no, I don't know him, who is he, and they pushed me away. Simon, here's a coward begging you to save your soul! You've given us help before, you won't deny it; give Pilate gold, he likes money —

JOHN. God forgive you, but you're babbling.

SIMON. Go home. You're an old man and you shouldn't rush about the streets.

(A clamor in the distance. Enter Ruth)

JOHN. Too late. I see nothing as yet, but they are coming. God will crucify himself today for the sake of the world that shall be judged presently in mercy but in terror. *(He kneels to one side)*

RUTH. Why is that beggar kneeling in front of my house? Drive them away, Simon. Today's no day for trouble.

PETER. Woman —

RUTH. Do you call me woman? I call you vagabond. You should be ashamed to carry on in the streets like an old ragamuffin. Leave us alone.

SIMON. Now . . .

RUTH. You're trouble, I tell you. They come to town without a pair of shoes to their feet, they take charity from families that work for their bread, and then they tell us how we should live.

SIMON. That will do. Go back inside, and peace! And you, believe me when I say nothing can save him. Don't endanger my house.

PETER. I'm ready, John. There's no help for you or me. God's will be done.

SIMON. Peter. Don't watch him with the cross on his shoulder. If God loves him, he'll be dead before he reaches Calvary.

PETER. Don't meddle with us.

(Peter and John leave. Voices in the distance. Simon covers his face with his hands. Gabinius watches Peter and John departing)

SERON. Can we help?

SIMON. I gave him very good advice, and yet he is no younger than I am. It's all a question of nerves, and I have strong nerves, thank God.

BACCHIDES. I suggest we retreat into the house for a while. As you said yourself just now, why look? And they're coming closer and closer.

RUTH. You see, it's not a woman saying it, but your friends. Come into the house. (*To Seron and Bacchides*) He is rude to you, keeping you outside when you've traveled a long journey.

SIMON. Woman, *you* go in. My guests understand.

BACCHIDES. Of course. But the danger to you —

SIMON. I will stand here and watch the man who must die. He will raise his eyes toward me and notice Simon standing aside: standing aside; but not striking; and that is better than swaddling him after he is dead. And when it is all done, we'll return to business like reasonable men, like adults.

GABINIUS. Simon!

SERON. Who is *this*?

SIMON (*to Ruth, fiercely*). Away! Into the house!

(*Ruth withdraws but remains visible*)

GABINIUS (*laughing*). Away! Into the house! Away with the women when a Roman appears! Good day to you, my dear sir. And I greet your friends, the two strangers. I am Gabinius, a Roman. Now Simon, I couldn't help overhearing your little meeting with Peter and John on my way to duty. Yes of course we know their names. And who they talk to; and who gives them a little money now and then — out of charity of course! What a pity our Emperor doesn't like charity for rebels. He calls it collusion, conspiracy — well, *I* don't know what he calls it, I'm only a soldier. But *he* knows! Far away though he is, he knows, Simon, in spite of your influence with the authorities. Well then. Why don't you speak to me? And why do your friends stare at me? You *are* Simon, aren't you, the father of Alexander, yes? who snatched the emblem of Tiberius out of my hands, yes? and tore it up in the street?

SIMON. You nothing. (*To Seron and Bacchides*) But here even a nothing has a cause. His swagger is so sweet to him he'll boil children alive to please this Tiberius of his.

GABINIUS. *This* Tiberius! Wait — you think I'm joking. Open insults against the Emperor. Conniving with known rebels. Father of a fanatic enemy of the State. There's your record. Let me warn you, merchant —

(*Enter Marcellus*)

MARCELLUS. Gabinius! I'm looking for you. (*Whispers aside to him*) Where in blazes have you been? You were supposed to report to me. There's an uproar and you're gossiping in the street.

GABINIUS. Shut up, you fool. I was after big game. All right, let's go. Well, look who's here. The flashing patriots.

(Enter Alexander, Mathias and Zadok)

RUTH. Alexander!

ZADOK. Marcellus and Gabinius. And without escort. You've left your moronic soldiers alone to hold down the mob.

GABINIUS *(hand on sword)*. But they're not far off. I think you're fond of your life. Clear the way.

ZADOK. There's three of us. Not helpless either. *(Draws his knife)*

(Simon rushes in between and roughly seizes Alexander, while the Romans laugh)

SIMON. Into the house! Away, all of you! Fight elsewhere! Ruth!

RUTH. Here! Don't go back!

ALEXANDER *(stuggling)*. Take your hands off! *(But a couple of servants appear, and along with Ruth and Simon manage to get Alexander indoors.)*

SIMON. Tell the servants to hold him! Tie him up if he tries again!

GABINIUS. Wisely acted, Simon. Keep your puppy out of my way. And watch who I see you talking to, in spite of your money and your connections. *(To Mathias and Zadok)* You too. I'll deal with you later. Clear the path. Clear the path I say! *(Mathias and Zadok stand aside and sullenly let the two Romans pass)* I'll see both of you in a noose. *(Exeunt Marcellus and Gabinius)*

SIMON. Go away! Don't come near my house again!

ZADOK. You'll be asking us and your son to protect you when the time comes. We'll see you then. *(Another clamor is heard, much closer)* Good hunting! Come on.

(Zadok and Mathias leave)

BACCHIDES. Almost here. Simon, you're trembling. Come into the house.

SIMON. I'll see it all. Trouble and all. I'll stand aside but I'll see.

(Now the crowd is close)

GABINIUS *(off-stage)*. Keep them back! Soldiers!

(Enter Gabinius, Marcellus, soldiers, and Christ carrying the cross)[1]

MARCELLUS. Disengage! I want the man disengaged from the mob!

SOLDIER. Keep away, Hebrews!

(Some of the soldiers form a line and keep the crowd at bay with their weapons)

SERON. God help us.

MARCELLUS. And you. Why don't you crawl? Gabinius, prod him. Push him, men, the man is a weakling.

GABINIUS. Up, King of Hebrews! Nobody's hurting you now. We're here

---

1. Whether the crowd appears on stage or not will depend on the resources available. In any event, additional crowd noises and speeches can be introduced in this area "ad libitum". As for Christ, he must appear in a state of ultimate pain and exhaustion. He is a beardless thin man in his thirties. The cross he drags is huge and so heavy that it will take two soldiers or even three to remove it from his shoulder.

to protect you. What's the matter with him? He's stopped again.

SIMON. He can't.

RUTH (*at the door*). Simon, don't look. Let me take you away.

MARCELLUS. Beat him, men, apply the Roman law to his back!

RUTH (*to Seron and Bacchides*). A woman begs you, tell him to come in.

SERON. He won't. He stands at the edge. Avoiding is too easy.

MARCELLUS. Give him the mule treatment. Beat the mule. Make him move. Damn damn damn. Why did they put the cross on him? I'm sweating my guts out! Beat him, didn't you hear me? Is he moving?

GABINIUS. He can't feel those swords any more. We need a regular flogging here.

MARCELLUS. He's stopped again. Now what's he staring at?

GABINIUS. At his friend Simon!

MARCELLUS. Mother of my whore! He's paying a call on a friend. (*To Simon*) No spectators, my dear sir. I assure you I'm not responsible. I'm avoiding all the good houses as far as possible. I'd carry the cross myself. Go into the house, my dear sir. Move! Move! Can't you see it's too heavy for him? Why did you stop beating him? Nobody's listening to me!

GABINIUS. He's about to open his mouth.

MARCELLUS. So he is! Speak, King Jesus. We'll do anything we can for you. Well?

CHRIST. Father

SIMON (*rushing toward Christ*). Let him die in peace!

RUTH. Simon! Come back!

(*The Romans are speechless for an instant while Simon lifts Christ in his arms as if to protect him. At the same time Seron and Bacchides are struggling to restrain Ruth who cries and moans throughout this scene*)

SERON. Hold her! Hold her!

BACCHIDES. Ruth, come inside with us!

RUTH. Simon! Simon!

(*Simultaneously:*)

SIMON. Give him water! There's wine on my table!

MARCELLUS. These people are insane! I represent the Emperor!

(*The soldiers are irresolute*)

GABINIUS. Make him carry the cross, Marcellus.

SIMON. Roman, this is your son!

MARCELLUS. Shut your mouth! (*He strikes Simon down*) Make him carry the cross!

RUTH. Have mercy! He's an old man! Let me fall on my knees!

BACCHIDES. Ruth, come away!

SERON. You'll make it worse.

GABINIUS (*to the soldiers*). You heard the order! Wake him up! Put the cross on top of him!

A SOLDIER. On your knees, old man.

ANOTHER SOLDIER. We need your help.

GABINIUS. Get him up! Don't coddle him!

(A soldier roughly tugs Simon up)

SOLDIER. Come on, you fool.

RUTH. They'll murder him! Simon! I'm his wife! *(She breaks down completely)*

MARCELLUS. Get that hysterical female out of the way! At once, I say, at once at once at once.

(With the help of a servant, Seron and Bacchides now succeed in pulling the sobbing Ruth into the house. At the same time the soldiers load the cross on Simon's shoulders with a mixture of shouts and friendly encouragement)

MARCELLUS. Everybody lend a hand! *(To a soldier)* You — help King Jesus. Wipe the blood out of his eyes.

GABINIUS. Forward! Move, move! *(He strikes Simon)*

MARCELLUS. Whores in hell! He's almost as weak as the other one. Let's walk; walk walk walk walk.

(Simon begins to move)

GABINIUS. Soldiers! Form around them!

MARCELLUS. At last I see the light! March, march, march, march, march, march, march. *(They are gone. Bacchides reappears)*

BACCHIDES. Alexander is with her. What happened?

SERON. They've led him off, not saying another word, under the cross, on his knees, crawling, his hair in his face.

(Enter Alexander)

ALEXANDER. Have they taken him away?

SERON. Yes.

ALEXANDER. What will they do to him? He's not accused of anything. He never meddled. They'll release him and he'll come back.

BACCHIDES. And your mother?

ALEXANDER. She is unconscious. The maids are with her. But I won't leave her.

(Seron and Bacchides sit down. Alexander remains standing irresolutely)

ALEXANDER. Is there something I should do?

(They do not answer. A long while, and then Zadok and Mathias appear, carrying Simon's body. They place it at the feet of Seron and Bacchides)

MATHIAS. Gabinius thought this would be a good joke.

ZADOK. He made five soldiers hook us out of the crowd, five against two, and told us to carry him back to you.

MATHIAS. We would have done it anyway.

ALEXANDER *(kneeling beside the body)*. He's only exhausted.

MATHIAS. No, my boy, he's dead. He's dead of volunteering for the Romans.

ALEXANDER. Maybe he's only hurt. They cut him with the swords.

MATHIAS. Not the swords. He broke down. His heart.

ZADOK. An old man, after all.

MATHIAS. You'll get even with them.

ZADOK. The day is coming, Alexander. You'll get a bucket of blood for every drop of his.

(He and Mathias leave. Darkness falls. Long, long silence. Seron and Bacchides are standing on either side of the body. Alexander kneels over it. What follows is spoken in almost total darkness)

SERON. Cruel and stupid men, you are not worth the spilling of a single drop of blood of a wise man's finger.

BACCHIDES. Cruel and stupid men, you need so much pity.

SERON. Oh Simon, reckless pity, erroneous death.

BACCHIDES. Care, cries your death, we must care.

SERON. I don't know.

BACCHIDES. I don't know.

ALEXANDER. We'll avenge you, father. A bucket of blood for every drop of yours.

SERON. On an evil day we came.

BACCHIDES. On an evil day we leave.

THE END

ADAM ADAMSON

On a bien le droit d'avoir une
opinion sur sa propre mort.
Céline

CHARACTERS

ADAM ADAMSON

ROBERT TAVRAC

STELLA TAVRAC

CAPTAIN OLLENDORFF

CAPTAIN JAHMANN

PRIVATE KALK

PRIVATE LEMBO

COLONEL FRANK

THE JAILER

GENERAL FANTOCHKA

LIEUTENANT RUUZ

SUPERINTENDENT BEQUAT

THE FLUTE PLAYER

The action takes place in a territory invaded by the Germans in World War II.

(An abandoned barn. Captain Ollendorff is sitting behind a small table set up for the occasion. The two prisoners, Robert Tavrac and Adam Adamson, their wrists tied, are standing in front of the table, guarded by Private Kalk. As the curtain rises, there is a period of immobile silence, followed by a burst of shots outside. Tavrac does not wince. Adamson moans)

CAPTAIN. Number two. *(He crosses a name off a sheet before him, and affects to rummage through a few documents)* Next. Mister — let me see — Tavrac — Robert Tavrac. Tavrac?

TAVRAC. Yes.

CAPTAIN. I repeat my questions. Where is Boris Selvinsky? Where are his accomplices? Where did they go after leaving the Center Garage?

TAVRAC. I don't know. I demand to know why I was pulled out of my bed at three o'clock in the morning.

CAPTAIN. *You* were pulled out, Tavrac, make a note of that. We left your wife on the mattress. I hope you won't force us — to go further?

TAVRAC. I can't tell you what I don't know. I heard the explosion like everybody else. I didn't know what it was. Next thing I was arrested.

CAPTAIN. Not exactly next thing. In between, Selvinsky and his men found their way to your garage, and were conveyed out of it again to a destination you know. Why deny it? We have our friends in town, and they report to us.

TAVRAC. I've never seen Selvinsky. He's just a name, a name I respect. I respect him, but I've never set eyes on him. You're trying to get speech out of stones, Captain.

CAPTAIN. Our political officers have ways of making even stones talkative, my friend. Consider yourself lucky you are in the hands of a regular soldier like me. I am reluctant to turn you over — sheer humanity! Come now, let's start again. Four of you knew the whereabouts of Boris Selvinsky. Now only two of you know. Are we agreed so far?

TAVRAC. No.

CAPTAIN. What do you mean? I see only two of you left.

TAVRAC. None of us knows a thing.

CAPTAIN. Us? None of *us*? You *know* that the two corpses outside knew nothing? You *know* that your friend here knows nothing?

TAVRAC. I know *I* know nothing.

CAPTAIN. You're the peaceful manager of a garage, Robert Tavrac. You hate us, but quietly. Your record is downright virginal, not a blot on it. Yet in three minutes you will be dead in a ditch. In an hour or two your Stella will be informed, but she will not receive your body. Your body belongs to us. It will vanish. And Boris Selvinsky will be drinking his whiskey ten years, twenty years from now with *his* Stella — or even yours, why not? A widow, after all. He will wipe a tear off a corner of his eye and say: "Those fine comrades who died for me!" And you will be delicately decomposed in the sour ditch. Unrecognizable! Bones with a few shreds of flesh, while the world is having dinner! Look at me, Tavrac. I'll make peace with you. With both of you. You tell me where to dig out Selvinsky, quietly, nothing in writing, and I'll let it be known that it was number two — what was her name? Anna Tommasini — who talked. She talked, and we removed her, sent her to prison in Germany. And number one, well, he was shot. Reprisals. Forgotten already. There are so many human beings in the world, gentlemen. I take an oath, as an officer of the German army. Nobody will know. I'll send you both home, you'll go back to bed and sleep it all off. Your friend, now, I can see he realizes I'm talking sense.

TAVRAC *(grim, to Adam).* Don't let Fritz wheedle you. A mess of words.

CAPTAIN *(suddenly shouts).* Where is Selvinsky?

TAVRAC *(shouts back).* Go to hell!

CAPTAIN *(to Kalk).* Hit him!

(Tavrac falls)

TAVRAC. Go to hell!

CAPTAIN. Hit him! Where is Selvinsky?

TAVRAC. Go to hell! Go to hell!

CAPTAIN. Hit him!

ADAM. Stop — stop —

CAPTAIN. Where is Selvinsky?

(Tavrac is almost unconscious)

TAVRAC *(weakly).* Adam. We don't know. We don't know nothing.

ADAM. Have pity.

CAPTAIN. I'm through with him. *(To Kalk)* Call Lembo and take him out.

KALK. Excuse me, sir. Same as the other two?

CAPTAIN. Yes. Go on.

KALK. All right, you. Get up.

TAVRAC. Adam!

ADAM *(to Ollendorff).* Don't send him out! He doesn't know; I see him every day, and I swear he doesn't know!

CAPTAIN. Kalk! Don't just stand there.

KALK. No, sir. Come on. March. Out. *(Calling)* Lembo! *(Private Lembo enters the barn)* Same as the others. *(Lembo grabs Tavrac)*

TAVRAC. Let me write to my wife!

CAPTAIN. Take him away.

TAVRAC (*struggling*). Adam — tell her —

ADAM. He doesn't know! Don't kill him!

(*Tavrac is dragged out. The barn door is banged shut. Kalk returns to Adam. Another frozen silence. Then the voice of Tavrac: "Swine! Dirty butchers! Long live —" interrupted by a burst of fire*)

CAPTAIN. Number three. (*Adam moans. Ollendorff crosses out a name*) One moment a man. Next moment, a nothing. Horrible. Now you: Adam Adamson.

ADAM. I don't know anything — I've got nothing to say — believe me —

CAPTAIN (*soothingly*). Come, come. We are alone now. The witnesses are gone, eh? (*He winks*) Kalk, move along to the door and stay there. You are safe, Adamson. There is no shame when you are not watched by somebody. And I'm nobody; a nameless foreign officer who'll flit out of your life as though he'd never existed. Do you understand me, Adamson?

ADAM. Yes.

CAPTAIN. Nobody will ever know who talked. We'll send you to a camp deep in Germany. It will not be pleasant. It will be far from pleasant. But I sense that you wouldn't want it pleasant. Call it your penance. When the war is over, you can return clean to your people. Just a word, Adamson, the name of a street, a house, a village; one word, and all's over.

ADAM (*low*). I don't know anything. What's the use of killing me?

CAPTAIN. A train blew up. We lost eighteen men, and an enormous amount of petroleum. We have to shoot hostages anyway.

ADAM. But why me? Suppose I did know —

CAPTAIN. Ah.

ADAM. Suppose it — that's all I said — then if you killed me, you'd never find out. But if you don't, there's always a chance that I'll — don't you see? Do you follow my reasoning? There's always a chance for you —

CAPTAIN (*still mild*). A reasoner! But if you reason with me, I'll have to reason right back with you. Reason tells me to turn you over to our political officer. Shall I tell you about our Captain Neihart?

ADAM (*low*). I already know.

CAPTAIN. Sometimes one doesn't know whether to cringe or laugh. This pumping air into you with a bicycle pump, or making you swallow gallons of water, or ripping your nails out, or burning out an eye. Sometimes it isn't funny anymore.

ADAM (*almost inaudibly*). Be human, I am a human being.

CAPTAIN. What did you say? But after all, that is what you yourself were asking. To be kept alive just in case. Whereas my way is more honest. Kalk, come here. Take Mr. Adamson to the window. Allow

him to see his three friends, so undignified in a heap.
(Kalk pushes Adam to the window)
KALK. Come along. Open your eyes. I said open your eyes!
CAPTAIN. Bring him back, soldier. We are not bluffing, are we, Adamson?
KALK. Answer the captain.
ADAM. No.
CAPTAIN *(changing his tone)*. No what?
KALK. Answer!
ADAM. You are not bluffing.
CAPTAIN. You are not bluffing — what?
ADAM. I don't understand.
CAPTAIN. You're talking to an officer, you scum!
ADAM. Sir.
CAPTAIN. You are not bluffing, sir!
KALK. Repeat, damn you.
ADAM. You are not bluffing, sir.
CAPTAIN. That's better. And now I am going to ask you my question for the last time. Where is Boris Selvinsky?
ADAM. ——————————
CAPTAIN. Call Private Lembo.
ADAM. No — wait —
CAPTAIN. For what? If you don't know, I don't need you. Call Lembo.
KALK *(at the door)*. Lembo! Come on. Number four.
(Enter Lembo)
CAPTAIN. Relish your last seconds, Adamson.
LEMBO. Reporting, sir.
CAPTAIN. Carry out the execution.
LEMBO. Yes, sir. All right, you.
ADAM. Wait — not yet —
LEMBO. Get going.
ADAM. Wait! Wait!
(Captain Jahmann dashes in)
CAPTAIN. Jahmann!
JAHMANN. Ollendorff! Information! *(Ollendorff points toward Adam as though to advise caution)* Never mind *him* — you won't need him now. Come here! *(He takes Ollendorff aside and whispers to him)*
CAPTAIN. I'll be damned! Well, congratulations! While I'm wasting my time here!
JAHMANN. Get rid of him with the others.
CAPTAIN. I just gave the order. Thanks, Jahmann.
JAHMANN. Report to Colonel Frank, will you, when you're done with your patriot. I'm off with the hunting party.
CAPTAIN. Right.

(Exit Jahmann)

CAPTAIN. Well, my little man, it appears that we located Selvinsky without your help. *(To Lembo)* All right, take him away. And when you're done, get a detail from the third platoon to bury them all in the usual place.

LEMBO. Yes, sir. All right, that's all this time.

ADAM. Captain, don't let him take me! What's the use if you already know? Show your generosity —

CAPTAIN. Don't be a bore. You should have talked five minutes ago.

LEMBO. Come on.

ADAM *(struggling)*. Don't — I don't want to — Ah!

LEMBO. Here. Your pals are waiting. *(He has dragged Adam to the door)*

ADAM. I'll talk! I'll talk! I'll tell you details!

CAPTAIN. Well, so he *does* know! But I don't need you anymore! *(He collars Adam)* All right. Where is he?

ADAM *(stunned)*. You don't know!

CAPTAIN. Shoot the monkey!

LEMBO. This time —

ADAM. The farm! The Pines! Highway 31 —

CAPTAIN. Come here. Is it the whole gang?

ADAM. I don't know. I think so. Oh God, oh God. *(He is near collapse)*

CAPTAIN *(to Kalk)*. Get Captain Jahmann. On the double. *(Exit Kalk, running)* All right, take him to the infirmary — keep him there — and give him a bowl of soup.

ADAM. Oh God, what did I do?

LEMBO. On the level, sir?

CAPTAIN. Sure. Cheer up the little man. You can untie him, too.

LEMBO. Yes, sir. Come on, on your feet. *(He drags Adamson away as Jahmann enters)*

JAHMANN. You did it!

CAPTAIN. The Pines. Highway 31. Don't waste a second.

JAHMANN. The engines are running. We'll drink to this later, Olly! *(He goes. We hear him shouting orders off-stage. Ollendorff wipes his brow, gathers up the papers. Enter Colonel Frank)*

CAPTAIN. Sir.

FRANK. At ease, Ollendorff. Sit down. Cigarette? *(He sits on the table)*

CAPTAIN. Thank you, sir. This is one I'm going to enjoy.

FRANK. Ollendorff, you're a magician. I was really skeptical this time. All that psychological bunk. I kept asking myself why didn't we turn the whole damn mess over to Neihart and have done with it.

CAPTAIN. I'm glad we kept him as a last resort, sir.

FRANK *(lifting an imaginary glass)*. "Cried the German troopers"—

CAPTAIN *(falling in)*. "Hang the Party snoopers!" *(They laugh)*

FRANK. All the same, when you began to shoot your witnesses, my gut was in my mouth. All that information down the bloody drain.

CAPTAIN. Four informants were too many, sir. They kept glaring at each other. I felt I must narrow down to one.

FRANK. Which one was it, by the way? The fellow with the children and grandchildren?

CAPTAIN. No, sir. The one who is all alone in the world. Adam Adamson.

FRANK (extremely surprised). You don't say so! You gambled on a man who's got nothing to live for?

CAPTAIN. I gambled on the man who's got everything to live for.

FRANK. Ollendorff, I'll be sending out a report on this that will make your mother happy. If my voice carries at headquarters — this is between us, Ollendorff — but I've got you down for a citation.

CAPTAIN. I appreciate this, sir.

FRANK. Never mind. One Hessian to another. I hope I can still tell a good man when I've got one. You're a professional, Ollendorff, long live the professionals!

CAPTAIN. Amen. (Sings)

> "Shine your buckle and your boot,
> Share the lasses and the loot,
> Give Von Kluck a smart salute
> And the French a bloody snoot."

FRANK (laughing). Von Kluck?

CAPTAIN (laughs too). Yes, Von Kluck. That was my father's favorite song. First World War. And General Von Kluck was — a general.

FRANK. Not bad. Write that song down for me. I'll recite it to our Major von Eben dash Eckenbach when he comes back.

CAPTAIN. Where has the major gone, sir, if I may ask?

FRANK. Oh, to the railroad station. Suddenly it became necessary to hop-hop and oversee the unloading of small weapons.

CAPTAIN. I'm sorry. I'm sorry about the whole affair. It shouldn't have happened.

FRANK. It's a mucky situation all right.

CAPTAIN (offering Frank a cigarette). Will you try one of mine, sir?

FRANK. Thanks.

CAPTAIN (lighting the cigarette). And yet I think I can understand Major von Eben-Eckenbach's — eh — reluctance. I beg your pardon, it's really none of my business.

FRANK. Well I'm making it your business, damn it. Fact is, I need my staff's advice. Goddamned insubordination. (Ollendorff makes a gesture of protest) I mean it, Ollendorff. Make no mistake. And I'm gagging over it.

CAPTAIN. Baron von Eben-Eckenbach is a splendid man, though. The best connections in Berlin. And an old name, which he didn't want to besmirch.

FRANK. But you and me without the best connections or the stinking old name can besmirch and beshit our names all we want — is that what you're trying to say?

CAPTAIN. Not what I'm trying to say, sir!

FRANK. I'll tell you this much, an order's an order and I'll make him eat his hyphen for disobeying it. Do you know what our baron said to me? "Colonel Frank," says he politely. You know? He ought to wear a monocle. "If I decline to obtain information from our hostages by any method not stipulated in the Geneva Convention, will you or will you not have me shot?" (*Ollendorff whistles*) "No," says I, just as polite as him, "no, I will not have you shot; but I won't answer for anything else." "That's all I want to know," says he. "I cannot undertake the interrogation." And if that isn't disobeying an order, I'm a Polish Jew.

CAPTAIN. "Stipulated in the Geneva Convention." I don't know what to say, sir, except that you were damn patient.

FRANK. Listen, join me about ten tonight, will you? Informally, over a cognac. As I said, I've got to sound out the staff.

CAPTAIN. I'll be there, sir.

FRANK. Well, let's move along. Better set up a reception committee for the Selvinsky gang — in case Jahmann brings 'em back alive.

CAPTAIN. In case.

FRANK. What did you do with the informer?

CAPTAIN. Sent him to the infirmary. I told Lembo to feed him before we send him back to town.

FRANK. All right — but — what condition is he in, Ollendorff?

CAPTAIN. Alive, sir, alive. (*They leave*)

SCENE TWO

(*Adamson crouches inside a wire cage. An "unreal" light shines on him; other lights illuminate the bare stage. Voices are heard far and near. Adamson listens and lives them*)[1]

---

1. The cage may be suspended. There is, needless to say, no objection to actually staging the episode of the voices.

VOICE INSIDE (*loud whisper*). Selvinsky, I see them. Curse God.

VOICE INSIDE. Over there! I told you! There! There! Selvinsky!

SELVINSKY'S VOICE. Keep away from that window.

VOICE OUTSIDE (*through megaphone*). Selvinsky! The farmhouse is surrounded! We know you're in there! Come on out, all of you, the whole gang, hands high, one by one, through the front door. We're giving you five minutes!

VOICE INSIDE. You, get out of the light!

VOICE INSIDE (*at the same time*). Get out of the light, damn you!

SELVINSKY'S VOICE. Steady, all of you.

A SECOND VOICE OUTSIDE. Selvinsky! Come on out, one by one, hands in the sky. You're surrounded! Four minutes and we'll make a bonfire of the lot of you!

VOICE INSIDE. The bastards, oh God oh God.

VOICE INSIDE. I can just make him out. If I could get a crack at him —

VOICE INSIDE. What about the kitchen door?

VOICE INSIDE. Too late.

VOICE INSIDE. Selvinsky, why don't you say something?

VOICE INSIDE. Another spotlight!

ADAM (*feebly*). Get out of the light . . .

VOICE INSIDE. Selvinsky's given up. Me too. I've done my job, to hell with it and good-bye, sweet universe.

VOICE INSIDE. Shut up, shut up!

VOICE OUTSIDE. Three minutes, Selvinsky! Get moving. We'll fry you alive, we'll make torches of you. I'm not bluffing, Selvinsky. Come on out the front door, one by one.

VOICE INSIDE (*hysterical*). What do we do, Selvinsky? Why don't you think of something again?

ADAM (*moaning*). Please! Think of something . . .

VOICE INSIDE. Will they shoot if we come out?

SELVINSKY'S VOICE. They will, my boy.

VOICE OUTSIDE. Two minutes!

VOICE INSIDE. Maybe they won't —

VOICE INSIDE. We've got to take a chance! Somebody yell we're coming out. Selvinsky! You.

VOICE INSIDE. I'm for getting out too — but drilling their guts till we drop — finished.

VOICE INSIDE. Sure — with four toy pistols between us. Lemme out of here right now —

VOICE INSIDE. Hold him!

VOICE INSIDE. Get down — you'll do like the rest of us.

VOICE OUTSIDE. One minute, Selvinsky! Your last minute. We're ready to go!

VOICE INSIDE. Curse God.

VOICE INSIDE. Tell 'em to wait! Another minute!

ADAM. Selvinsky — tell them to wait . . .

VOICE INSIDE (*hysterical*). Tell 'em we're thinking it over — we're deliberating!

SELVINSKY'S VOICE. Friends, it doesn't matter anymore.

(*Orders are shouted outside*)

VOICE INSIDE (*hysterical*). This is it. Aaah! They're throwing something! We'll burn alive! Open the door!

ADAM. Don't go out the door! . . .

VOICE INSIDE (*in terror*). Selvinsky!

SELVINSKY'S VOICE. All right. (*Shouting*) We surrender! You out there! Do you hear me?

VOICE OUTSIDE. We hear you. Keep talking.

SELVINSKY'S VOICE. We've got enough ammunition to blast you to hell, fire or no fire. Do you guarantee our safety if we pledge to throw away our weapons?

VOICE OUTSIDE. Right you are. We do.

ADAM. Don't go out . . .

VOICE INSIDE. Father, be with us in the agony of death . . .

VOICE OUTSIDE. You've got sixty seconds, Selvinsky! Come on out, one by one, hands up!

SELVINSKY'S VOICE. We are coming out! Repeat that you guarantee our safety!

VOICE OUTSIDE. Don't play with us, Selvinsky! We guarantee your safety.

VOICES INSIDE. Be with us in the agony of death . . .

ADAM. Take them alive! Why not? Why not?

VOICE OUTSIDE. Thirty seconds!

(*A door is thrown open*)

SELVINSKY'S VOICE. I'll go first. You men follow, one by one. Heads high, do you hear? So long.

ADAM (*loud, holding out his arms*). Must it happen?

(*Silence*)

VOICE OUTSIDE. Open up!

(*Fusillade and cries. Adamson collapses. Silence. The lights change. From the distance comes the mild resigned sound of a flute. Adamson raises his head*)

ADAM. Again. (*He listens*) I wonder if I dream this. Again. (*He listens*) I could ask the jailer whether he hears it too. No, I'd rather not know. (*The flute is no longer heard*) Today I think it is August. The month of lice. I've counted six hundred and thirty-six zealous intersections of wire in my cage since the eagle chirped this morning, that is to say, yesterday or tomorrow morning. I am excellent in counting, bravo and alas. Ten fingers too. Do nails grow indefinitely if you don't bite them off? If they do, I could pick the lock with a fingernail five feet long. But the jailer would notice it before that no doubt no doubt. Yet I could bury it in the sand whenever I heard him coming. Provided he wore shoes you can hear. But wouldn't he wonder at my single fingertip happening to touch the sand vertically every time he came? Well, why would he? It's an inconspicuous gesture, a fingertip reclining gently upon the ground while the body rotates around it in twenty-four hours. Oh God, will I be in jail long enough to think every thought my brain could ever think?

(Enter the jailer)

JAILER. Here's your soup, Adamson. (He unlocks and opens a small "window" of the cage and hands a bowl to Adam)

ADAM (plaintively). My spoon broke at the handle.

JAILER. Show me. (Adam shows him a wooden spoon in two pieces) So that's what the banging was.

ADAM (innocently). What banging is that?

JAILER. Don't flibble me. You was banging against your cage half the morning while I couldn't figure out where the noise was coming from. So that was it.

ADAM. I am a killer of people, so it's normal for me to bang on cages.

JAILER. Don't be funny. You'll just use the half spoon till the end of the month if you don't mind. And then thank God you'll be on the pavement again and out of *my* sphere and domain.

ADAM. Are my forty months up?

JAILER. Why do you ask me the same stupid question every day? Listen Adamson, General Fantochka is coming round for an inspection. (Solemn) The Superintendent himself is showing him the grounds in his own person. In consequence thereto I want you to play dead. Not a word. No banging, no drumming, and not a syllable. And tell 'em you get treated right in this place. I mean right. I mean not too rough, because that wouldn't be democratic, but not too soft neither because that wouldn't be just. All right, give me the bowl and remember what I said.

ADAM (who has been eating his soup). The soup was very tasty, thank you. Will you send the boy to take away my pot later?

JAILER. If you don't bang on nothing and behave. (He goes)

ADAM. Jailer!

JAILER (comes back). What do you want?

ADAM. Are we winning the war?

JAILER. The radio says the enemy is suffering enormious casualties; which means we're retreating again.

ADAM (frightened). Are the Nazis advancing this way?

JAILER. I hope not, but we're digging trenches again. All right, son, I've got other babies to burp. *(He goes again)*

ADAM. Jailer!

JAILER. Christ on the Mount! What now?

ADAM *(timidly)*. You forgot to bring my letters.

JAILER *(laughing)*. Well, that's a new one. Your letters! What a sense of humor! And who you got writing letters to *you*, I'd like to know?

ADAM. Maybe the authorities are keeping my mail from me.

JAILER. Sure, sure. Your mail is stacked up to the ceiling in the Chief's office all from your admirers and girl friends and your dad and mom and uncles and aunts. Love and kisses! *(Severe)* Look here, that's enough out of you, Adamson. You're just smacking your tongue about, but I happen to be on duty and the Superintendent and the General is expected any minute. Goodbye. And don't by Jesus call me back.

(Leaves)

ADAM. I'll write a letter to me in the sand. Dear Adam. *(He scratches with his spoon-handle)* How are you? We are all doing very well in town. Many of the boys have died, and they are beginning to take the younger ones now, but the rest of us are doing very well. We are all pulling in our belts because food is getting scarcer all the time, but otherwise we are doing very well. As long as we all work together, each for all and all for each, all will be well. Some fight, others work in the factories, the old men are air raid wardens, the old women are nurses, and everybody does his bit to the best of his abilities, and that is why we are all together and very well. We hope that you are rotten. You bastard. Curse you to hell. Signed Everybody.

(The flute is heard again in the far distance. Adam lulls himself half to sleep. Enter General Fantochka, his adjutant Lieutenant Ruuz, and Superintendent Bequat)

FANTOCHKA. And this, I understand, is your Third Tier.

BEQUAT. Exactly, General Fantochka. We run our establishment with moral precision. I am only a tool, of course. The powers above me regulate our facilities: classification, discipline, amenities, diet, even the geometry and dimension of our cells.

RUUZ. They look too comfortable. Seems to me you're running a regular hotel.

FANTOCHKA. Lieutenant.

RUUZ. I beg your pardon, sir.

BEQUAT. In our First Tier you saw the lowest category of criminals. The final brutes. Those who collaborated with the Nazis because they were believers. The sincere types. Burn the books. Exterminate the

Jews. The master race. The thousand-year Reich. We limit them to 6 by 6 cells. Six feet, that is. No windows, no heat, no bunk. A single meal a day — watery gruel with stale bread floating in it. One by one they stand trial and they are shot.

FANTOCHKA. That part will have to be sped up, Bequat. Just in case — this is between ourselves, of course — but just in case we've got to withdraw again. Don't keep confirmed Nazis around.

BEQUAT. Only a dozen are left anyhow, General Fantochka. In an emergency it won't take us long. Well, then, I proceed to the Second Tier.

RUUZ. Those who collaborated for profit.

BEQUAT. Exactly. A more redeemable breed. If lust for money or power prevailed on men to work for the Nazis, lust for money or power would prevail on them to be decent citizens. Meantime, twenty years of confinement. Cell furnished with a window. Exercise once a day. A female once a month. Two meals. Meat on Sundays. Mass for believers, showers for atheists. These are the rascals who betrayed us for thirty pieces of silver. The shoddy failures who caught their chance to rise to something they called the top. They looted, denounced, harried and murdered for the sake of a job with a title, an extra ration, a salary. But here we are in the Third Tier, that of the forgivable weaklings.

FANTOCHKA. I emphasize forgivable.

RUUZ. With your permission, sir, I emphasize weaklings.

BEQUAT. Those who collaborated with the enemy under the threat of death. Three to five years. Airy cell. Decent food. Treated not too harshly — that would be undemocratic — nor too kindly — that would be unjust.

RUUZ. This civilian mincing and measuring frankly disgusts me, Bequat.

FANTOCHKA. Come, come, Lieutenant Ruuz. Bequat is carrying out orders from the highest authorities, and I must ask you to be civil to him.

RUUZ. No reflection on you personally, Superintendent Bequat.

BEQUAT. Thank you, sir. I speak the words, but I am not the mouth.

FANTOCHKA. Well, what about the Fourth Tier upstairs?

BEQUAT. Most satisfactory. Three months of supervised community living. Plenty of sunshine. Meat for dinner. Slides and films. Directed discussion periods. For those who gave way under torture. Those who tried, but they broke.

RUUZ. But this, excuse me, this angers me. Others tried and did not break.

FANTOCHKA. You must understand, Bequat, that Lieutenant Ruuz was beaten by the Gestapo till his skull was fractured. He was tied to the ceiling by his thumbs, his body was burnt with cigarettes, his limbs were crushed with clamps, and still he didn't talk.

RUUZ. There must be justice. Rewards and punishments. A difference.

BEQUAT. Lieutenant Ruuz, I apologize. Let me take your hand and kiss it.

RUUZ. Do.

FANTOCHKA. Good. Now you will show me the famous Adam Adamson, Bequat? Where is the man?

BEQUAT. Here he is, general. Adamson, sit up. Shall I tell him to stand at attention, General Fantochka?

FANTOCHKA. Never mind. So this is the man Adamson.

ADAM. Who betrayed Boris Selvinsky to the enemy, while three of our heroic citizens: Kuypers, Tommasini, and Tavrac, went to their martyrdom, accepted death at the hand of the enemy rather than disclose the place to which the leader of our underground network had fled for safety. For what he thought was safety! Believing that this man, this Adamson, would be true, not to him! not to Selvinsky! because it was not of himself that Boris Selvinsky thought; but that he would be true to all the brave men and women fighting the hateful enemy, and daily sacrificing their lives for each one of us. Now Boris Selvinsky is dead, along with sixteen of our bravest fighters. The rest is well-known. The effectiveness of our underground operations was destroyed, the reconquest of this province was materially delayed, and torrents of blood were shed which might have been spared had this man, this Adamson, made the sacrifice that thousands and thousands of our citizens have made in these heavy years without a moment's hesitation.

BEQUAT (confidentially). He is reciting the Prosecutor's summation.

RUUZ. Like pulling his tongue at us?

FANTOCHKA. No. I think he is serious. And I am a little moved. I suspect my mission here will not be unsuccessful. His intentions, after all —

RUUZ. Permit me, sir. His intentions were to be a sniveling coward. The Nazis are advancing again, and they can thank men like Adamson for opening their doors for them.

FANTOCHKA. Well, that's a little sweeping.

BEQUAT. A little sweeping, perhaps. Adamson isn't one of our dangerous inmates.

FANTOCHKA. He does look like a meek little person.

BEQUAT. Take it from me, general. Quite self-abased and — ready for anything — hungry in fact. (Confidentially) Besides, what is he going to do in the world, even supposing he doesn't get lynched, without papers, without rights, without citizenship? Try him, General Fantochka.

FANTOCHKA. I intend to. Step to the side, you two. (He approaches the cage) Adamson, I am General Fantochka. Tell me why you betrayed Selvinsky. Are you a friend of the Nazis?

ADAM. A friend of the Nazis?

FANTOCHKA. I know you're not. Were you merely afraid to die?

ADAM. Yes.

FANTOCHKA. Was that all? Many others have died.

ADAM. Yes.

FANTOCHKA. It is the cowards who make evil prevail in this world.

ADAM. I was only one.

FANTOCHKA. Everybody is only one. Think of all the ones in Germany at this very moment. Each one who sees a neighbor in his own house arrested and who says next day "Oh? the upstairs has always been vacant." Each one who sees the trains that carry the innocent to death camps and who says, "What can I do? I am only one." Each one who hears of the gas chambers, the pitiless experiments on human beings, and who is afraid to speak up. He didn't want it to happen. He didn't mean it that way when he voted for Hitler years and years ago. Are you a man like these people, Adamson?

ADAM (low). Yes.

FANTOCHKA. Where will you go when you're released?

ADAM. Home.

FANTOCHKA. There is a memorial to Boris Selvinsky and his men in the main square. There are widows and sons.

ADAM. I'll go elsewhere.

FANTOCHKA. To your family?

ADAM. No.

FANTOCHKA. Why not?

ADAM. —————————

FANTOCHKA. You will be a kind of outlaw all your life, Adamson.

ADAM. Yes.

FANTOCHKA. But would you like to see this brand on your flesh burned out, erased, as though it never existed?

ADAM. Yes.

FANTOCHKA. There is one way. Shall I tell you?

ADAM. Yes.

FANTOCHKA. Work for the army. A dangerous, a very dangerous mission. But your name will be cleared, your rights restored.

ADAM. What is the mission?

FANTOCHKA. To blow up the Scandella Bridge.

ADAM. Are the Germans nearby?

FANTOCHKA. Hours away.

ADAM. How does a civilian blow up a bridge? I only know something about motors.

FANTOCHKA. Destroying is not so difficult. We'll teach you quickly.

ADAM. Why do you ask me of all people?

FANTOCHKA. I need a civilian, and a man who is cautious, inconspicuous, and absolutely desperate.

ADAM. Is it that dangerous?

FANTOCHKA. It is.

ADAM. I will die?

FANTOCHKA. Maybe.

ADAM. My rights will be posthumous?

FANTOCHKA. Perhaps.

ADAM. Probably?

FANTOCHKA. Probably.

ADAM. Almost certainly?

FANTOCHKA. Almost certainly. Well, Adamson? Time is short. Your country calls on you.

ADAM. ⸻

FANTOCHKA. I could have you shot, do you understand that?

ADAM. ⸻

RUUZ. Sir —

FANTOCHKA (*waves him away*). Just a moment. Adamson! The second time? You'll stab your people a second time? Once was not enough? What grudge do you bear against your country?

ADAM (*piteously*). I want to live . . .

FANTOCHKA. The man is a coward! A pure, neat, flat coward! Each atom in his body is a coward. Why shouldn't I drag him before a firing squad this very minute?

BEQUAT. General Fantochka! (*Leads him aside*) The law, sir — allow me — the prisoner in question is to be released —

FANTOCHKA. Released! The law! The law was made by cowards for cowards! Bloated civilians! I don't know why we bleed for you! It was you — Bequat — you who led me to this mangy dog in the cage! And I pitied him! Let me get to the front. There I have enemies I respect! (*Stalks out*)

BEQUAT. General Fantochka! I can show you a dozen brave prisoners — (*Follows the general out*)

RUUZ. You're yellow around the muzzle all right, my friend. Upset? Here, have a cigarette.

ADAM. Thank you, sir.

(*He reaches out of the cage with his hand. Ruuz strikes it violently with his swagger stick. Adam cries out*)

RUUZ. You'll remember that next time you shake hands with a German. (*He leaves*)

ADAM (*holding his hand*). Why was I born? Why was I born?

(*He weeps. In the distance the flute player resumes. Gradually Adam becomes quiet. Enter Stella Tavrac, preceded by the jailer. She is dressed in black*)

JAILER. Anything for Mrs. Tavrac. 'Tis a privilege to be of help to the bereaved widows of our heroes. (*To Adam*) You. Hey you. Here is Mrs. Tavrac good enough to pay you a visit. Mind your manners, d'you hear? I'll leave you, Madam. Fifteen official minutes. But for you — you understand —

STELLA. Thank you.

(*The jailer leaves*)

ADAM (*hopeful*). Stella. Mrs. Tavrac.

STELLA. I wanted to see you.

ADAM. I'm — I'm glad.

STELLA. Our friend. And this is the cage.

ADAM. How are you managing, Stella?

STELLA. I have a pension. I am treated with consideration, even after three years. My husband improved my social position.

ADAM. Why have you come here?

STELLA. I wanted to talk to a fine, proud, impudent traitor.

ADAM (*wretchedly*). Why do you bother to taunt me? I was always a weakling. I was always afraid of pain.

STELLA. I suspect it's you who do the taunting. You look humble, you play weak; clever! and all the time you're chuckling under your breath, "You bitch of a world, I've beaten you at your game. The heroes are dead and I'm alive, hurt but alive enough to be hurt!" Isn't that what you're saying? The truth!

ADAM. No, it isn't. Chuckling? What has happened to you, Stella?

STELLA. Why did you talk to the Germans?

ADAM. Again, again, again! I was afraid to die.

STELLA. Didn't you hate them?

ADAM. Hate them? I'd kill them one by one — sometimes I choke with it — the hatred — and yet I was afraid. That's me and that's all of me, nothing of chuckling.

STELLA. And you're ashamed?

ADAM. Yes, I'm ashamed. Stella, why are you here?

STELLA. I'll tell you. On the day you are released, Adam, look and you will see me standing alone at the gate.

ADAM. Yes?

STELLA. I will offer you my hand.

ADAM. Offer me your hand — ? And then — ? If I take it?

STELLA. Face it out at your side.

(*Silence*)

ADAM. Stella. He was dragged away begging me to keep silent.

STELLA. Let no man be required to will his life to other men.

ADAM. Required! I don't know. But expected — in decency?

STELLA (*wild*). Let no one expect it! Each life for itself!

ADAM. Robert gave his!

STELLA. He chose to! Fine decent man! So decent to die for us! Applause! All that self-respect down there in the grave! I don't know where he lies, but I hope he enjoys his decency. He wanted to be a hero. Applause, applause! But don't let this swine of a world demand it of a man! He had the right not to die! Like you! I discovered it! Life gave you the right to your life, like an animal, hugging it, cowering, and running. Fools who don't know it!

ADAM. Stella!

STELLA. But I do know where he lies! What was I thinking? Here's his coffin! *(She shows a box)* And here he is! A medal in its box! Come out, Robert. Leap up to your wife. Kiss her. My hero, my patriot, hug me!

ADAM. Put it back, you're raving.

STELLA. And who made this filthy world where a man has to die for others? Did he? Did you? You simpletons! Were you a Prime Minister? A Chief of Staff? Did you write treaties or editorials? You dust! I'll tell you what. Stella Tavrac has made a law: Next time a war breaks out, on that same day, "regardless of age," as they say, "regardless of rank or physical condition," every official, every journalist, every director of television, every general, every lord and president and minister and king and every last member of every last house of representatives will march to the front-line: rifle on his shoulder, helmet on his head, biscuit in his pocket, mud in his face, and forward march into the bullets! *We'll* be giving out the medals then! Adam and Stella will stay home and cheer on the senators at the front!

ADAM. Stella! At the trial — you didn't speak like this.

STELLA *(suddenly droops)*. I haven't forgotten.

ADAM. You were clawing my face, God knows what —

STELLA. And you were handcuffed. I told you, I haven't forgotten —

ADAM. The policemen finally tore you away.

STELLA. Robert had just died.

ADAM. He's still dying. I hear him shouting at me, "Don't tell them! Adam, don't tell them!" And then I broke down. And Selvinsky rushing into the garage that night — the sky seemed to be burning —

STELLA. Did you promise to die for him?

ADAM. He came to us because he knew — he thought — he could count on us.

STELLA. He had only the right to hope. No man owes his life to another, nor to ten others, nor to a million others.

(There is a long silence)

ADAM. Is it true they built a memorial to Selvinsky?

STELLA. Yes. It shows a large muscular man. For some reason his torso is nude, but he wears trousers. He carries a rifle and his foot is on a snake. It doesn't resemble Selvinsky but it stands for him. And underneath there's an inscription. First some Latin which I don't understand, then "For Those Who Freely Gave Their Lives," and then it talks about "The Grateful Nation." And then there are names, many names, including my husband's.

(Enter the jailer)

JAILER. Pssst. Mrs. Tavrac. It's almost time for the daily check. I'm sorry.

STELLA. I'll go. One moment.

(The jailer leaves)

STELLA. I shall wait for you, Adam. The country hates you forever. Let us help each other.

ADAM. I don't know.

(Stella leaves)

ADAM. Who came here? Good or evil spirit, who spoke?

SCENE THREE

(A clearing in the wood. Irregular terrain. In the center, a boulder. Pathways off into the wood in several directions. Artillery fire in the distance. Occasional gun-fire at closer range. Enter Captain Jahmann and Privates Kalk and Lembo)

KALK. Wait. Quiet. There!

JAHMANN. Where?

(Kalk fires, and rushes into the wood)

JAHMANN. Is he going out of his mind?

LEMBO. Oh, I don't know.

(Kalk returns)

KALK. I guess I was wrong. Sorry.

LEMBO. It must have been a deer or something.

KALK. I could have sworn —

JAHMANN. All right, all right. So you wasted a bullet. Where are we?

KALK. I'd say a matter of five miles from Scandella Bridge, due south. This is the third time in four years I'm fighting for this wood, Captain Jahmann. It's getting to be like home to me.

JAHMANN. All right. Let's push on. We're too much in the open here. And next time you shoot remember Major Ollendorff wants him alive.

KALK. Yes, sir. One enemy general coming up!

(They vanish. General Fantochka, who has been hiding in a tree, comes down. His uniform is torn, and he is disarmed except for his swagger stick)
FANTOCHKA. Alive? Never.
(Exhausted, he leans against a tree. A humming voice is heard. Fantochka conceals himself behind the trunk. Enter the flute player, tall, blond, strong, dressed in a rustic cape, and walking with a long staff. He sits down, props himself up against the boulder, eats a piece of bread and cheese, drinks out of a canteen, and then plays on his flute while the guns roar on. Fantochka peeks, then comes out)
FANTOCHKA. You're one of our boys, anyway.
FLUTE PLAYER. I guess you wouldn't see a Nazi playing the flute in a wood.
FANTOCHKA. Why aren't you home?
FLUTE PLAYER. Too dangerous, my friend. Every house is a target, so I try surviving in the open. I'm so obvious, I hope nobody will notice me.
FANTOCHKA. Why the flute?
FLUTE PLAYER. Why not the flute?
FANTOCHKA. There's a war on, haven't you heard? Why aren't you in the service?
FLUTE PLAYER. In whose service?
FANTOCHKA. Your country's, damn you.
FLUTE PLAYER. Oho. You're about to ask me to do something for you. Aren't you a general?
FANTOCHKA. I am General Fantochka, supreme commander of this sector.
FLUTE PLAYER *(ruefully)*. Of this ex-sector. You're retreating again.
FANTOCHKA. We won't retreat far. Not if I can get out of this uniform, and slip back into our lines.
FLUTE PLAYER. Are you that important?
FANTOCHKA. Frankly, I am. Every table of organization is imprinted in my brain, I know what is where and who is when, I have studied the enemy's manpower and deathpower, I know his mortar emplacements and ours, the degree of his fatigue and the number of his grenades, and I have worked out an unbeatable strategy; we feign retreat and turn with a furious counter-offensive which takes advantage, one, of his over-stretched lines of communication, two, the losses I mean to inflict on his depots by aerial bombing, and three, the attrition of his initial impetus.
FLUTE PLAYER *(whistling)*. Good God! How come they let you get lost?
FANTOCHKA. The Germans?
FLUTE PLAYER. No, us.
FANTOCHKA. Nobody let me get lost. We fell into a classical ambush. My men stood their ground to cover my escape. Myself and two staff officers got away with the papers, but of the three, only I am left. Now let me ask you. First, your name.

FLUTE PLAYER. I am called the Flute Player.

FANTOCHKA. I am placing you under my direct command.

FLUTE PLAYER. I am honored.

FANTOCHKA. The Germans are searching the forest for me. If they find me alive, I'll swallow a poison which I keep in the hollow of my ring in the best tradition. But that means the end of our counter-offensive, and then I tremble for our country. I proceed.

FLUTE PLAYER. Do.

FANTOCHKA. We'll swap outfits. You know your way about. You'll make it back to your cottage safe enough, where you can burn my uniform and put on new clothes. This will give *me* at least a fifty-fifty chance of escaping.

FLUTE PLAYER. Dear general, that is a very dangerous assignment for me.

FANTOCHKA. What kind of a comment is that? Of course, it's a very dangerous assignment for you! We're at war, remember? And look at you — young, tall as a tree, bulging muscles — are you scared?

FLUTE PLAYER. Yes.

FANTOCHKA. Animal!

FLUTE PLAYER. Yes again.

FANTOCHKA. I order you to take off your clothes. General Fantochka is giving you an order. Do you hear?

FLUTE PLAYER. I hear, but I won't do it.

FANTOCHKA. We'll see about that.

(*But the flute player suddenly slams his staff against Fantochka's forearm. Fantochka drops his stick and cries out*)

FLUTE PLAYER. Stay away from me!

FANTOCHKA. Dirty collaborator, we'll meet again. But if we don't, the blood of your country sticks to your hands. (*He leaves*)

FLUTE PLAYER (*alone*). I am sorry for my country, and I love my country, I really do, but I am another Adam Adamson, and besides I am a flute player. (*He plays. Gun-fire*) I am an animal, and therefore I am reluctant to die. But I am also a man, and therefore I have principles, like honor, loyalty — let me see, and several others. But how is a man to have principles if he is not alive to have them? So if I am an animal, I want to be alive. And if I am a man of principle, I want to be alive too.

(*He plays again*)

FANTOCHKA (*running in*). I think they've seen me! Have you got a hiding place around here? You'll do that much, I hope!

FLUTE PLAYER. This boulder is hollow. Creep in. Make yourself small. Hurry.

(*Fantochka goes behind the boulder, which the flute player then covers with his cape. He swiftly erases Fantochka's tracks nearby, climbs onto the boulder, takes a relaxed supine position, and plays his flute. Reenter Captain Jahmann and Privates Kalk and Lembo. The flute player sits up)*

KALK. All right, let's see your hands!

JAHMANN. We're turning in circles. Who the hell are you?

FLUTE PLAYER. I am the district flute player.

JAHMANN. An artist in the woods!

KALK. Must be a Jew.

JAHMANN. All right, Jew flute player, how long have you been piping here?

FLUTE PLAYER. Half a day, sir, wandering to and fro in the woods.

LEMBO *(aside to Jahmann)*. I warn you he's a guerrilla, sir.

JAHMANN. Why isn't a civilian like you under his bed at home?

FLUTE PLAYER. A house is a target these days, sir. I am trying to survive in the open.

JAHMANN. Have you seen any of your officers hiding or running?

FLUTE PLAYER. I've seen soldiers, sir. I can't tell you what level.

LEMBO. He's trying to be funny. You want me to knock your teeth down your throat maybe?

JAHMANN. Are you trying to be funny, flute player?

FLUTE PLAYER. No! I wouldn't dare.

JAHMANN. Get off that rock. Kalk, keep your finger on the trigger. Lembo, take his stick away.

(Lembo carefully examines the staff)

FLUTE PLAYER. Why are you doing this?

JAHMANN. Talk when you're talked to, all right? We're looking for a high officer of yours. A general. It'll pay you to cooperate with the German Army. We'll shoot you if you don't. Have you seen your general?

FLUTE PLAYER. I don't know. I've seen so many persons. Is he tall and thin, and around fifty or fifty-five years old?

JAHMANN. I don't know.

FLUTE PLAYER. Does he wear a moustache by any chance? A grey silvery sort of moustache?

JAHMANN. I tell you I don't know. But since you do, where is he? Where did you see him? Talk, by Christ!

KALK. Talk, you dog, or I'll blow your guts to hell.

FLUTE PLAYER. Please, gentlemen, I'm trying to help. The tall thin officer I saw running into the woods over there, and the officer with the moustache took the winding path back of you.

(Jahmann stares speechlessly at Kalk and Lembo)

KALK. He's a commando, a guerrilla, a spy, I don't care what, but they've got them in the woods already. Let me shoot him, Captain Jahmann.

LEMBO. He's right, sir.

JAHMANN *(still astonished)*. The impudence!

KALK. Come on, Captain Jahmann, give me the order. We haven't got

time to fool around and I'm not planning to leave this bird behind
when I go.

(*Gunfire very close*)

LEMBO. Down!

JAHMANN. Cover!

(*As they fall down, the flute player leaps aside and runs away*)

KALK. Stop!

LEMBO (*at the same time*). Where's it coming from?

KALK. The bastard! (*He rises and runs after the flute player*)

JAHMANN. Kalk, come back! Idiot!

(*Kalk is hit and falls*)

KALK. Gah. I told you —

JAHMANN. It's coming from all sides! (*Gunfire continues*) Let's get out
of here, Lembo. (*They run away*)

KALK. Don't leave me. Hey! I'm only wounded. Captain Jahmann! Lembo!

(*The firing abates. Fantochka emerges and seizes Kalk's rifle*)

KALK. The general! I've got him!

(*Reenter the flute player*)

FLUTE PLAYER. General Fantochka!

FANTOCHKA. Thanks for holding out, friend. Look what I've found. A
German who has recognized me. What's your estimable advice,
flute player?

FLUTE PLAYER. Shoot him.

KALK. No! I don't know you! Wait — I have a mother!

(*Fantochka shoots. The flute player bends over the body*)

FANTOCHKA. Hold it. Let me take his ammunition. (*He does so*)

FLUTE PLAYER (*dragging the body behind the boulder*). Sons of the dark,
return to the dark.

FANTOCHKA. We seem to have odds and ends of friends scattered in the
wood. If only I could rally them and give them a brain. Meanwhile
I'm still in uniform.

FLUTE PLAYER. But you've got a rifle now. You could aim it at me, and
force me to change with you this time.

FANTOCHKA. I should, you clown. Don't I know that in another moment
you would have given me away?

FLUTE PLAYER. You're beginning to understand.

FANTOCHKA. I am. So. I'm *not* aiming the rifle at you, flute player.

FLUTE PLAYER. I noticed. Thank you.

FANTOCHKA (*examines the rifle*). Now that I've got a friend, I can cope
with the brutes. I'll lie in a ditch till nightfall — you'll give me that
crust of bread — and then I'll slip out of this trap.

FLUTE PLAYER. There's a better way for you.

FANTOCHKA. Namely?

FLUTE PLAYER. Look.

(Adam and Stella enter hand in hand)

FANTOCHKA. A dream!

FLUTE PLAYER. Adam and his woman, like two quiet animals of the wood.

ADAM. We meet again, General Fantochka.

FANTOCHKA. What in blazes are you doing here, Adamson?

FLUTE PLAYER. They live farming a plot of ground by the bend of the river, in the cross-fire of two enemies. They work hard, they earn little, they want nothing. Today, General, you can be their hired man. Adam will give you an old suit, and you will be allowed to stay until the way for you is safe.

FANTOCHKA. Adamson! You? You will conceal me and defend me?

ADAM. I will.

FANTOCHKA. And when the Germans knock at your door?

ADAM. I will call you my servant.

FANTOCHKA. And if they notice that the clothes are not mine?

ADAM. I will say, "This is wartime. We buy the clothes we can."

FANTOCHKA. And if they promise you a great reward for information about me?

ADAM. I will know nothing.

FANTOCHKA. And if they threaten to burn down your house and destroy your crop unless you find me for them?

ADAM. I will let them burn down the house and destroy the crop.

FANTOCHKA. And if they offer to kill you, or kill this woman?

ADAM. I will betray you.

STELLA. Will you come with us, General?

FANTOCHKA. I will come with you.

ADAM. Wait until we are gone, and then follow us at a small distance. The farm is a mile away, the path to it is narrow and rugged. Do not lose us.

(Adam and Stella, still hand in hand, leave)

FANTOCHKA. And yet I — Lucas Fantochka — I, without boasting, I would die for my country.

FLUTE PLAYER. That, my dear sir, is why the world made you a general.

(Fantochka leaves)

THE END

OF ANGELS AND ESKIMOS

CHARACTERS

JOHN SEBASTIAN TALBOT

DAISY TALBOT, *his wife*

ALICE TALBOT, *his daughter*

JIM CASH

TENNYSON CASH, *his son*

REGINALD BUCKINGHAM

INUK[1]

THE BLACK SHADOW

AN ANGEL

A POLICEMAN

AN AMBULANCE DRIVER

A DOCTOR

1. Pronounced as "in nook."

Act One

A used car lot.
Used cars.
A pretty office.
Bunting.
A banner which reads: DON'T BE RASH; DEAL WITH CASH.
Reginald Buckingham is polishing up one of the cars. Jim Cash and his son Tennyson are sitting on the office steps. A transistor radio at their side is broadcasting one of Scarlatti's sonatas. Jim is reading aloud from a book.

CASH. "And St. Francis goes behind the altar and kneels down in prayer. And as he prayed he was inspired by the divine presence with fervor so exceedingly great that his whole soul was burning with love for holy poverty; in such wise that what with the hue of his face and the strange yawning of his mouth, it seemed as if flames of love were bursting from him. And coming thus aflame towards his companion —"

REGINALD. Here's a customer, Mr. Cash.

CASH. Eh? So it is. Look, Tennyson. You can tell — the chin tilted up, the corner of the mouth thrust into the cheek, the eyebrow lifted — an air of expectant pessimism, and you know it's a customer. Will you take care of him, Mr. Buckingham?

REGINALD. Of course, Mr. Cash.

CASH *(to Tennyson)*. We'll go on reading inside the office, son.

REGINALD. Don't go for *my* sake.

CASH. No, Mr. Buckingham, but there's something private, mysterious and tender between a salesman and his customer which no man should intrude upon. Why, I might glance at his left lapel and destroy the vital atmosphere. Come along, Tenny.

TENNYSON. Shall I turn off the radio?

CASH. What do you think, Mr. Buckingham?

REGINALD. Well, sir, he might be fond of Scarlatti, and then again he might prefer something by one of the modern gentlemen with saxophones and electric guitars. One never knows. Indeed —

CASH. You're right, Mr. Buckingham. Silence Scarlatti, my boy, and let's take St. Francis into the office. Mr. Buckingham, I wish you good luck.

REGINALD. Oh, after ten years with you, sir — but thank you anyway.

(Cash and his son disappear into the office. Enter John Sebastian Talbot. He looks at the banner to make sure he is in the right place.)

TALBOT. Mr. Jim Cash?

REGINALD (*giving Talbot his card*). No, sir. Reginald Buckingham, chief salesman. Can I be of assistance?

TALBOT (*reading the card*). "Reginald Buckingham. Integrity backed by eleven centuries of aristocracy. 97 Myrtle Street." (*Holding out his hand*) My name's Talbot. John Sebastian Talbot.

REGINALD. Pleased to meet you, Mr. Talbot. I hope we can accommodate you this morning. Anything in particular?

TALBOT. I'm not sure. Maybe you can offer a few suggestions. I stopped at Cutright's car lot earlier today —

REGINALD. Our roughest competitor, Mr. Cutright. Dear man. Impeccably in business for twenty-nine years.

TALBOT. I know, but then again he told me he didn't have a single car on hand that he could recommend.

REGINALD. I'm surprised.

TALBOT. He said, for some reason or other all his cars were gargling today.

REGINALD. Gargling?

TALBOT. Or gurgling. They go glg-glg-glg-glg on the road. Mr. Cutright thought it might be due to the southwesterlies we've been having lately. He said they carry sand particles into the differentials.

REGINALD. That's odd. We haven't experienced anything like it. Perhaps the General Motors plant across the way keeps the wind out for us. And so?

TALBOT. And so Mr. Cutright said I could of course take a chance, because in time some of the cars might grow out of their gargle — or gurgle — but for the moment he would take it upon himself to recommend Mr. Cash. I'm quoting.

REGINALD. I see. Of course, this places quite a responsibility on our shoulders. About how new or how old a car were you thinking of? And what sort, speaking in a general way?

TALBOT. I was thinking of something about three years old. Or two, or four, or somewhere in between.

REGINALD. I see.

TALBOT. And the car should be friendly, even a little on the — on the witty side, if you know what I mean. We're a humor-loving family.

REGINALD. Nothing too — compelling — too — authoritarian —

TALBOT. Or too solemn.

REGINALD. I have it. I think I know what you need.

TALBOT (*looking around*). Actually, most of your cars look pretty attractive.

REGINALD. Oh, you mustn't let appearances deceive you, Mr. Talbot. We polish them, true; our dignity demands it; but sometimes underneath these shining bodies, shocking blemishes lie concealed.

TALBOT. You don't say. Well, I'm in your hands, Mr. Buckingham. Frankly, I'm a cretin as far as automobiles are concerned. I'm in real estate myself.

REGINALD. A very interesting line, Mr. Talbot. But let me show you a car which may suit you. This one, for instance.

TALBOT. Not bad. It's the color of Daisy's eyes. Daisy is my wife.

REGINALD. A good omen, Mr. Talbot.

(Reginald lifts the hood)

TALBOT. Spic and span. Even *I* can see that.

REGINALD. Well now, not quite, not quite. A used car is a used car, Mr. Talbot; don't entertain too many illusions about it even under the best of circumstances. Here, for instance, the generator is none too efficient.

TALBOT. Still, I'm sure —

REGINALD. Oh, of course, the car *will* do its duty, if you are firm with it. It will move, both forward and backward. The valves and pistons, I might add, are in tip-top shape, the spark plugs are clean and decent, and the oil filter filters the oil. But now and then the crankshaft tries to move sideways.

TALBOT. Don't we all.

REGINALD. Let me turn the ignition on. *(He is inside the car)* Are the headlights delivering? *(He turns on the lights)*

TALBOT. Yes, they're fine.

REGINALD. Here goes. *(He turns on the engine)*

TALBOT. Sounds good. Putt-putt-putt. Sounds normal.

REGINALD. What's that?

TALBOT. I said, "Sounds normal"!

(Reginald reappears)

REGINALD. Normal, Mr. Talbot! What is normalcy? An open invitation to trouble. *(He listens to the motor)* I suppose the engine will do. Wait — there's a ping. Can you hear it?

TALBOT. No.

REGINALD. Listen carefully. *(He accompanies the rhythm of the motor)* There — there — there — ping — ping — ping —

TALBOT. Oh, I don't know. Nothing is perfect. You've got to make allowances. *(Reginald plunges in with a wrench)*

TALBOT. You shouldn't get yourself dirty.

REGINALD. There! How is it now? Hush . . . I can still detect it. My ear is attuned, you see. It's nothing dangerous; but this is a ping which will have to affect the price of the car. *(He listens again)* Ping ping. Unquestionably.

TALBOT. Really, I can't see why —

REGINALD. What are you saying, Mr. Talbot? I hope you trust me. *(Turns motor off)*

TALBOT. I do.

REGINALD. You admitted that you know next to nothing about automobiles.

TALBOT. Still —

REGINALD. This *may* be the car for you, Mr. Talbot, but only if we can agree on a price.

TALBOT. The more I look at it, the better I like it.

REGINALD. The body is a little squat.

TALBOT. Plump. Cute and plump. All right, Mr. Buckingham, cards on the table. How much?

REGINALD. Cards on the table, Mr. Talbot. For you — we'll say a thousand dollars.

TALBOT. That's ridiculous. A thousand dollars! For this car?

REGINALD. A thousand dollars is a reasonable price. Remember the dubious generator.

TALBOT. I remember it; but what about the healthy valves? And the clean spark plugs?

REGINALD. What about the ping ping?

TALBOT. Far-fetched.

REGINALD. Believe me —

TALBOT. No, Mr. Buckingham, I've been in business too long to be fooled with. Let's say twelve-hundred, that's what the car deserves, and we'll call it a deal.

REGINALD. That would be robbery! I don't mean to offend you. But Mr. Cash wouldn't stand for it. It's not an offer I could even show him.

TALBOT. If that's your last word (*he moves away*) — maybe another time.

REGINALD. Wait! You're a hard bargainer, Mr. Talbot. Let's split the difference. The car will need a new clutch within the year, I'm sure; I'm almost sure. Eleven hundred.

TALBOT. I don't like to rob anybody. You people are squeezed from all sides. I know the profit margin is minute.

REGINALD. Minute? We'll live like feudal kings on your eleven hundred, Mr. Talbot.

TALBOT. Pooh.

REGINALD. Like Byzantine emperors!

(*They laugh*)

TALBOT. I'm a pushover for a good sales talk. Here.

(*They shake hands*)

REGINALD. You won't regret it, Mr. Talbot. She's really a healthy little car.

(*A band nearby is heard playing a rousing fanfare*)

TALBOT. Good God, that's more than —

REGINALD. What did you say?

TALBOT (*louder*). I said that's more than I expected. Do you always celebrate a deal with music?

REGINALD. Ha, ha, ha, very good! No, Mr. Talbot, just a coincidence. It's the General Motors band. Wait. They're bound to have somebody out singing too. They always do in warm, sunny weather.

INUK *(singing off stage while the band accompanies him; Reginald nudges Mr. Talbot and encourages him to pay attention)*

> Let every voice in industry be raised;
> The mercy of the Lord be praised;
> With meteors dreadful destroy us he might,
> Yet daily he spares us the heavenly blight.
>
> And let us sing of heaven's mighty grace
> Which orders the moon "Stray not from thy place,"
> Which keeps down the sun to a civilized heat
> When broil us it could with most horrible speed.
>
> Amen

TALBOT. That's what I call a fine baritone. He ought to go far in the automobile industry.

REGINALD. I'm glad you think so. He's a friend of ours.

TALBOT. The baritone?

REGINALD. Yes. His name is Inuk. He's an Eskimo.

TALBOT *(impressed)*. An Eskimo? You don't see many of *them* here in town. I guess the climate's too warm for them.

REGINALD. This one is a Negro Eskimo, he doesn't mind the sun.

TALBOT *(more impressed)*. And he's a friend of yours?

REGINALD *(confidential)*. Not only that. His mother was Jewish. Before she passed on.

TALBOT. I'll be damned! What does he do at the plant?

REGINALD. He's a foreman. That's why he gets the solo parts, you know.

TALBOT. You don't say!

(Enter Cash and Tennyson)

CASH. Inuk was booming like a happy bull this morning.

REGINALD. Oh, Mr. Talbot, I want you to meet the owner and my employer, Mr. Jim Cash. And this is his son, Tennyson.

CASH. Glad to meet you, Mr. Talbot.

TALBOT. The pleasure's mine. Hello, my boy.

TENNYSON. How do you do.

CASH. Well, Mr. Talbot, has Mr. Buckingham fitted you with a car you can live with?

TALBOT. Yes he has. I'm buying this supersonic job right here. Oh, I forgot — the money. Money-money-money. We said twelve hundred . . .

REGINALD. Eleven hundred, Mr. Talbot.

TALBOT. Oh yes. *(He counts out the bills)* Here you are. Byzantine dollars.

REGINALD. And here's your certificate of ownership. I do hope you're happy with the car.

CASH. Remember, we stand behind our merchandise.

TENNYSON. Impartial censure we request from all,
        Prepared by just decrees to stand or fall.

TALBOT. Aha. So that's how it is. Poetry.

TENNYSON. Yes, sir. William Congreve.

TALBOT. Is your son studying to be a poet, Mr. Cash?

CASH. Yes he is. I want him to do something practical, and not toil his life away like his stupid father. What do *you* do, Mr. Talbot, if I may ask?

TALBOT. I'm like yourself, Mr. Cash — except that I scrounge in the real estate line. Work work work. It's an insult to heaven.

CASH, REGINALD and TENNYSON. True.

TALBOT. Well, I'd better be on my way. I'll drive the car up and down a few hills.

REGINALD. Any time we can be of help. It's been a genuine pleasure.

TALBOT. It has. You know, the more I look at the three of you —

CASH. Yes?

TALBOT. I like your faces, damn it.

CASH. We like yours too, Mr. Talbot. What's on your mind?

TALBOT. I wonder if I could interest you in a deal.

CASH. Why not?

TALBOT. I mentioned that I'm in real estate.

CASH. Yes.

TALBOT. All right, here's the story. I've had my eyes on a property in the outskirts — a vacant piece of land crying out to be developed. Mind you, this is inside information. I'm looking for a few partners to raise the necessary cash with me. And beyond that, I'm simmering up a scheme, a scheme, in a word, a scheme, a good scheme, as sound as the first bleat of the newborn lamb. This is sudden, I know, call it a gush of sympathy, anyway I wonder if you gentlemen might be interested.

CASH. We might.

REGINALD. Sounds jolly.

TALBOT. A windfall, gentlemen.

CASH. Tell us more.

TALBOT. I've got a better idea. Let's see. It's ten-thirty now —

TENNYSON. Ten-thirty? How about our coffee break, dad?

CASH. In a minute, son. Don't interrupt Mr. Talbot.

TALBOT. That's all right. Coffee breaks must be taken seriously. But here's what I suggest. Come over to my house at three or four this afternoon. Wait. Let me give you my card, here's the address. Close shop early; you'll drink coffee again, we'll talk business, and you'll get to meet my wife and daughter. How about it?

CASH. I'm willing. How about you, Mr. Buckingham?

REGINALD. Women, coffee, and business: I'll be there, Mr. Talbot.

TALBOT. Well, that is that. Open the door, Mr. Buckingham. I'm driving off.

CASH. Why don't you join us for our coffee break before you go?

TALBOT. Thanks, but I'm overdue for the one at my office.

REGINALD. Here you are, sir. The keys are in the ignition. Go easy on the fuel pump, Mr. Talbot. *(He brushes the car seat)*

TALBOT. Good springs. I feel at home with the beast already. Fine. I'll see you all between three and four.

CASH. We'll be there, ready to deal and dally. Good luck!

TALBOT *(driving off)*. I'm off!

ALL *(waving)*. So long!

CASH. Watch the fire hydrant! ... He made it.

(Talbot is gone)

CASH. Well, Mr. Buckingham, you've done it again. Another car sold, another entry in the ledger, another vacancy on the lot, and another commission for you.

REGINALD. Thank you, sir.

CASH. How much did you ask for the car?

REGINALD. A thousand dollars.

CASH. You should have started at nine hundred. I hope you are not endangering your soul.

REGINALD. I hope not, Mr. Cash. I do my best.

CASH. Well, your best, I must admit, is very good indeed.

TENNYSON. Coffee break, dad.

CASH. All right, Tenny, go get the coffee. Here. *(He gives money to Tennyson)* One with and one without. And a lemonade for you.

(Exit Tennyson)

CASH. In fact, Mr. Buckingham, I think we should be looking into the question of a promotion for you.

REGINALD. Oh really —

CASH. I mean it. I read in the paper this morning that Fred Spalding is on the road again.

REGINALD. Spalding? The president of Chase National?

CASH. That's right. Left the bank yesterday at three in the afternoon with a satchel over his shoulders and a staff in his hand, and headed for the countryside, patting dogs and children as he went.

REGINALD. Not a week goes by —

CASH. As you know, I keep a walking stick in the garage, and satchels can be bought. At my age, St. Francis was dead. I am a widower; why shouldn't I walk into the woods? I'll take Tenny along; the beauty of the poet's trade is that you can ply it on the road almost as well as in the office.

REGINALD. I don't know what to say.

CASH. You've been chief salesman for six years, Mr. Buckingham; a faithful disciple, in short. Now I've been studying a proposal, which I drew up myself, to create the post of executive manager for my business, and to appoint you to fill the vacancy. You'll send me ten per cent of the gross care of General Delivery hither and yonder, wherever oaks and poplars abound and the cows look satisfied. This is no mean promotion, Mr. Buckingham.

(Tennyson has returned with the coffee)

REGINALD. Thank you, Tenny. I'm overwhelmed, Mr. Cash; and yet, as promotions go, I had hoped —

CASH. Go on, don't be afraid to speak.

REGINALD. What I'd really like is — more vacations, Mr. Cash. Two months instead of six weeks.

CASH. You're pushing me against the wall, Mr. Buckingham. May I borrow your spoon? Very well, take the two months. Either I'll close shop while you're gone or I'll delay my pilgrimage.

REGINALD. I wouldn't worry about St. Francis, sir. You've plenty of time. The medieval life-span was a good deal shorter than ours.

CASH. I don't know. I love my used cars, but I need to be drenched on the open road, and my mouth wide open to the wind.

TENNYSON. Look, there's Mr. Inuk! Mr. Inuk, come over here, I'll get you some milk.

CASH. Here. *(He gives Tennyson a coin)*

INUK. Morning everybody.

CASH and REGINALD. Good morning, Mr. Inuk.

TENNYSON. Milk?

INUK. The usual, my boy.

(Tennyson leaves)

CASH. Roll up a chair, Mr. Inuk. You were in fine voice this morning. I was in the office reading aloud, and the trucks going down Broadway, but I heard you all the same.

REGINALD. A rich throat, Mr. Inuk, mellow thunder.

INUK. Nature has been good to me. Do you gentlemen realize, by the way, that 3,466 days have gone by without a detectable meteorite damaging this city? There's not been so much as a bump on a sparrow's head.

CASH. Is that the reason you're strolling about at 11 A.M. instead of terrorizing the assembly line?

INUK. Terrorizing is good, ha, ha, ha! No, seriously — Muffle, you know, the vice-president, he came over to me and said, "Inuk, you were in fine voice today; take the morning off; we're turning out too many

damn cars anyway." So here I am. The men have gone bowling.
(*Tennyson returns with the milk*)

INUK. Thank you, Tenny.

TENNYSON. Your voice was round as a melon this morning, Mr. Inuk.

INUK. Oh, I don't know. How about you, Tenny? Committed any good poems lately?

TENNYSON. I hope so, sir. Would you like to hear my latest?

INUK. I certainly would.

TENNYSON. Good! Gather round, everybody.

CASH. Is it a poem I know, Tenny?

TENNYSON. Nope. Hot off the typewriter; and I mean hot.

REGINALD. This is going to be a treat. We're ready, Master Cash.

(*Enter a customer. He has a pair of wings growing out of his back through slits in his shirt. We only catch a glimpse of these wings, however, because the customer tucks them in and puts his coat on over them*)

CUSTOMER (*to the audience*). Ask no questions. I have been sent to examine Inuk.

TENNYSON (*who has taken a sheet of paper out of his jacket*). The title —

REGINALD. Wait a moment, Tenny. Here's another customer.

TENNYSON. Oh no! This is our coffee break.

INUK. The boy is right, Mr. Cash.

CASH. Don't anybody get excited. (*He walks over to the customer*) Sir, my name is Jim Cash. Are you shopping for a car?

CUSTOMER. I am, but there's no hurry. I'll look around quietly —

CASH. I won't hear of it. Join our little session. My boy Tennyson is about to recite one of his new poems. Here's a comfortable fender — sit down, and we'll look at cars afterwards.

CUSTOMER. Thank you.

INUK. Go on, Tenny.

TENNYSON (*reading*). "To Glycinta." That's the title, G-l-y-c —
    "I am weary, oh Glycinta, of thy raven kisses —"

INUK. Raven kisses? Excuse me for interrupting.

TENNYSON. That's all right.

INUK. Why raven kisses?

CASH. Yes, Tenny, why raven kisses?

TENNYSON. Because a raven is a bird of ill omen and because it is predatory. You'll see; the kisses I'm talking about are of ill omen and they're predatory too. And then, raven reminds you of ravenous, which fits too.

INUK (*whistling with admiration*). I'm answered all right.

REGINALD. Isn't the raven a kind of crow, Master Tennyson?

TENNYSON. Yes, they're related. The raven is a poetic crow; or you might think of the crow as a pedestrian raven.

REGINALD. I was thinking that the crow is supposed to be an intelligent bird.

CASH. That's correct.

REGINALD. Perhaps this adds something to raven kisses too.

INUK. Ill-omened, predatory, ravenous and intelligent kisses?

TENNYSON. I doubt it.

REGINALD. It was only a thought.

INUK. Go on, Tenny.

TENNYSON. I'll start again, otherwise it's like jumping over a ditch without a headstart.

TO GLYCINTA

I am weary, Oh Glycinta, of thy raven kisses,
I have lain between thy pudgy breasts, thy hungry thighs, too long,
And having wasted, flame by flame, the holy fires of my youth,
And lost my teeth embracing thee, I seek the grave where I belong,
My flesh is eager for its worm; and yet I cannot pass away,
For still thy bawdy venom doth sustain my hated breath:
Thy tyrannous beauty beats me with soft hands away from death.

(*Applause*)

CUSTOMER. Very pretty indeed.

INUK (*enthusiastic*). Did you all catch those paradoxes? Come on, Tennyson, read it again.

(*Tennyson reads the poem again*)

INUK. Fantastic! The venom that keeps him alive, the beauty he hates because he loves it, because because he loves it he can't die. Fantastic!

REGINALD. I liked that bawdy venom.

TENNYSON. Did you notice the pun?

REGINALD. What pun?

TENNYSON. Bawdy, body.

REGINALD. Oh, very good, very good.

CASH. And "my flesh is eager for its worm" — a shrewd reversal, I thought. But I don't know about "pudgy breasts."

INUK. No, "pudgy breasts" is good. I mean, it doesn't really fit, Tenny, not here, your dad is right; but it's nice in itself. Realistic. Nice and homely and squishy.

REGINALD. Sexual and yet friendly.

INUK. It stays in the family, so to speak. No, the line I object to is where you lose your teeth embracing the girl.

TENNYSON. I guess that's not right, is it?

CASH. Take it out, Tenny. Makes the girl sound like a piece of leathery steak. Or, come to think of it, like the crow you were just talking about.

TENNYSON. I only meant that the poet has grown old.

CASH. We know what you meant, Tenny, but that's not what you achieved.

TENNYSON. I'll change it, dad. But you liked "my flesh is eager for its worm"?

REGINALD. Magnificent!

INUK. And those hungry thighs! (Whistles)

TENNYSON. You see, they go with the raven kisses. Everything fits.

CASH (to the customer). What is your opinion, sir?

CUSTOMER. For a boy of fifteen —

CASH. It shows a lot of experience, don't you agree? The rhyme scheme, to mention nothing else.

REGINALD. When did you write this, Master Tenny?

TENNYSON. I finished it yesterday after the ball game. I was lapping up an ice cream soda with Sharon Goldberg when the bawdy venom struck me and I rushed home to put it down. In five minutes it was all over.

INUK. Fantastic. Who's the girl, Tenny? Somebody real?

TENNYSON. Oh yes, it's Sharon Goldberg. She's in my Spanish class. She was mad because I don't come right out and mention her name.

INUK. Well, I hope you're not really all that tired of her.

TENNYSON. No, I'm not. I'm only fifteen, you know. But I'm old and weary for the poem's sake. And I told Sharon, "If the poem is good, to hell with the truth."

CUSTOMER. Well said, Master Cash. (to Cash) I predict your boy will go very far.

TENNYSON. Thank you, sir.

CUSTOMER. I came to look at used cars, but all I can think of now is love. A pleasant improvement. No offense meant to your cars, Mr. Cash.

INUK. I'm all quivery too. Those hungry thighs! But I've got to go back to work. So long everybody. Thanks for the milk and poem.

CASH. Come again tomorrow, Mr. Inuk.

INUK. I will; and I'll bring a few doughnuts.

(Enter Alice Talbot, holding a couple of parcels. Inuk stops)

ALICE. Excuse me — Mr. Cash?

CASH. I am he. What can I do for you? A great deal, I hope.

ALICE. My name is Alice Talbot. I'm looking for my father. Mr. Cutright told me I might find him here.

CASH. Delighted to make your acquaintance, Miss Talbot. Your father left a few minutes ago after buying one of our cars. I think you'll like it. He also summoned us to a business conference at your house this afternoon. With coffee and sugar.

ALICE. How nice! Well, since he's gone — I was going to invite myself to lunch with him — after gadding about all morning — but I'll go home instead. Thank you so much.

CASH. Are you walking, Miss Talbot?

ALICE. Yes, I am.

CASH. Not any more. Allow me to give you a lift in one of my many cars. *(Pointing at the customer)* Tenny, Mr. Buckingham, take care of this gentleman while I'm gone. *(He opens a car door)* Miss Talbot.

ALICE. Thank you.

(She is standing at some distance from the car. She has already caught a glimpse of Inuk. Reginald gives Inuk a brick; the latter advances resolutely between Alice and the automobile, and places the brick on the ground. Alice takes a long look at him; she looks at the brick; and then deliberately inadvertently stumbles over it and drops a parcel.)

ALICE. Oh!

INUK. Let me help you. Dear me, you might have hurt yourself. *(He picks up the parcel. They hold hands for a longer time than is customary)* I'm afraid you've scuffed your shoe.

ALICE. And I almost fell. But thanks to you I didn't. I'm very grateful, Mr. —

REGINALD. This is Mr. Inuk. A prince among men. Single. Excellent baritone.

TENNYSON. Loves good poetry.

REGINALD. Mad about mechanical engineering. He works for General Motors.

ALICE. It must be very interesting.

INUK. Oh yes. Thumping machines, great echoes of metal, hammers and rivets going all day, whistles and wheezes, it's tremendous.

ALICE *(shyly)*. They must like you.

REGINALD. Everybody likes him. My name is Reginald Buckingham. Executive manager.

ALICE. I'm glad to know you. *(But she doesn't see him)* Shall I take my parcel again?

INUK. I have a better idea.

ALICE. Yes?

INUK. Let me hold the other one for the time being. Until you're completely recovered.

ALICE. Actually it's very light. Two lace handkerchiefs.

INUK. Still, one never knows. After almost taking a fall.

ALICE. I suppose so. *(She gives him the second parcel)*

INUK. Miss Talbot —

ALICE. How do you know my name? Oh yes, I mentioned it.

INUK. I even know Alice.

ALICE. Yes.

INUK. I have a substantial income; suitable for — for anything.

ALICE. I'm so glad. I mean, it's pleasant for you.

INUK. After all, I'll have to settle down. It's natural. Did you know that baritones are professionally less demanding than tenors?

ALICE. Really?

INUK. It's a fact. Domestically too. They tend to help around the house.

ALICE. The baritone's a more restful voice, anyway, like a cello.

INUK. Exactly! May I ask, Miss Talbot, do *you* do anything for a living?

ALICE *(laughing)*. O yes, I breathe regularly.

(Inuk laughs)

INUK. You're fond of jokes.

ALICE. Only silly ones.

INUK. Looking at you — I would like to remark that you are more beautiful than an angel, an archangel.

CUSTOMER *(aside)*. Gently!

INUK. I say to myself, she must be tremendously engaged to somebody.

ALICE. Oh no.

INUK. Not even a little?

ALICE. Not even. I had never met the man I wished to marry.

INUK. How would you know if you did?

ALICE. How would I know? I'd meet him suddenly, out of nowhere. He'd do something, and say something, it would taste like fresh water when you're parched, and then suddenly I'd want to be fascinating and irresistible, only it wouldn't matter, because at the same time I know what he'd like to be —

INUK. A Greek God shooting about the clouds — for your sake —

ALICE. Well, not in the clouds. But he's not a god, and I'm not fascinating, so it fits together, and then his knowing what I felt and my knowing what he felt would make a circle around us, but it's very difficult to explain.

INUK. I suppose I'm asking too many questions.

ALICE. One doesn't mind from a stranger.

INUK. Oh, I'd forgotten.

ALICE. Forgotten what?

INUK. That I *am* a stranger to you.

ALICE. It's better than —

INUK. Than?

ALICE *(very softly)*. Not being even that.

CUSTOMER. My children, I advise you to join hands again.

CASH. I have a feeling I won't be driving Miss Talbot home.

ALICE. Inuk . . .

INUK. Alice, Alice . . .

(She touches his lips with two fingers and brings them to her own)

INUK. And now?

ALICE. My shoe is scuffed, Inuk. Remember?

INUK. By the grace of God, I know a shoemaker three blocks away.

ALICE. Please show me where he is.

(*They walk away, hand in hand*)

REGINALD (*cries after them*). Bless you, lovely creatures!

CASH. Now the earth is two, or even three loves richer than it was. There may be a presence haunting the neighborhood.

TENNYSON. I *thought* I smelled feathers.

CASH (*to the customer*). My dear sir, you must be thinking it's about time we applied our faculties to your used car.

CUSTOMER. No, no, not at all. I'm somehow no longer in the mood for a car. For the moment, you understand.

REGINALD. *I* certainly understand. Lovely creatures!

CUSTOMER. Besides, I have other means of conveyance. But I'll be back.

CASH. If only to hear one of Mr. Buckingham's sales pitches. They are prize-winners. But you're right. Today — I don't know what.

CUSTOMER. Another day, Mr. Cash. Gentlemen. And Master Tennyson, keep composing; at eighteen, at twenty-one — heaven knows!

(*Tennyson bows; the customer leaves*)

CASH. Well, Mr. Buckingham, we've heard Scarlatti on the harpsichord, we have had a poem read to us, we've drunk coffee in peace and good company, we have witnessed the beginnings of a marriage, and I've come close to falling in love myself, but how many cars have we sold?

REGINALD. One, Mr. Cash.

CASH. That's plenty. Let's all go for a walk.

ACT TWO

Chez Talbot.
A neat interior.
A window.
One door leading to the entrance hall, another door leading to the rest of the house.

Daisy Talbot is sewing and listening to dance music over the radio.

DAISY (*humming*). Alice Alice Alice has done it has done it.

RADIO. We interrupt your afternoon concert to bring you a late bulletin. A series of volcanic explosions has rocked the island of St. Barabbas. Within five minutes of the first explosion, the village of Granitti was engulfed by a flood of lava. Early reports put the toll at twenty-one dead and at least three times as many injured. We are extremely sorry to disturb you with this tragic report. More bulletins as they come in. *(Daisy is crying. Organ music on the radio. There is a honk outside, then John Talbot enters)*

TALBOT. Come out and meet the new car, Daisy! Why — you're crying — what's the matter?

(They kiss)

DAISY. Oh John — it's the radio —

TALBOT. What now?

DAISY. One of those awful volcanoes. Why do they have to exist?

TALBOT. Where did it happen, Daisy?

DAISY. The island of St. Barabbas.

TALBOT. Where's that?

DAISY. I don't know. I thought you'd know.

TALBOT. Never heard of it. St. Barabbas? Sounds far away.

DAISY. Twenty-one people died. *(She cries again)*

TALBOT. Twenty-one! *(He wipes an eye too)* And here I come with a brand new car, all chipper and all. Poor devils!

DAISY *(trying to carry on)*. Did you find the car you wanted?

TALBOT. Yes, I did. You'll like it, Daisy-maisy. It's the same blue as your eyes. Shall we go look at it? It'll cheer us up a little.

DAISY. First let's say a prayer, John.

TALBOT. That's a wonderful idea.

(Both stand with bowed heads, facing the audience)

TALBOT.   Hear me, wicked mountains, cruel seas,
      Storms and fire and grim disease:
      God shall assuage the bitter pain
      Of every soul that you have slain,
      Of every soul that you have slain.

DAISY. My Lord, take our brothers and sisters of St. Barabbas under your special mercy, and especially the children.

TALBOT. And extinguish the volcano which revolted against you.

DAISY. And do better next time if you possibly can.

TALBOT. Amen. Give me your hand, Daisy, it's a blue car and it likes us already.

(They go out. The music plays on a while, and then the thief enters. While he goes about his business, the music stops and the announcer's voice is heard again)

RADIO. We interrupt this program to bring you another news bulletin. Washington. The War Department discloses that the 17th Infantry Division launched another assault on the rust-covered Potomac Bridge before dawn today. Armed with scrapers and benzene, the division's thirty-eight men succeeded in clearing several more steel girders without meeting with more than token resistance. It is reliably reported, however, that reinforcements will have to be flown in before the main cable tower can be handed over to the painting crew. We asked War Secretary McBoodle to comment on the report. *(Voice of McBoodle)* "We're still appraising the situation, Sam. Our boys are doing a heroic job." *(Announcer)* Is it true, sir, that the Russians have embarked on a major bridge-painting project throughout the Soviet Union? *(McBoodle)* "Uh, all I'm free to say at this point, Sam, is that the Potomac Bridge is damn rusty." *(Announcer)* Now back to our regular program of flimsy music.

THIEF *(shaking his head).* Trouble, trouble. You can't believe anybody any more. *(The dance music resumes. All this time the thief has been active. He is dressed in the conventional manner of a thief — cap, old leather jacket, black mask — and carries a full bag over his shoulders. He appeared either from another room or through the window, calling out "Anybody home?" Now he is in the living room, looking about carefully, opening doors and drawers and examining every object he sees. Outside a couple of honks are heard. The thief finally opens his bag and takes out a silver candlestick. Just as he is about to place it on a credenza, he notices that the Talbots already possess a silver candlestick. He replaces his own in his bag, from which he now extracts a silver teapot. As he does so, his bag knocks over a vase. Startled by the noise, he dives under a table. Another honk is heard. Emerging, the thief places the teapot on the table, and compares it with a coffee pot he has found in the credenza and which he replaces where he found it. He admires his handiwork for a moment, then, hearing the front door, slinks out and vanishes)*

DAISY. I like it, I really like it. And it hasn't got a vulgar honk, like most cars, but a pretty kind of toot toot.

TALBOT. I'm glad I hit it right. Well, I hope Alice likes it too.

DAISY. Alice! Our daughter Alice!

TALBOT. What's the matter?

DAISY. How could I forget? Where's my brain? Oh, it was that awful earthquake. Alice called an hour ago —

TALBOT. Look! Daisy! *(He points to the teapot)*

DAISY *(simultaneously).* John! Look! *(She points to the pieces of the broken vase)*

(They look at each other, then huddle in each other's arms)

BOTH. The Black Shadow!

DAISY. Oh John, he must have been here a minute ago — while we were looking at the car. Maybe he's still in the house. Why do you suppose he left us a teapot? I'm trembling all over.

JOHN. Who knows? So now it's become our turn. You always think it only happens to the other fellow. But why did he break the vase? He's supposed to be —

DAISY. I'm sure it was an accident. John — look for him — please — catch him and make him take the teapot away, and call the police.

JOHN. Oh, all right, I'm rushing right out. How do you talk to a criminal?

DAISY. I don't know. Be polite. Hurry up!

(Talbot walks out without great hurry, and we hear him rummaging next door)

DAISY. See anyone?

TALBOT *(off-stage)*. Not a trace.

DAISY. Try the back yard.

(She examines the teapot, takes her coffee service out of the credenza, notes with approval that the teapot matches. Then she sweeps up the broken vase, not without a suspicious look here and there)

DAISY. John?

(The excited voice of the radio announcer suddenly breaks in on the music. Daisy pays no attention to him)

RADIO. Ladies and gentlemen — I have just been handed the following late-breaking story. Boulder, Colorado: Professor Norman T. Harrington revealed today at 11:06 A.M. that the final effect of Chaucer's "Merchant's Tale" is not comic at all, but sardonic, a dark and unsettling view of an aspect of man's experience. Questioned by newsmen who arrived on the scene at the University of Colorado, Professor Harrington asked *(voice of Professor Harrington)* "What about the prologue? What about the prologue? You must not read the Merchant's Tale outside the dramatic context of its prologue! We must fight the tendency to ignore the strong, viable presence of the narrator!" As soon as further particulars are available — *(Daisy absentmindedly turns the radio off. Talbot returns)*

TALBOT. Not a sliver of him anywhere. I guess we'll have to call the police. What a nuisance. Good God, don't tell me he was here again!

DAISY. No, silly, that's our own coffee set. Look — a perfect match.

TALBOT. You see the value of experience — even in crime.

DAISY. Do you realize that the Black Shadow has struck our neighborhood three times this month?

TALBOT. But now he's gone too far. We're well-off, damn it, we don't need his bric-a-brac.

DAISY. I wouldn't call it bric-a-brac. It's Victorian silver. John, let's be fair to the man.

TALBOT. Daisy, look into my eyes! Are you planning to *use* it? I knew it! What about the police? *(Solemn)* And what about your conscience?

DAISY. Oh, I don't know. You did have to stir it up. Wait! An inspiration! Daisy, you've done it again!

TALBOT. What now?

DAISY. It's divinely simple: we'll give the entire set to Alice for a wedding present.

TALBOT. A *wedding* present?

DAISY *(clutching her head)*. My head is spinning — I haven't even told you — every second another crisis!

TALBOT. Haven't told me what? Daisy, take hold of yourself.

DAISY. It was that awful Black Shadow, just as I was going to tell you — Alice called — that's it.

TALBOT. She's married!

DAISY. Almost.

TALBOT. To whom? When? What happened? I saw her at breakfast this morning. She was as unengaged as a baby. To the point of saying she'd let me take her out to lunch.

DAISY. Well, between breakfast and now, eight hours have gone by. It takes only thirty seconds to get engaged. Besides, it was you who practically introduced them.

TALBOT. Say that again?

DAISY. Alice went looking for you at the car lot for that famous lunch, but you were gone; instead she ran head-on into your son-in-law, a young man by the name of Inuk —

TALBOT. The General Motors baritone! I'll be pummeled!

DAISY. You've seen him?

TALBOT. No, but I heard him. He was singing two blocks away. Buckingham, the salesman, told me all about him. A splendid voice, Daisy, a *solid* voice.

DAISY. Well, they met, and it was love at first sight. They went rowing on the lake —

TALBOT. Fast worker.

DAISY. She fell into the water, and he saved her life. Of course — this is not for anybody else to know, John — she leaned over and pushed herself a little.

TALBOT. The minx!

DAISY. Whereupon they decided to get married.

TALBOT. For good?

DAISY. For good? What do you mean? Do you take your daughter for an idiot, John Sebastian? For good!

TALBOT. Young people go wild sometimes. For how long is it then?

DAISY. They decided on a decent five years. And then they'll see.

TALBOT. Five years is sound. It's long enough and yet it's not eternity either.

DAISY. John.

TALBOT. Yes?

DAISY. Are you remembering — that's the way we did it, the first time round?

TALBOT (*fondly*). I remember. And look at us now. (*They kiss. Daisy giggles happily*)

DAISY. He sounds like a very sensible young man.

TALBOT (*suddenly grave*). Inuk. Yes. This reminds me, Daisy. I don't know whether Alice told you. Who and what he is.

DAISY. Yes, she did. I wanted to discuss it with you. I *am* a little worried, as a matter of fact.

TALBOT. No clouds on your pretty face, Daisy-maisy.

DAISY. No clouds, darling.

TALBOT. What did Alice tell you exactly?

DAISY. Well — first of all — he's a Negro.

TALBOT. As brown as a ripe coconut.

DAISY. And then — this is really wild — he's an Eskimo.

TALBOT. A very unusual combination. But is that all she mentioned?

DAISY. Oh dear, is there more?

TALBOT. Yes. Daisy, he is a Jew. His mother was Hebrew.

DAISY. Oh dear. I guess she forgot to mention *that*.

TALBOT. Let's face it, half of him is Negro, half is Eskimo, and half is Jewish.

DAISY. Oh dear, oh dear.

TALBOT. I'm sure he doesn't make a *display* of anything, Daisy.

DAISY. Still, look at him, and then look at us. Episcopalians with pink cheeks.

TALBOT. I thought we were Congregationalists.

DAISY. Well, whichever.

TALBOT. Come on, Daisy, cheer up. Inuk's not marrying the Talbots but Alice, and Alice is a charming girl, almost a beauty. You're not giving enough credit to her solo charms, so to speak.

DAISY. She *has* blossomed, hasn't she?

TALBOT. She's past the pigtail stage, anyway.

DAISY. And the freckles! Remember the lemons she used to rub on her cheeks?

TALBOT. Oh God, those lemons! (*They laugh*) Well, well, I've got a hunch that Inuk is no snob. Besides, we'll see to it that she gets a suntan before the wedding day. No — there was something that made me trust him the moment I heard old Buckingham talk about him. And don't forget the voice and the music.

DAISY. Yes, that's a good point.

TALBOT.　　　　　"In sweet music is such art,
　　　　　　　　Killing care and grief of heart . . . "

(*The doorbell rings*) Who's that? Oh, it must be the gang from the car lot. I asked them over for coffee to discuss the property — you know.

DAISY. Fine! Open the door, I'll put the coffee on. *(She leaves one way, Talbot the other)*

TALBOT *(off-stage)*. Hello there!

REGINALD *(same)*. How d'you do, Mr. Talbot.

TALBOT *(same)*. Come in, come in; hang your hat here; follow me.

REGINALD *(same)*. Thank you. *(Both enter; Reginald is holding a bouquet of flowers)* I had to come alone, Mr. Talbot. The chief was detained at a special knapsack sale. He sends his regards, and hopes you'll allow him to call on you another day. Meantime I'm to report our business conversation to him.

TALBOT. Good good good. I'll make a point of contacting him myself. Daisy! Coffee for one guest! Mr. Cash couldn't come!

DAISY *(off-stage)*. All right. I'll be with you in a minute.

TALBOT. Sit down, Mr. Buckingham. Wait — I'll take these. *(He relieves Reginald of the flowers)* Not necessary, you know.

REGINALD. Oh . . .

TALBOT. But Daisy will be delighted. *(He places the flowers in a vase as Reginald sits down)*

REGINALD. Before anything else, Mr. Talbot, I want to ask you whether you're satisfied with the automobile so far. I saw it snugly parked in the driveway.

TALBOT. No trouble so far, Mr. Buckingham. An unblemished record from your lot to my driveway, by way of my office.

REGINALD. If there's any indecency in the engine, you *will* let us know, I trust.

TALBOT. Certainly.

(Enter Daisy with coffee, cakes, etc.)

DAISY. Coffee everybody?

TALBOT. You bet. Daisy, this is Reginald Buckingham. Mr. B., my wife.

REGINALD *(very much impressed)*. Delighted! *(He kisses Daisy's hand)* More than I can say!

DAISY *(also favorably impressed)*. How do you do, Mr. Buckingham. I do like the car.

REGINALD. I'm so happy.

TALBOT. Daisy — look. *(He points to the flowers)*

DAISY. Oh, they're beautiful! But you shouldn't have, really! A silly cup of coffee!

REGINALD. Please don't mention it.

DAISY. They're beautiful. Wait! Here's a pitcher of water. *(She waters the flowers)*

TALBOT. Do you want me to pour, my dear?

DAISY. Oh no, I'll take care of everything. One thing at a time. Sugar and cream, Mr. Buckingham?

REGINALD (*who can't take his eyes off Daisy; at first forgets to answer*) Oh! Black, if you please, and no sugar. Thank you.

DAISY (*not unresponsive to his attention*). A tiny slice of chocolate cake?

REGINALD. Tiny. Oh, this is too much.

TALBOT. Nonsense. You can afford to put on a bit of flesh. A big one for me.

DAISY. Piggy!

(*Jollity*)

TALBOT. I must notify you, Mr. Buckingham, that romance has blossomed in your car lot. (*Reginald, who is still staring at Daisy, is a little startled*) My daughter and Mr. Inuk —

REGINALD (*enthusiastic*). I know what you're going to say! I knew it! We all guessed it, even Tenny. I offer you my congratulations, your daughter is a lovely person. And now, I might add, I know why. (*He plunges his eyes into Daisy's*)

DAISY (*lowering hers*). Do you think they'll be happy, Mr. Buckingham?

REGINALD. I know they will. And I can vouch for Mr. Inuk. A prince. We've all known him for years; benevolence and peace in every vein and artery.

DAISY. I'm so glad. (*Blushingly*) I do believe in love at first sight.

REGINALD (*meaningfully*). I believe in nothing else!

TALBOT. Now that's going a little too far. Pour some more stimulant for Mr. Buckingham.

REGINALD. Thank you. No, Mr. Talbot, love at first sight is the most reliable of all — and also the most thrilling — of course. The most reliable, because it flares up naturally, you see, without calculations. Let's say that a maybug is walking on your arm. It tickles you. Instantaneously, you see, without your interfering with reasons and suppositions and evaluations. It touches, it tickles. Utterly reliable, utterly true and real. That's how it is with love at first sight.

TALBOT. Like a bug crawling over you, eh?

REGINALD (*protesting*). Oh no!

DAISY (*modestly*). I understand you, Mr. Buckingham.

REGINALD (*pregnantly*). I was sure you would.

DAISY. Do you think that Mr. Inuk feels as you do?

REGINALD. I know he does; we have had many conversations about these wonderful feelings. Besides, remember that he is a working man. Did Mr. Talbot tell you?

DAISY. My daughter did.

REGINALD. He works with his hands, he builds cars, he handles wrenches and drills. Such a man is, how shall I put it? palpable; you trust him; he is concrete.

TALBOT. Well, I'm glad Alice showed so much sense the very first time.

REGINALD *(amazed)*. The very first time?

DAISY. Yes.

REGINALD. Even more exciting! Historical! And with a man of Inuk's tremendous experience and — vitality. Splendid!

TALBOT. That's Alice for you. Always practical.

DAISY. And yet always a dreamer too, like her mother, always looking, looking . . .

REGINALD. Are you a dreamer, Mrs. Talbot?

DAISY. A little . . . I'm afraid so.

TALBOT *(patting her hand)*. And the softest heart in the world besides, like a newborn robin.

REGINALD. I hoped — I thought as much.

DAISY. Let's not talk about me. I keep thinking about my little girl. It all happened so suddenly.

REGINALD. Suddenly and yet, I'm sure, with every step in place. Even an avalanche is well-ordered, if you think of it sympathetically. I feel as though I could reconstruct in my mind the decisive scene between Inuk and your charming daughter. I see them walking hand in hand through the streets, oblivious to the world, interpenetrating each other's beings like two confluent rivers.

DAISY. Beautiful . . .

TALBOT. I'll have another slice.

REGINALD. They sit down in the park under a flowering chestnut tree. Inuk is the first to speak: "Our love is sudden, but it is as true as a fire ignited by lightning."

TALBOT *(his mouth full)*. Longer-lasting, I hope. But I'm glad you brought up the subject of parks, Mr. Buckingham, because, if you'll remember, that was precisely —

DAISY. Oh John, can't you let your park wait five minutes? I want to hear what happened, or what might have happened, between Alice and Inuk. "Our love is true," he says . . .

REGINALD. As true as the river is portly under a summer rain. And she replies ecstatically —

DAISY. As fine as the flower's start when an unrepentant bee pecks it for honey.

TALBOT. Good little Alice, always ready with an answer! Would you reach me the cream, Mr. Buckingham?

REGINALD *(absent-mindedly giving Talbot the cream, his eyes fixed on Daisy)*. And he comes back with: As splendid as a landscape alighting out of the fog.

DAISY. And she: As delicate as the sun at dawn, removing its grey scarf, and brushing every field awake.

TALBOT (*eating more cake*). Umblgffrmf. (*Aside*) Daisy's right, I'm making a pig of myself.

REGINALD. I feel, he says, like Adam waking upon Eve, there she stood, and his lips envied his eyes because his look outsped his kiss.

DAISY. And I, she said, I am Eve, newborn, child, and wife together.

REGINALD. He must have wanted to fall on his knees before her.

TALBOT. In the park?

DAISY. She must have wanted him to ask her, to dare, to wait no longer —

REGINALD. Shall we flee? Shall we escape?

DAISY. Yes, my beloved — she answered — at once, anywhere, I will kiss your mouth as many times as there are galaxies in heaven.

TALBOT. Why should they flee and escape? They have our blessing, don't forget, and I intend to pay for their honeymoon, the best hotels.

REGINALD. My happiness is like a storm of all the elements — he said — my body is a feather — I could leap over this table — I mean these trees —

TALBOT. Oh I don't know; this is not the first time for Inuk, as you said yourself. Daisy, this was one of your better cakes; but take it away before I devastate it.

REGINALD. *You* baked this cake, Mrs. Talbot? This delicious cake?

DAISY. I did. You see, I have my practical side too.

REGINALD (*enthusiastic*). I do see! (*He snatches another piece, and eats it devoutly*)

TALBOT. All right, now, away with the dishes, Daisy. I want to talk business with Mr. Buckingham.

REGINALD. Allow me. (*He helps Daisy*)

DAISY. Please don't, I can manage. I'll leave you two alone. (*She removes the coffee things and takes them shakily to the kitchen*)

REGINALD. Splendid, splendid woman.

TALBOT. I should say so. Been married to her nineteen years; off and on, that is. Shall we get down to business?

REGINALD. With pleasure.

TALBOT. Cigar?

REGINALD. Thanks.

TALBOT. I'll be brief and blunt; all my cards are on the table.

REGINALD. Good; mine too.

TALBOT. There's a piece of undeveloped land going up for sale on the outskirts of town. A death in the family — land has to be unloaded — and I can get my hands on 200 acres provided I scrape together fifteen thousand dollars in cash. I've got half the money myself, and I'm looking for the other half, and another 500 a month thereafter.

REGINALD. Sounds interesting. But what will you do with the property? And do I smell a plot?

TALBOT *(chuckling)*. This is confidential, old man.

REGINALD. Padlock on my lips.

TALBOT. A park, Mr. Buckingham. That's why I was trying to interrupt you. I plan to convert the land into a park. Gardens, grasses, trees — the works. All the way. Let the fur fly and the windows rattle. A duckpond. Lawn chairs.

REGINALD. Like London.

TALBOT. Puppet-shows.

REGINALD. Like Paris.

TALBOT. Open-air cafés —

REGINALD. With wicker chairs?

TALBOT. With wicker chairs, and waiters in black tie. Playgrounds. Fountains designed by mad sculptors. Statues.

REGINALD. Of naked goddesses!

TALBOT. Woodsy paths for lovers. Bicycle paths for children. Peacocks. Wasps in the yoghurt. You get the idea?

REGINALD. I do.

TALBOT. So far so good. Then — say in five years — we strike.

REGINALD. We strike. How?

TALBOT. Donate the park to the city. Bang! Every competitor left gasping. Overnight we're civic benefactors. Overnight, Mr. Buckingham. Civic.

REGINALD *(whistling)*. Deep.

TALBOT. Everything foreseen. Practically no risk. All we need is money to get started.

REGINALD. Very deep.

TALBOT. Brain at work twenty-four hours a day. Files available for inspection.

REGINALD. Oh, hardly necessary.

TALBOT. Interested?

REGINALD. Indeed.

TALBOT. What about Mr. Cash? What do you anticipate?

REGINALD. Don't worry about him. The best nose in town for a fragrant opportunity.

TALBOT *(rubbing his hands)*. Good good good. Next question: how much have you personally got?

REGINALD. Oh, about three thousand, if I sell this and that.

TALBOT. Not bad. How about Mr. Cash?

REGINALD. Plenty.

TALBOT. But I don't want either of you to come to any sudden decision. Talk to Mr. Cash. Think it over. And we'll all get together again in a few days, visit the property, look at the papers, and all the rest. Daisy, where are you?

DAISY *(off-stage)*. Slaving over the dishes.

TALBOT. Come back in. I've been haranguing Mr. Buckingham about my park.

(Enter Daisy, in her apron)

DAISY. What do you think of it, Mr. Buckingham?

REGINALD. If it helps to bring me nearer —

TALBOT. Hold on, hold on, friend; I don't want you to participate for sentimental reasons. You're one of us anyway, we've adopted you, park or no park. The rest is strictly business.

REGINALD. It is. And it looks fabulous. Off-hand, of course. I *will* study the documents by and by. I'll come here to study them.

DAISY. Wait — here's Alice at last. Oh dear, I'm so excited!

(Noises in the hallway. Daisy has removed her apron. Enter Alice and Inuk.)

ALICE. Mother! *(She flings herself in her mother's arms)*

INUK. Sir. My name is Inuk.

TALBOT *(embracing him)*. Son.

ALICE. This is Inuk, mother. We're married. We got married an hour ago.

INUK. Baruchim hanimtzaim.

TALBOT. That is to say?

INUK. Blessed are you who are here.

DAISY *(half-crying)*. I don't know what to say. I guess I'll kiss the groom. Blessings on you both. Be happy.

INUK. I'll take good care of your daughter, Mrs. Talbot.

TALBOT. Mrs. Talbot! She's your mother now, Inuk!

INUK. I know, but it feels odd. You're too young. I'm thirty myself, you see.

DAISY. Well then, call me Daisy. Sit down, sit down. This is all so sudden, so wonderful. An hour ago?

INUK. Yes. We decided not to wait.

REGINALD. Bravo!

INUK. Mr. Buckingham! I didn't even see you!

REGINALD. Don't mind me. I'm really one too many in this family scene. *(Protests)*

INUK. I'm glad to find you here. *(To the Talbots)* We've known each other for years. *(Patting Reginald's back)* A prince!

ALICE. But *I* haven't really met Mr. Buckingham.

TALBOT. That's right!

INUK. Sorry! Mr. Reginald Buckingham, Mrs. Alice Inuk, born Talbot.

REGINALD. We did meet briefly this morning.

ALICE. Yes, of course.

REGINALD. That lucky purchase of yours, Mr. Talbot! My abundant felicitations to both of you.

INUK and ALICE. Thank you.

DAISY. May I ask you, Mr. Inuk — Inuk — is this your first *and* your last name?

INUK. Yes, it is, Mrs. Talbot.

TALBOT. Daisy.

INUK. Daisy. It'll be a little difficult at first. But enjoyable.

DAISY. I think Inuk is very nice. Sweet, short, and simple. Inuk. It has authority too.

TALBOT. Well, children, let's smash a bottle of champagne, and when you're reeling we'll meditate on a wedding gift. *(He leaves, we hear a bottle popping, and then he returns with champagne and glasses)*

DAISY *(meantime)*. Don't worry about a wedding present, Alice. I've got one here all ready for you. *(She shows the silver set)*

INUK. Pretty!

ALICE. Oh no, mother, this is yours.

DAISY. But I want you to have it.

ALICE. I've never seen this teapot before. When did you buy it?

DAISY. I didn't buy it. The Black Shadow was here while we were out, and this is what he left behind.

REGINALD. The Black Shadow! When will that fiend be caught at last? Why, the teapot matches the rest of your set!

INUK. That's the way he works.

DAISY. And that's what made me think it would be lovely for the children.

TALBOT. Good idea. Illegal, though. Well, here's to a full five years of relentless bliss, and maybe a renewal or two!

EVERYBODY. Amen. *(Bride and groom embrace)*

ALICE. Oh, if you all knew how I love him! I wish I could run out into the street and hug everybody and cry "I married Inuk!"

INUK. Alice! *(He kisses her again)*

TALBOT. Does this awaken something in you, Mr. Buckingham?

REGINALD *(ardently)*. Oh, it does, it does. Oh, it does. Aaah.

TALBOT. Is anything the matter? Your glass is shaking.

REGINALD. No, nothing — *everything!*

ALICE. You *are* pale all of a sudden, Mr. Buckingham.

INUK. Tell us what's the matter.

REGINALD *(to Daisy)*. Shall I? Now?

(She nods demurely)

TALBOT. Shall you what? Speak up, Mr. Buckingham! Has love bitten you too?

INUK. That must be it. He has the same delirious look as mine.

REGINALD. This is — I propose — I am about to make a significant statement.

(Daisy mutely encourages him)

TALBOT. Steady now.

ALICE. I know it's going to be exciting! (*She kisses Inuk*)

REGINALD. Mr. Talbot, your wife and I wish to spend four weeks in Acapulco.

(*General surprise. Even Daisy is a little surprised*)

ALICE. Mother!

INUK. Fantastic!

TALBOT. Daisy! Is this true?

ALICE. In Acapulco?

TALBOT. I'm dumbfounded.

DAISY. Isn't that in Mexico, Mr. Buckingham?

REGINALD (*ardently*). In tropical Mexico.

(*Daisy and Alice embrace*)

TALBOT. Daisy, you're taking me by surprise! When did all this develop?

DAISY. Now — somehow — with magnetic waves and things.

ALICE. You're wonderful, mother, every day another trick.

DAISY (*modestly*). I'm a little surprised myself.

INUK. So much fire! And you, Mr. Buckingham, a volcano!

TALBOT. One moment, everybody! All these events in a single day. Alice — Inuk — our new car — the Black Shadow — and now Daisy — all heaven is breaking loose. (*Reginald pours him a glass of champagne*) Thank you, old man. Son, there's another bottle in the refrigerator. (*Inuk goes out and returns with another bottle*) Reginald — Daisy — you are splendidly mature human beings — I hope you know what you're doing.

DAISY. It's only for four weeks, John. And only if it's not inconvenient to you. Otherwise we can postpone it.

REGINALD. Quite.

TALBOT. Oh no, no inconvenience at all, that's not the point. I simply want you two to be sure.

ALICE. Four weeks, dad . . .

DAISY. Alice is right, you mustn't have fits of anxiety over us.

TALBOT. Well, you know I'm concerned about you. (*He takes her hand*) After all — nineteen years, off and on.

DAISY. I'm never wrong in my loves.

REGINALD. She's adorable.

DAISY. My only worry is your being in the house by yourself for a month, now that Alice is married.

TALBOT. Wait, wait, there's a solution for everything. When are you two leaving for your honeymoon?

ALICE. We were going to start tomorrow, and do the Grand Canyon.

TALBOT. What about General Motors?

INUK. The usual three weeks honeymoon leave. No difficulty. Warm personal note from Muffle — our vice-president.

ALICE. But we could postpone our trip, couldn't we?

INUK. Sure. And you'll move in with us for a month. When everybody returns home, who knows? The Black Shadow will have filled the house with silver and crystal to the rafters.

ALICE. Silly!

TALBOT. You're a dear girl, Alice. But now that I've had a moment to think about it, I see the way clear for everybody. I've had a few — talks — as you know, my dear — with—

DAISY. Mrs. Glimmer, that's right! Her husband's the famous skindiver. And she is a beauty.

TALBOT. This might be a good time — four weeks — yes, my lovely people, I don't foresee any trouble. Glimmer's been wanting to skindive Rhode Island. It's all settled. Mr. Buckingham, your hand.

REGINALD. And yours, Mr. Talbot.

TALBOT. A magnificent final idea! As I'll be home for the next four weeks — or a few blocks away, to be precise — take my car, drive to the Grand Canyon with it, I'm paying all the bills, and when you're at the bottom of the canyon, Inuk, sing "John Talbot's a jolly good fellow," but loud, make my name John Sebastian Talbot bounce from wall to wall, let the sound print itself into the granite.

INUK. To John Talbot, may he thrive!

ALL. To John Talbot!

ACT THREE

The angel, formerly the customer, appears after the intermission in all his glory.

ANGEL. Inuk is dead. I announce his ascent to heaven with genuine professional satisfaction, not forgetting, however, that those who remain below are, as usual, more aggrieved by their own loss than responsive to the new happiness of the departed.

How did he die? It was raining. The wet highway curved while Inuk was telling Alice who knows what fine stories. The car rolled off the road. It broke into many pieces. What can angels do?

Inuk is dead. And you, my dears, are going to die too. So it goes. You know, of course, that for you too heaven is waiting with open arms and that your nostrils shall be filled with perfume. But still, it is a wrench. In spite of heaven, you die reluctantly. You are attached to the beautiful earth which we made for you in its nest of time. Believe me, we are flattered.

I ask you, however, to consider our Creator's quandary. He longs for every conceivable human being, for every human being who can be conceived, to partake of his creation. Therefore fresh babies leap day and night into the world, bright new guests of life. But your globe is small. Most of it is water, because that is what the fish need. How can we house God's innumerable children? Where shall we move the old so that the young can breathe? God pondered and puzzled, until one day he smiled and invented death. "This is clever of me," he said; "but," he added, "it is not perfect."

Fortunately, heaven is not lazy. We think, we brood, we fence with problems, we engineer little improvements. Why, friends, are we flinging you into outer space with roars of metal and fire? A bright display of high spirits, you think? Not entirely. We are working, my dears, on the suppression of death. Find a few temperate planets under distant suns, settle on their surprising meadows, build new cities, and to these the overflow from earth will journey instead of dying, and man shall live as long as he chooses.

We mend our faults, you see, but not overnight, there is no hurry in God. And meantime Alice is offended with us. Though I am about to tell her that Inuk has preceded her to a better world of spirits, where she will be reunited with him, she will refuse this consolation at first. However, we look on our speech as a seed, it does take root and with time it bears flowers.

(The angel now approaches Alice, who is kneeling beside Inuk's body with her eyes closed and her hand on his eyes)

ANGEL. Alice, I have come to take his soul away.

ALICE. I know. I felt your coming. I am angry with you. Where, tell me, is the beautiful world your master is supposed to have made?

ANGEL. All around you. He made it as beautiful as he could, my poor master. It is still vexed by accidents.

ALICE. Blunders! Your blunders!

ANGEL. Alas.

ALICE. Do you say alas? Then let me go with Inuk. Look, I'm injured too.

ANGEL. No. Not now. Time must be satisfied. But on time's other side you will meet Inuk in a world still better than this one, and there you will hold him again, him and the others.

ALICE. Angel of God, don't speak to me of better worlds. I knew him for only twenty little days. What evil game are you playing with me? You drove me to love him, and a moment later you stole him from me. This is stupidity.

ANGEL. One day soon you will be reconciled.

ALICE. Never! I hate you!

ANGEL. We love you.

(The Angel now plants a tall hyacinth near the body, and, making a gesture toward Inuk, leaves. Shortly afterward we hear the siren of an ambulance, and then the ambulance driver enters)

ALICE. Leave him alone! He's mine!

AMBULANCE DRIVER. No use, lady. The hyacinth, you see. Excuse me. Bad luck, dumb luck. *(He picks up Inuk's body and takes it out)*

ALICE. Inuk . . .

(The ambulance driver returns)

AMBULANCE DRIVER. Now you come along. You're injured too. Here. I'll be taking you to a hospital, though it don't look serious to me. Hopsa! You know, five thousand million trillion zillion people have died ahead of your boy friend. What bothers me is how they've all managed to find room, considering the earth ain't bigger than it is. Lean on me some more, lady, I'm only trying to distract you with funny stories. *(He takes her out. We hear him say, "Wrap a blanket around her, Tom." Then he returns once again, and plants a little headstone behind the hyacinth. He reads off the epitaph)* "Here died Inuk of an automobile accident. Great singer. Great lover. May he enjoy the apples of heaven." *(He taps the headstone with his shovel, blows off all the dust, sprinkles the hyacinth with a watering-can, and leaves. We hear the ambulance driving off. After a little while, enter Jim and Tennyson Cash as pilgrims — cloaks, satchels, staves, sandals)*

TENNYSON. Dad, I'm tired, my feet are still wet from that awful downpour, and one of my toes is swollen.

CASH. Don't say "awful downpour," Tenny. Think of the strawberries and the barley growing because of it.

TENNYSON. Well, it was awful for me. I also feel the sniffles coming on. And one of my toes is swollen.

CASH. St. Francis never had a swollen toe.

TENNYSON. He was more experienced than me. Can I sit down for a few minutes?

CASH. Sure. Here's a headstone you can sit on — the grass is still wet. But don't forget it's a long way to the next motel. Watch that hyacinth!

TENNYSON. Whew! I don't know that I'm the type to become a pilgrim, dad. My socks are drenched.

CASH. Take off both sandals, Tenny. And here's a change of socks.

TENNYSON. We've gained a solid ten pounds apiece ever since we started being mendicants. Everybody has got his hands stretched out with cherry pies and chickens and potatoes. We can't ever walk off all those calories.

CASH. Not to mention my knapsack and pockets full of money. I don't know how to refuse without offending people. Well, cheer up, Tenny, and breathe in this lovely wind, done to a turn by that lazy cook of a sun.

TENNYSON. Wind or no wind, I'd like to be in the ball park or the ice cream parlor.

CASH. And yet when Buckingham went on his leave of absence to Acapulco and I decided to close shop for a few weeks, you were itching to go.

TENNYSON. My feet weren't sore then. Itching is one thing, sore another.

CASH *(seeing the wreckage)*. Hey!

TENNYSON *(busy with his feet)*. What now?

CASH. A car smashed up! Still warm and the oil dripping! *(Tennyson is too tired to care)* Rubble! Everything gone!

TENNYSON. Speaking of parks, I'm looking forward to the one you're buying with Mr. Talbot. I'll do my pilgrimming there instead of on the highways.

CASH *(puttering amidst the wreckage)*. I hope nobody was hurt. Seems to me I recognize the car.

TENNYSON. All cars are brothers. I mean nature is sublime, but not with swollen toes. I bet Wordsworth never had swollen toes.

CASH *(still puttering)*. I bet he did, wandering over hill and dale ... The steering wheel's split in four ... Do you realize what the rain is like in England? You say a word — wham, the rain falls on you. You keep still — wham, the rain falls on you again. If you ask me, Wordsworth must have had dripping socks weeks at a time.

TENNYSON. Maybe that's when he wrote his bad poems. My ankles —

CASH *(holding up a piece of car)*. Devils in hell! This is the car I sold John Talbot!

TENNYSON *(turning around at last)*. What? Let me see.

CASH. I recognize it! My God, what happened? Where's Talbot?

TENNYSON. Don't you remember? He lent the car to Inuk and what's her name, his daughter.

CASH *(thunderstruck)*. Alice! Alice! Let me see that headstone! *(He reads the epitaph)* Inuk is dead! *(He gapes)* And what about Alice?

TENNYSON. She must be safe, dad. It doesn't mention her.

CASH. My knees are giving way. Here he died — here! where we stand.

TENNYSON. I'm frightened, dad. I was sitting — Oh, I feel sick.

CASH. Come here, my boy. Here's some brandy. Inuk gone! What could have happened? He must have been too happy, and that made him reckless. And Alice? She's angry. I feel it, Tenny. She's angry. Maybe it was the car's fault. Was something wrong with the car?

TENNYSON. We overhaul all our cars, dad. Nobody can blame you.

CASH. This morning I was thinking of them. And then I stepped on a caterpillar.

TENNYSON. Let's turn back, dad, let's go home. You ought to say a few right words to the Talbots.

CASH. And our pilgrimage?

TENNYSON. It was never a real pilgrimage, since we weren't heading for anywhere in particular.

CASH. It was the going that mattered, Tenny, not the getting anywhere.

TENNYSON. They must have brought Alice home after the accident.

CASH. Do you think so?

TENNYSON. I'm sure.

CASH. I don't know what's right.

TENNYSON. We ought to return, dad.

CASH. I'll call up from the nearest house. Say a few words over the headstone before we go, Tenny. Give him your best.

TENNYSON. I will. Let's bow our heads, father.

> Inuk was a singer bold and strong;
> When he died, he died too young.
> He would have died too young at ninety-seven.
> Therefore receive him, angels, into heaven.

CASH. That was nice, Tenny. Poor happy fellow. Heaven is heaven, but he couldn't have wanted to go so soon.

(*They stand silent over the headstone*)

TENNYSON. Dad, you know what?

CASH. What?

TENNYSON. I wouldn't object to having a mother. Even if she wasn't all that much older than me.

CASH. Let's turn back, Tenny, my boy. I want to say a few right words to the Talbots.

ACT FOUR

The Talbot residence, as in Act Two.
On the table, a tall potted hyacinth.
John Talbot, Daisy, and Reginald Buckingham are sitting and nervously looking at the door leading to the next room. For a while no one says anything.

TALBOT (*he has obviously said this before*). Am I glad I finally located you between Acapulco and Whatsitepec or wherever it was.

DAISY. Hush, my dear.

(*Reginald squeezes Talbot's hand*)

TALBOT. Why is it taking so long?

DAISY. It hasn't been long at all, John.

REGINALD. It always seems that way. Anyway, I'm sure he knows his business.

DAISY. Of course he does.

TALBOT. I didn't mean to imply that he doesn't.

(*Another silence*)

REGINALD. Peppermint?

TALBOT. No, thank you.

REGINALD. Daisy?

DAISY. Thank you, dear; later.

(*Another silence*)

TALBOT. They were difficult days. She didn't smile once from breakfast to midnight snack. At first I tried to make light of it. But after three unsmiling days I had to stop pretending and face the brutal fact: Alice was sulking. That's when I called you.

(*Daisy begins to cry*)

DAISY. I never saw Alice sulk since that fox-terrier ran off with her doll when she was seven years old. And then it only lasted an hour.

REGINALD. Don't, Daisy. Now we'll all have something else to think about.

TALBOT. He's right, Daisy. Do you remember? It was the Glimmer's fox-terrier. That's how we became acquainted.

DAISY. Here he is!

(*The door opens, all three jump up, and the doctor comes out, followed by Alice*)

DOCTOR (*peacefully*). A child will be born.

ALICE (*unsmiling*). Inuk has a child.

DAISY. Alice, come here.

(*General excitement*)

TALBOT. My girl.

REGINALD (*shaking the doctor's hand*). I knew we could rely on you, doctor.

DOCTOR. I did my best.

DAISY (*to Alice*). Sit here; I want you to relax from now on.

REGINALD. Wait; this one is more comfortable.

DOCTOR. Don't overcoddle her now! Let her exercise! Tennis, roller-skating, shopping in the best stores. We don't want a weakling born into the family, do we?

TALBOT. We'll make her exercise, doctor. But today she'll be coddled. We'll be the three Magi, and bring her gifts. Let the incense fly!

DOCTOR. I recommend the incense of roast beef, medium rare. But right now I'd like her to lie down for an hour.

DAISY. I'll put her to bed. Thank you, doctor.

ALICE. Thank you for everything.

DOCTOR. No more moping.

ALICE. I'll try.

(Daisy takes Alice out of the room)

DOCTOR. Have her come to my office once a week, will you?

TALBOT. I'll see to it.

DOCTOR. Well, I'll be on my way. Don't move, I know where the door is. Mr. Buckingham, a bit plump.

TALBOT. Doctor, before you go . . .

DOCTOR. Yes?

TALBOT. You noticed the moping yourself, didn't you?

DOCTOR. Sure.

TALBOT. She hasn't unmoped once, so to speak, since the accident happened. Don't you think it's unnatural?

DOCTOR. Oh, I don't know. To have her husband dispatched so soon — it's irritating.

TALBOT. How did she respond when you told her she was going to have a baby?

DOCTOR. Nicely.

TALBOT. But —

DOCTOR. No smile. Not yet.

REGINALD. She was having such a wonderful time.

DOCTOR. That's what you have to understand, John. I examined Inuk once for General Motors, and I know he was no slouch. Suddenly bang, he's in the next world. Very nice for him, but damned inconvenient for Alice.

TALBOT. What do you suggest we do?

DOCTOR. Come on now, you're not children!

TALBOT and REGINALD (looking at each other). Another man!

DOCTOR. Two intellects.

TALBOT. I don't know. Alice is fussy.

DOCTOR. The world's aswarm with lovable candidates.

REGINALD. The doctor is right, Mr. Talbot.

TALBOT. I suppose he is. But we'd better be tactful with Alice. She's fragile.

REGINALD. I agree, but tact will do it. I remember, when my mother left us, the last words she whispered to my dad were: "Algernon, the boy loves haggis, and I want him to eat it twice a week." I was standing by her bedside at the time.

TALBOT. What's that got to do with Alice?

REGINALD. Tact, that's all. My father couldn't boil an egg, the dear man, and where do you go for haggis in this town? He took the hint and married again two weeks later. She managed it, you see, by not seeming to push.

TALBOT. A nice woman.

REGINALD. Oh, a saint.

DOCTOR. Well, you know what to do. Be tactful and grab the first good man who rings the bell —

(*The doorbell rings*)

CASH (*off-stage*). Anybody home?

TALBOT and REGINALD. Ha!

DOCTOR. Providence strikes again.

TALBOT. Coming!

DOCTOR. I'll slip in for another look at Alice and leave the back way. So long.

TALBOT. Thanks for the wisdom and bill me for it!

DOCTOR. I will.

(*He leaves while Talbot goes to the front door*)

CASH (*off-stage*). Greetings from the road!

TALBOT (*off-stage*). Shake off your dust, old bachelor!

(*Enter Jim Cash, still as pilgrim, and carrying a satchel fuller than ever*)

REGINALD. Good to see you again, Mr. Cash, very good indeed.

CASH. The feeling is mutual. You should have tramped with us, Mr. Buckingham. Getting a bit stocky, you know.

TALBOT. Daisy! Jim Cash is here!

DAISY (*off-stage*). I'm coming!

CASH (*to Reginald*). So glad you two came back.

TALBOT. Alice is resting.

CASH. I understand. How is she?

(*Enter Daisy*)

DAISY. Dear Mr. Cash! Welcome! When did you arrive in town?

CASH. This very moment, Mrs. Talbot. I know I'm unpresentable. I'll dirty your carpet. But I wanted to inquire . . . I was anxious . . .

DAISY. Who's worried about carpets? Alice is well, Mr. Cash. She's resting a little. John, pull up a comfortable chair for our guest. Where is Tennyson?

CASH. He's gone ahead to open the house. May I? (*He places the satchel on a table*)

DAISY. You must be exhausted.

CASH. Not at all. Only eleven miles today.

TALBOT. Why not take a bath upstairs? We want you to feel like one of the family. (*He nudges Reginald*)

REGINALD. I should say so. After eleven miles!

CASH. Not a bad idea.

DAISY. Fresh warm towels.

CASH. Wonderful. But as for the eleven miles, and it might have been twelve, don't forget, Mr. Buckingham, that I've got the habit by now, my legs move up and down like a pair of steamship pistons.

DAISY. I wish my men would take a lesson from you. John, give Mr. Cash a glass of milk.

CASH. Thank you. (He drinks) Ah, this awakens memories. Every day he'd stop with us and drink his pint of milk. We'll miss him.

(Enter Alice)

THE TALBOTS. Alice!

CASH (rising). Mrs. Inuk.

DAISY. You should have slept a little.

ALICE. I heard your voice.

CASH. Forgive me. But I needed to come here before going home. He was our friend. Never a cloudy word. Children followed him about.

ALICE. You knew him better than I did.

CASH. It was unfeeling of them to take him from you.

ALICE. To steal him from me.

DAISY. Alice! . . . Sit down again, Mr. Cash.

TALBOT (to Alice). And you, sit here. (He places her next to Cash)

REGINALD. Mr. Cash, I'd like to report that the car lot's in tip-top shape.

CASH. Good, good.

REGINALD. I reopened and sold three or four cars. I do think there was more fuel in them than when we left, but nothing alarming.

CASH. I don't suppose they've caught the Black Shadow yet, have they?

TALBOT. No, they haven't.

CASH. I've come as a sort of Black Shadow myself.

TALBOT. Oh?

CASH. Look at this satchel. A little unsightly, you've probably been saying to yourselves. Mr. Cash ought to have set it down in the hallway instead of parading it on the table like a trophy.

DAISY. I never noticed it, I swear.

CASH. Feel it. As hard and tough as a football. And yet, my friends, this bag is filled with soft paper money, bills and checks in high denominations.

REGINALD. You haven't sold the car lot, have you, Mr. Cash?

CASH. No, sir. This is what comes of being a neo-Franciscan mendicant. People fill your cup so fast, you all but need a bank clerk in tow. But, said I to myself, where shall I bestow these holy alms? And then I remembered the Talbot Park. And I stretched out my hand in the name of the park. Why not a corner for the animals Saint Francis was fond of? A good thought, said I to myself. Subject to your approval, of course, because it's the Talbot Park and none other.

TALBOT. This is an important idea, Mr. Cash, a special contribution, exactly the detail that was missing from our plan.

DAISY. Animals, Alice; aren't you glad?

ALICE (*quietly*). I think it's a lovely idea.

TALBOT. Mr. Buckingham?

REGINALD. Oh, you know me. Always in agreement with everybody.

CASH. I'll feed the animals myself, and talk to them, if I may.

ALICE. Mr. Cash . . .

CASH. Yes?

ALICE. I don't know whether Saint Francis mentions them, but would you allow one or two seals?

CASH. A flock of them! I assure you that he does mention seals, namely in his seventeenth chapter. (*He winks at the others*) A perfect thought.

ALICE. Thank you so much.

DAISY. Now that I think of it, we haven't told Mr. Cash —

REGINALD. Our good news!

TALBOT. What's the hurry?

CASH. Wait! Before you go on, I wonder, Mrs. Talbot, whether I could talk you into calling me Jim — such being my first name — I mean, now that I am in partnership with your husband.

DAISY. Why, of course! Let's all do it, shall we? We've known each other long enough.

TALBOT. Right, Jim, shake here. Reginald.

REGINALD. John, Alice. (*To Daisy*) As for you —

DAISY. All right, Reggie, you needn't blush.

TALBOT. At his age!

CASH. Mr. Buckingham.

REGINALD. Mr. Cash — this is a solemn moment.

CASH. Yes, after ten years — Reginald —

TALBOT. The rascal is blushing again!

REGINALD. It's such an odd feeling. Well, all right; here I go; shake here, Jim.

DAISY. Bravo! And I'm Daisy. It doesn't sound like much at first, but then it grows on you.

CASH. Daisy, I'm honored. And Alice — may I?

ALICE. Of course, Jim. You were Jim to me from the first moment, though you didn't know it.

TALBOT. She means it! I can vouch for that!

CASH. I don't know what to say.

DAISY. Wait till you hear the rest.

ALICE. Oh mother . . .

CASH. What is it?

DAISY. There is going to be a child.

CASH. Heaven be thanked! *(To Alice)* I was looking into your eyes, and I thought, yes, here is something blissful, in spite of everything, like a candle behind a smoky pane of glass. I am immensely happy.

TALBOT. Good man.

ALICE *(almost in tears)*. Thank you, thank you.

TALBOT. Children, I think we should be going to the garden now.

DAISY. Yes, this is a good time. Mr. Cash — Jim I should say — we are planting this hyacinth in our garden in memory —

CASH. I understand. Alice, may I carry it?

ALICE. Do.

CASH. Then on to the garden. I'll follow you all. And since I'm covered with dust already, I'll do the spading.

TALBOT *(to Alice)*. Take my arm.

REGINALD *(to Daisy)*. Take mine, Daisy.

(All leave. After a brief interval, the Black Shadow reappears. But this time he is secretly followed by a policeman. The Black Shadow surveys the room, clucks disapprovingly over its disorder, straightens it out a little, dusts a bit with a toy feather-duster he carries. He digs into his bag again looking for a suitable object to leave behind, rejects a frying pan, etc., and suddenly notices the money-bag on the table. He opens it, looks at the money, chuckles, and then deposits a money-bag of his own next to it. He is about to leave when the policeman pounces)

POLICEMAN *(throttling the culprit)*. Got you at last!

BLACK SHADOW. Aaaah!

POLICEMAN. Your career is over and done with, Black Shadow!

BLACK SHADOW. Let me go!

POLICEMAN. You'll take everything back now, Gol darn it, down to the last toothpick. Malefactor! Recidivist!

BLACK SHADOW. You're squeezing my windpipe, officer.

POLICEMAN. Oh, excuse me. But this is it, Black Shadow. What's your name, who are you, don't lie, and off with your mask!

BLACK SHADOW. Let me remain anonymous! I'll take everything back, I swear it on my mother's head, I'll rot in jail, but don't ask who I am.

POLICEMAN. Okay, I won't ask; I'll find out without asking. *(He rips off the Black Shadow's mask)*

BLACK SHADOW. Mercy!

POLICEMAN *(dumbfounded)*. Willifred P. Rockefeller! The plastic flower tycoon!

BLACK SHADOW *(meekly)*. Maybe I only resemble him.

POLICEMAN. Mr. Rockefeller — *(he doffs his helmet)* — I don't know what to say — but it ain't my fault that I happened to be the man on duty here — how can I apologize? But why? Why? —

(Reenter the Talbots et al. from the garden. General exclamations —

*"The Black Shadow!" "Willifred P. Rockefeller!" etc. The Policeman
blows his whistle)*

POLICEMAN. Ladies and gentlemen, the Police Department regrets this
unforementioned intrusion, but is pleased to announce the apprehen-
sion of the Black Shadow — I am terrible sorry, Mr. Rockefeller — in
the act of depositing a money bag in your domicile.

ALICE. Oh! *(She sits down, faint from the excitement)*

CASH. Water, Mrs. Talbot — Daisy — water, Reginald!

ALICE. It's nothing, Jim — too many things happening, that's all.

DAISY. Here, here, my love. You'll be all right.

(The Black Shadow tries to slink away)

POLICEMAN. No, Mr. Rockefeller, I don't know how to put it, but — you're
so to speak under arrest.

BLACK SHADOW. I'll be good.

TALBOT *(stepping forward)*. Now, Mr. Rockefeller, what in God's name
is the meaning of this? A man like you, who teaches Sunday school
two days a week, should know better than to break into people's
houses.

REGINALD *(whispering)*. Perhaps the poor man — *(indicates that Mr.
Rockefeller may not be in his right mind)*

ROCKEFELLER. Oh no, I'm rational, I'm only too rational, oh the shame,
the torment!

TALBOT *(to Daisy)*. Give him a drink, Daisy. Sit down, Mr. Rockefeller.

ROCKEFELLER. Thank you, Mr. Talbot. You're awfully kind.

TALBOT. Now tell us all about it.

POLICEMAN. I ought to be handcuffing him, Mr. Talbot.

CASH. Have a drink too.

POLICEMAN. No thank you, sir. I'm on duty.

TALBOT. Take a ten-minute break.

POLICEMAN. Good idea. *(He drinks)*

TALBOT. Proceed, my poor misguided friend. Unload your guilty conscience.

ROCKEFELLER *(groaning)*. I hope you enjoyed the teapot, Mrs. Talbot.

TALBOT *(severely)*. Don't change the subject, sir. The teapot goes back to
Mrs. Rockefeller. But why the money? Why all your depredations
in the city? What ails you?

ALICE. Dad, don't be too hard on him.

ROCKEFELLER. Oh thank you, Miss Talbot. If you only knew!

REGINALD. Knew what?

POLICEMAN *(stage whisper to the ladies)*. The confession!

ROCKEFELLER. If you only knew what it means to be the plastic flower
tycoon. Plastic flowers! I notice your look of repugnance. And
plastic rubber plants — a profitable sideline — plastic soil — another

source of miserable lucre — and now, on our drawing boards — *(he suffocates)*

TALBOT. What — what have you got on your drawing boards?

DAISY. What can it be? Make an effort, Mr. Rockefeller.

ROCKEFELLER *(in a hoarse whisper)*. Plastic snails. Genuine realistic effect.

DAISY. Tut, tut, Mr. Rockefeller, that really isn't nice.

POLICEMAN. Oh I don't know. My wife's got plastic pots of plastic flowers all over our bedroom — I'm speakin' off duty now — all kinds and all colors.

ROCKEFELLER *(groaning)*. And does she spray them with our imitation perfumes? *(Miserable)* Another thriving subsidiary.

POLICEMAN. Sure, a different perfume for each kind. She says the real kind asphyxicates you at night, while the plastic ones is harmless and they last a lot longer. We send them to the laundry once a month.

ROCKEFELLER. You see, you see. Millions of them, orchids, roses — floribundas and grandifloras — camellias, tulips, lilies, irises, with beards and without, all fakes, phonies and fiddlesticks, and masses of money rushing into my vaults from every florist in the country. But I try to make up for my filthy millions in a small humble way. I skulk from one house to the other, I unload, you see, it makes me feel better, and besides — it's fun. *(He breaks down and weeps)*

POLICEMAN. None of that, Mr. Rockefeller. Conduct unbecoming a criminal.

ROCKEFELLER. I'm sorry.

TALBOT. Is this believable?

CASH. As much as all the rest!

ROCKEFELLER. I swear it's the truth! And then, Mr. Talbot, I heard about your park.

TALBOT. Say no more! You thought, "Here's my chance."

REGINALD. A park without a single artificial flower in it.

ROCKEFELLER. Or snail.

DAISY. A chance to redeem yourself.

ROCKEFELLER. And to undermine the plastic flower market.

ALICE. He's a dear man. I like him.

POLICEMAN. Mrs. Inuk! I don't know if pre-trial sympathy is legal.

TALBOT. I'll keep an eye on her, officer.

CASH. Officer!

POLICEMAN. Sir?

CASH. Just now — didn't the party convey a smile to the culprit too?

POLICEMAN. Yes. She aggravated with a smile.

CASH. There!

TALBOT. Did you smile, Alice?

DAISY. Did you?

ALICE. Did I? Yes, I did!

DAISY. I knew she would! *(She embraces Alice)* She's back in the world!

TALBOT. Mr. Rockefeller, we owe our daughter's renovation to you. The Talbots offer you their thanks: all three of us, or all four, or all five, depending on developments. Logic dictates the next step. The Talbot Park goes into a quadripartite partnership. You sign on the dotted line, and the silver teapot becomes your original investment. Mrs. Rockefeller will have to use china. The money bag is an added contribution, and we drop all charges. Agreed?

CASH and REGINALD. Agreed.

ROCKEFELLER *(on his knees)*. Gentlemen, let me kiss the cuffs of your pantaloons.

TALBOT. Stand up, Willifred, we're all equal partners now, and the officer gets another drink — but in the tavern across the street, where he'll toast our healths. *(He puts money in the policeman's hand)*

CASH. With a special health for the ladies. *(He puts more money in the policeman's hand)*

REGINALD. Another for the unborn child. *(More money)*

ROCKEFELLER *(the tycoon again)*. And one for Talbot Park, my good man.

POLICEMAN *(saluting)*. Sorry once more for the intrusion, ladies and gentlemen. You know where to find me in case law and order breaks down again. And remember the Police Department's motto: "Every thief has a silver lining." *(He leaves)*

DAISY. Sit next to me, Mr. Rockefeller. You'll stay for dinner. And so will all of you, of course.

ROCKEFELLER *(kissing her hand)*. You're too kind. You too, Mrs. Inuk. My congratulations on the little one to come. As for me, I'll water the flowers in the park and teach their names to the baby.

REGINALD. Well, I'm glad that everything is somehow falling into place.

CASH. Not everything. Not yet. Alice . . .

ALICE. Yes, Jim?

CASH. My friends, I would like to ask a question, or make a statement — we'll see which.

TALBOT. It's about time.

DAISY. You look perturbed. What's the matter?

CASH. Is everything really falling into place? Does everyone have his — or her — appointed task? Daisy and Reginald, I realize, are going back to Acapulco for a week, the rest of us will busy ourselves with used cars, poetry, real estate, and parks, but you, Alice, dear Alice, what are you going to do? There is the summer to spend, the fall, part of the winter . . . Tell us.

ALICE. I'll be with my family. I'll sit in the garden, near the hyacinth and the goldfish, and I'll do nothing much of anything until my time comes.

CASH. Suppose I had a better idea? Suppose I said, marry me, Alice.
(*To his amazement, no one seems surprised*)

CASH (*resolutely*). I'm not a young man, I admit, but I'm as sturdy as a sapling, my pulse is strong, I'm not bad to look at, my principles are high, I'm well-read, musical, a good businessman; above all, I've a warm disposition, turn on the light and I melt; I've got a boy of fifteen in training to be an immortal poet who wants you in the family; and before the beginning and after the end of everything, I've yearned for you ever since you appeared in my lot that first day looking for your father. Not that it spoiled my appetite, and by the way I'm not fussy about food, I eat anything, nor that it blurred my vision, I'm not an idiot; on the contrary, it made a happy, fresh stir inside me; sharpened all my pleasures; something fine to think about, you see; and not jealous of anybody, God forbid; the best man took you, Alice, Inuk, a prince, many a time we've broken bread together and soaked our noses in the foam of a mug of beer, and he'd burst into a song that stopped the trucks on the asphalt —

TALBOT. You're weaving off course, Jim.

CASH. No I'm not. I know where I'm going. Alice, we'll be living and working on the spot where it all began. We'll raise the child, Tenny will have a brother or a sister, and *then* everything will have fallen into place.

DAISY. Alice, dearest, what do you say?

TALBOT. I accept! You can't become a spinster, Alice. Inuk liked you ripe and rich. If you let yourself shrivel for his sake, you'll be exactly the opposite of what he liked.

ALICE. I don't intend to shrivel, father.

TALBOT. Splendid. Cash, she's yours.

CASH. Does this mean yes, Alice?

ALICE. Of course it does.

CASH. Ah!

ALICE. A year from now.

CASH. Oh!

DAISY. A year from now?

TALBOT. Fiddlesticks! Why a year from now?

ALICE. For Inuk's sake.

TALBOT. Stuff! I'm a man of action. If later's good, sooner's better.

ROCKEFELLER. Leap before you look.

REGINALD. A girl without lover is a form without content.

DAISY. Reggie!

TALBOT. Talk to her, Jim! Don't run out of words now of all times!

CASH. What can I say? If that's the way Inuk would want it.

TALBOT. How do you know that's the way Inuk would want it?

REGINALD. He was always a sensible fellow.

ROCKEFELLER. If we could only talk to his ghost!

(*Whereupon an eerie whistle and uncanny music are heard, and darkness covers the room. Exclamations*)

ROCKEFELLER. What did I do?

DAISY. A manifestation!

REGINALD. Be still, everyone!

ALICE. Mother, hold me!

(*The ghost of Inuk appears, and as it does, the eerie music resolves itself into the second movement of Johann Mattheson's Trio for Three Recorders, Opus 1, Number 8. The ghost performs a charming dance to the music*)

GHOST (*as the music concludes*). Everybody marry!

ALICE. Inuk! Do you mean it?

(*The ghost vanishes. The lights come on again*)

REGINALD (*timidly*). What did he say?

TALBOT. Everybody marry is what he said. Though he seemed a bit out of breath. Funny for a ghost.

DAISY. I heard it too: Everybody marry. It was quite distinct, wasn't it, Reggie?

REGINALD. I thought I heard Everybody merry. Marry, merry. (*Daisy gives him an impatient look*) Marry! Everybody marry! That was it, of course!

TALBOT. What's the difference? Fate has opened its mouth, mortals must obey.

DAISY. Alice, you're not saying anything. You understood Inuk, didn't you.

ALICE. Of course I understood him. I love him unspeakably.

TALBOT. Well?

CASH. Alice?

(*Alice goes to him, puts her hands around his waist, and lets him slowly lead her out through the door*)

EVERYBODY. Hurrah!

ROCKEFELLER. The wedding's on me!

DAISY. Alice has done it, Alice has done it again!

TALBOT. God, this has been an exhausting day. (*He plumps down on the sofa*) I don't know whether the nervous system can take so much bliss. Sit down, children.

REGINALD. Not now, amigo. (*He produces a pair of maracas*) Off to Acapulco!

DAISY (*producing her own*). Off to Acapulco!

TALBOT. Inexhaustible! Send us a postcard!

ROCKEFELLER. And don't forget to come back!

(Daisy and Reginald dance off, singing a Mexican song)

TALBOT. Well, Willifred, that leaves only the two of us behind. I'm too tired to move. Hoo! Getting on, I guess.

ROCKEFELLER. What about Mrs. Glimmer?

TALBOT *(leaping up).* I knew the day wasn't finished yet! How did you know about Mrs. Glimmer?

ROCKEFELLER. The Black Shadow . . .

TALBOT. That does it. I'm off for the week too. *(He puts a flower in his buttonhole)* Willifred, can I leave you in charge till my return?

ROCKEFELLER. Yes, sir.

TALBOT. One. Call the nursery and tell them to start shipping the rhododendrons. Two. Modify the blueprints to make room for a flock of seals. Three. Summon the bulldozers and have them sharpen their fangs, because next Wednesday we churn.

ROCKEFELLER. Rhododendrons. Seals. Bulldozers. It'll be done; you can sleep easy.

TALBOT. Not with Mrs. Glimmer. So long, Willifred. Look after the house, will you?

ROCKEFELLER. Religiously.

(Talbot trips off, singing a ditty of his own. Left alone, Rockefeller chuckles with glee, and, after looking left and right, pounces on the vase from which Talbot has just picked a flower. He seizes the entire bunch, sniffs it with passion, tip-toes toward the door, changes his mind, and disappears out the window with his loot. An arm pulling the flowers out is our last glimpse of Mr. Rockefeller. Now the angel enters, peeks out the window, closes it carefully, pulls the drapes together, and switches off a lamp)

ANGEL. So ends another heavenly day.

THE END

APPENDIX

The tune for Inuk's song in Act One is that of an old hymn slightly modified:

"YE SERVANTS OF GOD, YOUR MASTER PROCLAIM"

LYRICS BY OSCAR MANDEL
MUSIC BY WM. CROFT (1678-1727)
ARR. BY HERMAN STEIN

LET EV' - RY VOICE IN IN-DUS-TRY BE RAISED. THE

MER - CY OF THE LORD BE PRAISED. WITH

ME -TE-ORS DREAD-FUL DE- STROY US HE MIGHT, YET

DAIL-Y HE SPARES US THE HEAV-EN-LY BLIGHT. A - MEN.

For the production of *Angels and Eskimos* at the Melrose Theatre in
Hollywood, we contrived a conclusion which the actors and the director
preferred, and to which I have no particular objection. Left alone, Rockefeller unpins a flower which Daisy had previously pinned to his lapel,
sits down with it, and formally introduces himself: "I am Willifred P.
Rockefeller." The flower whispers an answer into his ear, and the lights
go out on his ecstatic smile.

The director and his cast unanimously rejected an epilogue I had
written for the play, and which I give here. If used — and it had better
be used only when the production has been a success — it can be parcelled
out among the actors as indicated by the letters. The first speaker
reappears after all the bows have been taken and detains the audience as
if embarrassed. The others gain assurance as they proceed. The last line
should halt dramatically before the final "you," and on this "you" the
lights should suddenly come on.

EPILOGUE

A.　　Before we part, friends and mankind,
　　　We actors, fearing we may be maligned,
　　　Ask to be — in part — dissociated
　　　From the play our talent has created —
　　　A play which — no one can deny —
　　　Is merry, sweet, and spry —
　　　Deserves a kindly thought or two
　　　(Especially from the acting point of view) —
　　　But which exhibits, here and there, a shocking
　　　　　　　　　　　　　　unawareness of fact —
　　　Unlikely episodes — to be quite frank — in almost every act.

B.　　We Thespians, famous for our zeal
　　　In acting drama that is up-to-date and real
　　　Whether in the mode Absurd or Psychological,
　　　Socialprotestiferous or Scatological,
　　　Believe that every play ought to convey uncompromising lessons
　　　Concerning man's deepest existential essence.
　　　And though our playwright, I suppose,
　　　Has tried his best to paint the world he knows,
　　　He is regrettably short on information
　　　And somewhat immature about the actual world situation.

C.   Yet I myself have met him, up and down,
Peeking, pecking, poking through the town,
Busy with his facts and taking busy notes
In taverns, car lots, banks and ferryboats,
Trying, it would seem, to make his judgment ripe
Before sitting down to type.
And for this reason, when he lapses from the truth,
I personally blame it on his youth.
He's only fifty-four, you see,
And taking writing courses at the local university.

D.   Our next play, though, will strike you like a violent gale.
You shall see a young tough and his husband in the county jail,

E.   Spitting love and snarling hate, both in the relentless nude,
Racked by anguish, condemned, like all of us, to solitude.

F.   The heroin they crave for and to which they cling
Does not, you understand, come with a wedding ring.

G.   A bloodstained Black excites them wildly on the drum
While tortured by a drunken white cop swilling rum.

A.   We actors feel that, come what may, we must not shirk
From challenging the smug with this tormented work,
Written at white heat by a sensitive killer on Death Row
Whose genius seems with every new reprieve to grow.
Meantime — I speak in confidence — we're much relieved,
                               each time we finish here,
To drop back down to earth out of the stratosphere;
We're happy, when the house lights shine again, to see
                            before us — you know who —
Authentic, unmistakable, and realistic you.

Chronology

Most of the plays in these two volumes have been revised again and again over the years, and therefore exhibit several layers of composition. Since, however, the original conceptions not only remained alive but kept their predominance, I give the year in which the first draft of each play was written.

The Monk Who Wouldn't: 1954.

The Sensible Man of Jerusalem: 1956.

Island: 1959.

General Audax: 1961.

Professor Snaffle's Polypon: 1962.

Adam Adamson: 1963.

Honest Urubamba: 1963.

The Fatal French Dentist: 1964.

The Virgin and the Unicorn: 1965.

Of Angels and Eskimos: 1967.

Living Room With 6 Oppressions: 1968.

A Splitting Headache: 1969-1970.